The Ultimate Personal
Success Book

Dena Michelli,
Christine Harvey,
Alison Straw,
Jonathan Hancock and
Cheryl Buggy

Christine Harvey is an award winning speaker, and has addressed two parliaments plus audiences of 2,500. She's founder of Effective Presentation Seminars and Successful Selling Seminars taught to thousands in Europe, America and Asia, including corporations and the US Military. She has authored seven books published in 28 languages, including *In Pursuit of Profit, Secrets of the World's Top Sales Performers, Can a Girl Run for President?, Successful Selling In A Week, Successful People Skills In A Week, and Successful Personal Impact In A Week.*

Alison Straw is an independent consultant and executive coach. Her career has been devoted to helping individuals, groups and organizations develop. She is passionate about engaging and inspiring people and has worked with many senior executives, supporting them in developing themselves, their careers and their organizations.

Dena Michelli is an executive coach and leadership development specialist who works across cultures in business school and organizational settings. She is particularly interested in how people move through transition and change and undertook research to map this process for her PhD.

Jonathan Hancock gained two Guinness World Records for his remarkable memory and achieved the title of World Memory Champion. He used his learning skills to achieve a First from Oxford University, and has since published ten books on memory training.

Cheryl Buggy is a writer, lecturer and broadcaster. She runs a radio station in Portsmouth and writes programmes on emotional intelligence and releasing potential, for people of all ages.

The Ultimate Personal Success Book

Teach® Yourself

Make an Impact, Be More Assertive, Boost your Memory

Dena Michelli,
Christine Harvey,
Alison Straw,
Jonathan Hancock and
Cheryl Buggy

First published in Great Britain by Teach Yourself in 2023
An imprint of John Murray Press
A division of Hodder & Stoughton Ltd,
An Hachette UK company

1

Based on original material from *Personal Imapct In a Week*,
Networking In a Week, *Assertiveness In a Week*,
Successful Memory Techniques In a Week

A CIP catalogue record for this title is available from the British Library

Paperback ISBN 978 1 473 68937 4
eBook ISBN 978 1 473 68935 0

Typeset by KnowledgeWorks Global Ltd.

Printed and bound in Great Britain by Clays Ltd, Elcograf S.p.A.

John Murray Press policy is to use papers that are natural, renewable and recyclable
products and made from wood grown in sustainable forests. The logging and
manufacturing processes are expected to conform to the environmental regulations of
the country of origin.

John Murray Press
Carmelite House
50 Victoria Embankment
London EC4Y 0DZ

www.teachyourself.com

Contents

Part 1: Your Personal Impact Masterclass

Introduction   7

Chapter 1   10
    Conquer non-verbal power

Chapter 2   24
    Avoid embarrassment and discrediting
    yourself

Chapter 3   34
    Structure your presentation to prove your
    point masterfully

Chapter 4   52
    Make your point stick using incidents,
    analogies, and humour

Chapter 5   66
    Grasp 13 ways to 'grab and hold' attention

Chapter 6   82
    Build your fool-proof 'Presentation
    Planning Matrix'

Chapter 7   94
    Put icing on the cake of professionalism

7 × 7   110

Part 2: Your Networking Masterclass

Introduction   117

Chapter 8   120
Networks and networking

Chapter 9   134
Personal networks

Chapter 10   148
Organizational networks

Chapter 11   164
Professional networks

Chapter 12   180
Networking for career development

Chapter 13   196
Social networking

Chapter 14   212
Simple steps to networking success

7 × 7   228

Part 3: Your Assertiveness Masterclass

Introduction   237

Chapter 15   238
Preparing the foundations

Chapter 16   250
Creating winning scenarios

Chapter 17   264
    Dealing with the 'negative'

Chapter 18   276
    Creating a positive impression

Chapter 19   288
    Being assertive in public

Chapter 20   302
    Body language

Chapter 21   314
    Personal power

7 × 7   324

Part 4: Your Successful Memory Techniques Masterclass

Introduction   333

Chapter 22   336
    The right frame of mind

Chapter 23   350
    Your amazing brain

Chapter 24   366
    Think like a genius

Chapter 25   380
    How to remember anything

Chapter 26   396
    Learning to learn

Chapter 27   406
People skills

Chapter 28   418
Lifelong learning: your personal memory
improvement plan

7 × 7   429
Answers   435
Notes   436

PART 1

Your Personal Impact Masterclass

Introduction

When I was 21, I noticed that people who moved ahead the fastest in their careers were not necessarily the ones with the best education, contrary to my belief about success. Indeed not! Instead they were the ones who could put their ideas across most effectively. They were people who were not afraid to speak out at meetings, or even go up to a microphone.

This made me think. All the years of education are necessary. Yes. But there is more to getting ahead in life. I became a fervent student of the power of persuasion. What was it? What were the component parts?

I realized I had a long way to go. At my first professional job, I was afraid to even speak on the phone. Later I discovered that anything we throw ourselves into, we can achieve with practice. Soon I not only conquered the fear of the phone, but I bit the bullet and signed up for a course in public speaking! Again I discovered that pushing the edge of the comfort zone allowed me to achieve the unthinkable. In addition to raising my family, I started my own company – a huge risk and challenge. I had to learn to sell, and to motive people. I felt both were essential to success. Soon I had customers in Europe and America, and later in Asia.

But in the back of my mind was always this concept of education vs. personal projection. Why were the best-educated people not necessarily the ones making it to the top? The answer was clear. They hadn't learned the skills of personal projection, personal impact. They hadn't learned the importance of motivation, or how to do it.

I continued on with my business, and was later elected Chair of a London Chamber of Commerce – the first woman and first American to hold that position. I also decided I wanted to become a world class motivational speaker. I wasn't sure how I would measure that, but speaking before groups of 2500, at the likes of IBM, helped me to realize that goal. I always aimed to leave lasting impressions – ones that helped each and every person to realize their own inner potential. After all, if a gal who was once afraid of speaking on the phone can gain the competence and courage to address not one, but two parliaments, then surely anyone can do it. With the right information and the determination not to give up, I believed that anyone could achieve their highest potential.

In today's world, with the competition for jobs, promotions and customers, *plus* the visibility we have on Facebook, YouTube and social media, we need to take charge of our personal impact – it's essential to our success.

CHAPTER 1

Conquer
non-verbal
power

Whether you are giving your first presentation tomorrow, or you're a veteran speaker, it's essential for you to know that your non-verbal actions have tremendous power. It would be foolhardy to ignore this aspect of your impact.

Think about the presenters on television, on YouTube, people in politics and those at work. Think of people who win their point, time after time. Is it their actual words that win the point? Or... is it the way they use their voice to say their words? Or... is it the way they use their body to say the words, for example, their facial expression, the position of their body as they sit or stand, or perhaps the energy they exude?

In this chapter, you'll leave nothing to chance. You'll leave no room for embarrassment or lessening of your personal impact. To the contrary, this chapter shows you the importance of your *non-verbal impact* including:

- The power of eye contact
- The power stance
- Walking with purpose
- Magnifying your energy to vanquish fear
- Using gestures for high impact
- Projection of conviction

Three aspects of impact

Whether in a meeting at work, or on the stage for a presentation, certain things are critical to getting your point across and achieving success in your career. These include how you walk, how you move your hands, how you use your voice, even your eye contact – *all* are important!

The fact is that human beings process information through a number of senses. They are impacted with the tone, sincerity and conviction of our voice. We project varying degrees of credibility by the way we move, the way we hold ourselves, the energy we project, the conviction in our eyes, our face, our body.

Let's break down personal impact into these three categories:

1 Your words
2 Your voice
3 Your non-verbal movements and actions

What percentage impact do you think each category has on our listeners? There has been much research and much controversy among experts of the exact percentages to be attributed to each of the three categories. One of the most widely accepted findings are these. See if it surprises you. Three aspects of impact: Words 7%, Voice 38%, Non-Verbal Actions 55% = 100%.

Is it different from what you expected? Of course we need words to express our thoughts. At school we learn to put emphasis on words with little or no emphasis on the remainder of our personal impact.

So let's look at what makes up our non-verbal impact.

Five aspects of non-verbal impact

Eye contact

Stance

Walking

Gestures of arms, hands and face

Projection of conviction

The material ahead will contribute enormously to your authority, confidence, and leadership. You'll be surprised at its impact the moment you use it.

Power of eye contact

Eye contact is the king of non-verbals. In a recent rating of live audiences, presenters who had no eye contact with the audience were rated 40% less effective than those who had eye contact. Whether you want to make an impact in meetings, one to one, or to crowds of thousands, eye contacts is all important. When I train trainers and presenters, it's first on my list. Without good eye contact, your sincerity and impact is lost.

Since you don't have an audience as you're reading this masterclass, you'll need to practise through visualization. Perhaps you've heard about the highly successful experiment with ball players. They used visualization *without* the ball to dramatically short cut their learning curve. Subconsciously, before we do anything in life, we see ourselves doing it. What you'll do here is to speed up the process, consciously.

Perfecting 'eye contact' impact

Do this powerful practice now. Imagine you're in a group meeting at work. Your colleagues are around the same table. Imagine looking directly into the eyes of each person as you speak. See the person across from you. Then look left at the person next to you and do the same. See your boss at the head of the table and do the same.

Now see yourself making a presentation to 20, using the same great eye contact. Now to 40. Now 100. Keep going, letting the group get larger and larger, using the same powerful eye contact.

How does it feel? Does it feel ridiculous, awkward or inhibiting? If so, repeat the process. With six practices in total, you will feel like an expert. Then practise it tonight at dinner, or at lunch with your colleagues or family, as you talk about anything. *You shouldn't wait to give a presentation to practise good eye contact. Develop your skill now and remember to use it daily until it becomes a habit.*

Don't draw the wrong attention – use the power stance

Imagine, for a moment, an absent-minded professor pacing in front of his class. Conjure up a picture of him walking with a slight slouch, hands behind his back, pacing back and forth at the front of the classroom as he speaks, looking at the ceiling and floor. What do his students absorb? Do they hear his words or are they distracted by his movement?

Let's take a tip from television producers. They know that 'the eye of the viewer is greedier than the ear'. As humans we are more easily attracted by what we see than what we hear.

 Perfecting 'power stance' impact
Imagine giving a presentation, using great eye contact as in the last section. This time stand up, and keep your feet planted firmly on the floor.

- *Centre your weight evenly over both feet.*
- *Feel the power of your stance.*
- *Keep yourself 'planted' as you imagine speaking.*
- *Experience your power with this stance thus not distracting your audience from your message.*

How does it feel? Are you ready to build upon it? Let's take it further and study the impact of walking with purpose.

Walk with purpose

Do you think it would be good for a presenter to stand planted to one spot for their whole presentation? No, it provides no interest or variety. Should we pace like absent-minded professors then? No, that distracts our audience. What then?

The answer is to walk with purpose. Just as you choose your words, you'll choose your actions. What could those actions be? It depends on what kind of impact you want to create.

What if you want to create rapport with the audience, for example? You might walk up to someone in the first or second row, lean forward and say something while lowering your voice. What about a surprise element? You could walk to a table or podium and pound it with your fist just as you deliver an important line. They'll never forget it. Or perhaps you'll move to a flip chart or a screen. If so, walk with a sense of purpose, even a sense of urgency. Then your listeners will feel the importance of your message. Conversely, if you were to saunter across, you would give the non-verbal message of unimportance.

Remember that your non-verbal projection could account for as much as 55% of your impact. You've spent a lot of time preparing your subject – perhaps years of study and experience. We don't want you to negate your expertise now, through ineffective delivery.

Magnify your energy to vanquish fear

'You will always have butterflies before a presentation. Just make sure you keep them flying in formation.' That's the advice of Dale Carnegie, the legendary founder of Effective Speaking and Human Relations, a course delivered to millions all over the world. Simply think of the butterflies as valuable energy available to you that you can focus on your audience, your delivery and your message.

When you use energy, you radiate life. People feel your energy and are energized by it. They are drawn to you and to your message. Energy is not a perishable commodity. In fact, energy dissipates when not in use. Energy is rechargeable. The more you use, the more you get.

Have you heard the story about the petite woman who lifted a car off her son after an accident? She saved his life. The event triggered her adrenaline flow which gave her enormous power. Was that adrenaline always there ready to be on called upon? Yes, it was. Otherwise it could not be released in an instant.

We have the same power. Athletes release it for athletic events. You can release it for presentations or anytime you need it.

The secret of energy is one of the most misunderstood subjects of human nature. I often have audience members come up to me and say, 'Mrs Harvey, I really admire your energy.' What they don't know is that one hour before my talk, I may have felt completely unenergetic. Just as athletes get mentally prepared on the way to a match, we can do the same. Here's what I do. On the way to my presentation, I start to let my enthusiasm build. This lets the adrenaline flow and the energy follows.

Now let's master the next aspect of projecting your authority.

Using gestures for impact

Let's consider any movement of the body to be a gesture. Hands, arms, legs, face. Think of the face alone. What you do with your face, combined with the feeling behind your message, has more to do with conviction than anything else you can do.

Facial gestures

Many new presenters are surprised by this. They don't realize *what* their face does because it is so automatic. They don't realize they can control it or change it.

The best way to inspire change is by watching yourself on video. I studied television interviewing techniques with many BBC radio presenters who were moving into television. Most were shocked by seeing their facial features for the first time on the screen, and this shock provoked change.

Before that training, people often came up to me after my speeches and told me that I reminded them of Margaret Thatcher. After I saw myself on the television monitor, I discovered why – my facial gestures were so serious and emphatic. I could be talking about an issue as simple as cats having kittens and make it seem as grave as a 200% increase in the national deficit. After the training I didn't lose my ability to do that, but I immediately learned to be more selective in its use.

The point is this. When you know what you are doing, you can change it. If you don't have a video camera, sit in front of a large mirror while you talk on the phone. What you'll discover will be invaluable to you. However, if you are going to take your career seriously, you must see yourself on video. You'll notice some habits that you'll want to change. Everyone else sees them. Don't let yourself be the last to know!

Facial signals

You can also use your facial expressions to signal what's to come. You can be very serious before an emotional line. You can even pause and contemplate. Or you can smile or laugh before a humorous line.

Let your face be congruent with your message and let your facial expression precede your words!

Why would you bother to even think about this? If you watch television with the sound off, you'll see how important it is. As we said before, human beings take in information through all their senses. Their eyes take in your facial expressions and powerful messages about your intention, your sincerity, and your conviction.

Perfecting 'facial gesture' impact

Stop and think for a moment. What is it that triggers the face to do what it does? The main aspect is feeling.

1 Think of an issue you feel strongly about, then pick one sentence to describe it. For example, it could be, 'Our school system needs to be improved.' What feeling do you have? Is it a feeling of concern? A feeling of anger or rage or excitement? Let it show.
2 Look in the mirror and say the sentence three times.
3 First say it with no feeling.
4 Then say it with mild feeling.
5 Lastly say it with strong feeling and conviction – as if your life or your child's life depended on it.

 Impact Journal
What did you see in the three versions – no feeling, mild feeling, and strong feeling? Create an Impact Journal and jot down the difference in your facial expressions. Keeping the journal will allow you to review important points in the future to heighten your personal impact, before an important presentation or meeting.

Gestures of your arms and hands

We all use our hands and arms unconsciously when talking one to one, or in a group. The negative ways include fidgeting with your tie, necklace or ring, or jingling the keys or money in your pocket. Now it's time to consciously harness the power of gestures for positive impact.

Here's a rule of thumb. Simply magnify your gestures by the size of the group. Consider this. If you spoke to a group of 200 people using the same gestures as you would speaking to one person across a dinner table, the gestures would be practically unnoticeable. If you magnify your gestures to fit a group of 200 and use those gestures when you speak to one person, it looks equally absurd.

Here's how to magnify your gestures. Think of your arm first. It has three joints – the wrist, the elbow, the shoulder. Small gestures come from wrist movement, medium gestures come from elbow movement, large gestures come from shoulder movement. If you speak to any group larger than ten people, you should be using shoulder movements. Try it in the mirror and you'll see the difference in impact.

Perfecting 'arm and hand gesture' impact

Sit or stand where you are now. Say the same sentence you said earlier with feeling, such as 'Our school system needs to be improved.' Any sentence will do.

1 Say it once while moving your hand at the wrist.
2 Say it again moving your arm at the elbow.
3 Do it again moving your arm from the shoulder with a large emphatic movement.

Repeat the cycle until you've done each six times – small gesture, medium gesture, large gesture. After six times you will feel quite at ease with each.

Gestures to avoid

Most neophyte presenters do very well with gestures. It's simply a matter of being yourself, and using your hands in a more magnified way than you would when speaking to a friend.

However, some people want to be further forewarned about what not to do.

List of Don'ts

1 Don't distract your audience from your message with unnecessary non-verbal movements.
2 Don't let yourself indulge in jangling the keys or money in your pocket, twisting your tie or jewellery, or touching your glasses incessantly.
3 Don't stroll without purpose – this brings attention to you physically rather than to your message.
4 Don't fiddle with your hands – instead use them for conscious gesturing, as in showing the size of something, or the direction of something, or let them be still.

Now reflect on your progress. You've delved into one of the most powerful aspects of speaking, yet something we never study at school: your non-verbal impact. You've studied eye contact, power stance, walking with purpose, magnifying your energy and making an impact with gestures.

What creates projection of conviction?

Think about what causes the projection of conviction. There are three components:

1 The face, driven by feeling, as discussed above
2 Energy as discussed above
3 Emphasis of voice

When people speak with conviction, they are taken more seriously. If you want to speak with more conviction, be it to your peers or to an audience, apply the three principles above every day. You can use projection of conviction at the supermarket talking to the check-out staff, or at the bank, or at work. You'll be amazed at the difference in seriousness with which people receive you. When you learn to use it every day, you can draw upon it more easily in presentations of any kind.

Impact Journal

1 *Watch different presenters on television or YouTube. You'll see major differences in the way people project themselves.*

2 *Now think of the people you know of high credibility and impact who always win their points. What common thread do you see?*

3 *List what you notice in your impact journal. Keep this journal with you and record what you see in others that is effective over the next seven days. Watch face, hands, body angle, stance, movement, energy, eye contact. Note what you think is effective and ineffective. This will allow you to easily incorporate effective non-verbal actions into your own personal impact.*

Social media application

Direct eye contact with the camera is powerful and engaging, both in still and moving images. Whether on video, such as television and YouTube, or with still images such as Facebook, be sure to apply the eye contact principles.

With video, applied to all social media, the power stance will give you more credibility than bouncing around while standing or sitting. With video shots above the waist, be sure to magnify your energy through enthusiasm and emphasis in your voice plus facial expressions. Refer to the section on 'what creates projection of conviction'.

Remember too, the power of gestures. Using your hands and arm gestures creates impact. Take a moment to watch TV *without* the sound and you will pick up some great tips. Then adjust it to your personality for the effective use of non-verbals.

Although social media is meant to be quick and easy, often with a philosophy of 'just get it out there' and 'don't worry about perfection', we all know that human beings judge what we see and hear. Keep this in mind and let your personality come through naturally as you employ the methods above.

Most importantly, dare to utilize what you've learned in this chapter. For knowledge without action will lead nowhere!

Summary

In this chapter you learned about non-verbal actions that could account for up to 55% of your impact. These include eye contact, power stance, walking with purpose, magnifying energy to vanquish fear and using gestures for impact.

Research has shown that audiences give speakers a 40% less effectiveness rating when there is no eye contact. On the positive side, good eye contact, whether one to one, on television, YouTube or with audiences, makes more impact than any other non-verbal action.

You also learned that the 'absent-minded professor' habit of pacing back and forth causes distraction from our message. By using both the power stance, and walking with purpose, we dramatically heighten our impact.

Fear, you learned, is a form of energy that can be harnessed for positive impact. We all have a feeling of butterflies before a presentation but, by keeping the butterflies flying in formation, we transform the energy to our benefit.

Gestures of the face, hands and arms, are so automatic that we rarely think of them or of their impact, either as positive or negative. Yet, by knowing and practising the rules you've learned, you can eliminate the negative and greatly enhance the positive personal impact.

Fact-check (answers at the back)

1. What percentage of your impact is said to be based on non-verbal actions?
   a) 5% ❏
   b) 25% ❏
   c) 45% ❏
   d) 55% ❏

2. In ratings from live audience, the speakers received what percentage less effectiveness rating when there was no eye contact?
   a) 10% ❏
   b) 20% ❏
   c) 40% ❏
   d) 80% ❏

3. According to research done for television producers, what human sense creates the most impact for viewers?
   a) Hearing ❏
   b) Seeing ❏
   c) Feeling ❏
   d) Smelling ❏

4. Aimless pacing has proven to be a distraction from our message. Instead we should
   a) walk with purpose ❏
   b) take a power stance ❏
   c) both of the above ❏
   d) none of the above ❏

5. A legendary trainer of public speaking advised his students not to fear the feeling of butterflies before a presentation. Instead he advised them to
   a) keep them flying in formation ❏
   b) take a break before the presentation ❏
   c) take a stiff drink ❏
   d) cancel the engagement ❏

6. Which of the following is true about energy?
   a) It's not a perishable commodity ❏
   b) It dissipates when not in use ❏
   c) It's rechargeable ❏
   d) All of the above ❏

7. The best way to force change in your unconscious non-verbal actions is to
   a) look in the mirror when you talk on the telephone ❏
   b) watch yourself on video ❏
   c) scold yourself ❏
   d) ask a friend ❏

8. Which following non-verbal habits diminish your personal impact and should be changed?
   a) Walking with your hands clenched behind your back ❏
   b) Fidgeting with your necklace, tie, or ring ❏
   c) Jiggling the keys or money in your pocket ❏
   d) All of the above ❏

9. What causes us to project conviction?

a) Our face, driven by feeling ❑
b) Energy ❑
c) Emphasis of voice ❑
d) All of the above ❑

10. When using gestures with our hands and arms, the bigger the group, the bigger the gestures need to be. You should be using arm movements originating from the shoulder for groups larger than

a) 10 ❑
b) 20 ❑
c) 40 ❑
d) 80 ❑

CHAPTER 2

Avoid embarrassment and discrediting yourself

Have you ever heard anyone preface their statement like this? *'I don't know if this is important or not but ...'* It happens in meetings and in personal conversations every day.

What does that preface do? It sets up doubt in the listener's mind immediately. It's like a siren shouting: 'Not important, not important.' When this happens, both the statement *and* the speaker lose credibility.

In this chapter we'll look at how to compose your message for high impact and credibility. You'll also look at your personal experiences and rediscover the wealth of knowledge and strengths you can draw upon. This knowledge is essential to bringing credibility to yourself and to the points you're making. Without this, your listeners have no incentive to listen or take action. And without this, you have no personal impact.

We'll look at three keys for making your message powerful, even *before* you divulge your message. These include personal credibility, expert credibility, and reputable source credibility.

Also in this chapter you'll learn:

- How to avoid discrediting yourself
- How to create credibility prefaces
- How to draw upon your life experience and strengths for any subject

Create credibility prefaces

Many people discredit themselves unintentionally. If you do, stop immediately. It is a pity to have good ideas lost and ignored simply because of a discrediting habit.

Listen to yourself speak. Do you have other discrediting habits? Some people say, 'This may not be relevant but ...' Others say, 'I'm not an expert but ...' Or, 'Like John said...' All of these discredit you or your message. After all, why should they listen after you tell them it's not relevant, or that you are not an expert, or that they already heard it from John? Their brain then shuts your message out.

Here's a powerful way to change it. Use a credibility preface to tell the listeners why they should believe in your message. Try this at your next meeting or presentation and see the difference.

Your preface can take one of these three forms:

1 **Personal Credibility**
   Example: *'When I was chairman of the London Chamber of Commerce I discovered ...'* (make your point)
2 **Expert Credibility**
   Example: *'Susan Jones, founder of one of the largest direct sales organizations in the world believes ...'* (make your point)
3 **Reputable Source Credibility**
   Example: *'The Wall Street Journal stated in its January 22nd issue that ...'* (make your point)

Are you ready to try it? Good. Jump in. You'll see it's easier than you think.

Perfecting 'Personal Credibility Prefaces'

Think of any point you could make.

Now create your Personal Credibility Preface. It might sound like this. *'Over the eight years that I've been in this business, in three successful companies,* (that's your Personal Credibility Preface, now give your point, such as ...) *I've observed that the people who move ahead the fastest are the ones who have good people skills.'*

Combine your own preface and point and see how it sounds.

Don't confuse this with boasting about yourself. You are simply giving your point the credibility it needs to be taken seriously. Look at it this way. If you didn't want your message taken seriously, you wouldn't bother to say it. So why not give it the emphasis it deserves? Your ideas deserve to be taken seriously. When only a few people speak out with credibility, the world makes decisions based upon too few people. In this chapter I hope that you are going to change that balance by using credibility prefaces.

Perfecting 'Expert Credibility Prefaces'

Think of another point you could make.

Now create your Expert Credibility Preface. For example, *'Mike Smith, our new CEO* (that's your Expert Credibility Preface, now give your point, such as ...) *says that the people who move ahead the fastest are the ones who have developed good people skills.'*

Combine your own preface and point and see how it sounds.

Perfecting 'Reputable Source Prefaces'

Think of another point you could make.

Now create your Reputable Source Preface such as *'A BBC documentary on careers* (that's your Reputable Source Preface, now give your point, such as ...) *showed that the people who move ahead the fastest are the ones who display good skills working with people.'*

Combine your own preface and point and see how it sounds.

Well done. By using credibility prefaces before your statement, you are giving your listeners proof that your statement has widespread validity and is worth listening to.

Now let's look at your lifetime of strengths to add more power to your communication.

Draw upon your strengths to discuss any topic

Do you think you could talk for six hours straight on a string of subjects pulled from a hat? I didn't think I could, until I participated in a charity Talkathon in London. It made me realize that we all have a repertoire of experience that lies dormant in our minds until we are called upon to use it.

Why is this important? The answer is this. The greater your confidence in your repertoire of experience, the stronger your response will be when called upon in an impromptu situation, be it in front of the boss, in a meeting or in a formal presentation. Or even when asking for an increase in pay, or handling a job interview!

Although this is the longest exercise in this masterclass, the results you gain from it will be enormous. You'll be referring back to this section for sources of credibility, for proving your point, for incidents with high impact and even for humour. So dig in and enjoy. You'll be amazed at the wealth of experience and strengths you bring to every situation.

Strengths from types of organizations

In the exercises below, you'll discover the huge diversity of knowledge that you can bring to any situation. By referring to these personal experiences, you give yourself high credibility and make your comments interesting and memorable.

In your impact journal, list every 'type' of company you have ever worked for – paid or unpaid, part time or full time. Go back to your earliest job.

For example, mine looks like this:

- Computer Company
- Own Company – Property
- Own Company – Training
- Educational Institute
- Radio
- TV
- Publishing

List yours.

You are already getting a sense of the breadth of your experience.

Strengths from types of functions

Now list every function you had in any company or organization. For example, sales, administrator, finance, reporter, etc.

List everything you did, even if it was for a short time, or even volunteer work.

Strengths from recognition

Now list any awards or special recognition you gained in business, professional organizations, sports, hobby, music or school, even those not related to your career. Go back to early childhood, and come up to the current day.

Good. It's important to acknowledge yourself and see the lists of knowledge, strengths and experience growing.

Strengths from competence, interests and enjoyment

List your areas of competence. Include things at home, and in the community. For example: repair the car, wallpaper a room, keep people working as a team, etc.

Include all your interest areas, the subjects you have studied or enjoyed – school, seminars, books, lectures, sports hobbies, and activities.

Also list things you simply like to do, or volunteer to do – walk in the woods, be with family, do gardening, help at child's school, service organizations.

And anything else you excel in – teaching people, motivating people, creative, artistic, etc.

Reflect on the wealth of subject areas you have to draw upon to discuss any topic from your entries above.

 Impact Journal
1 *Pick any subject you might need or like to speak about.*
2 *From your lists above, choose three of your strengths or experiences that could link to it as a Personal Credibility Preface.*
3 *Record these in your impact journal.*

Perhaps you've heard it said that most people are more afraid of speaking in public than of dying. This won't happen if you concentrate on your strengths and background knowledge above. Instead you'll realize the wealth of experience, knowledge, interests and expertise that lies within you, ready to be called in to action. Keep these lists to refer to in the future.

Social media application

Let's consider your credibility first with regard to social media. Even with Twitter, a few words are enough to put across your credibility, along with a link to your message. For example, 'Find out what I discovered when I chaired the XYZ function', will draw more attention than not mentioning your position. The same is true with Facebook, LinkedIn, YouTube, etc.

Experiment with different ways of putting across your credibility and see which works best according to your field, but don't neglect it. When you find the best method, use it to your advantage.

Next, draw upon your background experiences to connect with people. Others will always be drawn to you by similar experiences. For example, if you want to connect with a certain author but you have no knowledge of their field, look to see what other interests they have that are compatible with yours, and connect through that. And if you have credibility in that compatible interest area, use that too.

Summary

In this chapter, you learned three key ways to give credibility to your points. You saw that before you make an important statement, you can preface it with a credibility point about yourself, or you can attribute it to an expert, or you can quote the source from which the point comes.

All of these prefaces make your listener take notice. They also prevent you from discrediting yourself. All of these bring credibility to you and heighten your image and impact.

Another important aspect of this chapter is learning to draw upon your strengths from the diversity of your background. Whether you are asking for an increase in pay, a promotion, or you are addressing a group about a subject close to your heart, the ability to quickly draw upon your strengths will bring you success and heighten your personal impact.

If you were tempted to skip writing the exercises, I urge you to go back and fill in the pages or your journal. Seeing your experiences in writing is a huge confidence builder, and will serve you surprisingly well in the future. Its impact is much greater in writing than seeing it in the mind's eye.

Fact-check (answers at the back)

1. When someone starts their sentence with a preface such as, 'I don't know if this is important, but...' the listeners think what?
   a) He/she is modest and I like them ❑
   b) It sets up doubt and lessens credibility ❑
   c) It seems friendly ❑
   d) It's a nice way to start ❑

2. There are three types of credibility prefaces that can enhance your image and your message. Choose the one below which is NOT a credibility preface.
   a) Personal credibility ❑
   b) Expert credibility ❑
   c) Reputable source credibility ❑
   d) Controversial credibility ❑

3. An example of personal credibility is
   a) When I was captain of the ABC Rowing Club ... ❑
   b) During my 10 years in the manufacturing industry ... ❑
   c) When I won the award for sales ... ❑
   d) All of the above ❑

4. Using personal credibility prefaces should not be confused with boasting about oneself. Which of the following are true with regard to credibility prefaces?
   a) People will take you more seriously ❑
   b) People will take your message more seriously ❑
   c) Your ideas deserve to be taken seriously ❑
   d) All of the above ❑

5. When you use an expert credibility preface, it could sound like this:
   a) Mike Smith, our CEO, says... ❑
   b) The successful chairperson of XYZ Company doesn't use this method, and neither should we ... ❑
   c) Susan Jones, founder of the ABC Foundation, has had great success with the method I am going to show you now ... ❑
   d) All of the above ❑

6. A reputable source preface could sound like this:
   a) The BBC special pointed out ... ❑
   b) The *Wall St Journal* quoted ... ❑
   c) The best-selling book, *XYZ*, said ... ❑
   d) All of the above ❑

7. When using either the expert or the reputable source preface, you are basically telling people
   a) that you have widespread proof that your statement is valid and should be taken seriously ❑
   b) that you have influence ❑
   c) that you are intelligent ❑
   d) all the above ❑

8. Listing points about your background will help you to
a) ask for a promotion ❏
b) address a group of thousands ❏
c) answer an impromptu question quickly and effectively ❏
d) all of the above ❏

9. Seeing the list of your background points in writing is more effective than
a) seeing it in your mind's eye ❏
b) telling your friends ❏
c) not doing it ❏
d) all of the above ❏

10. By making a list of your background points in the exercises above, which of the following is NOT true?
a) You'll be surprised at the diversity of your knowledge ❏
b) You'll spend time and find it useless in the end ❏
c) You'll discover things about yourself that you have long forgotten ❏
d) You'll see yourself in a new light, and discover the credibility you have to talk on numerous subjects ❏

CHAPTER 3

Structure your presentation to prove your point masterfully

Now we arrive at the exciting moment of our personal impact – what to say and how to say it! We can take a lesson from screenplay writers who make every scene and every line of dialogue count. There are no extraneous lines and no extraneous scenes. Everything is there for a reason. Everything leads to the final plot point and everything proves the point the writer is trying to make.

In presentations or in delivering any message, even one to one, it's the same. You have to know your message, like the plot of the movie. Then each point and connected proof must lead to and support the message. When you've set up your presentation like this, your audience will be left with a powerful message, for it will have moved them in some way.

In this important chapter you will learn how to prove your points masterfully by:

- Structuring your presentation for high impact
- Using the power of proof
- Developing logical and emotional proof
- Using numbers and statistics for power
- Using references for persuasion
- Using expert quotes for credibility
- Making your point stick
- Making smooth transitions

Logical and emotional proof

Getting our point across would be easy if everyone believed what we wanted to say without proof. But they don't. If you listen to a 10-year-old child, their conversation often sounds like this. 'My father is so strong, he can lift a car,' one child says. The other responds, 'Oh yeah, prove it.'

People never change. They like to have proof with everything they hear, but it doesn't stop there. There is not one, but *two* types of proof you need to provide. One is logical proof and other is what we'll call emotional proof, the intangible focusing on human needs.

With regards to emotional proof, perhaps Albert Einstein put it best when he said, 'I did not arrive at my understanding of the fundamental laws of the universe through my rational mind.'

Presenting our ideas effectively, whether to a group or one to one, is much like selling a concept. Most people start out thinking that all decisions are based upon logical needs.

On the logical level, the manager wants to buy machinery in order to increase productivity and stay within budget. But on the emotional/human needs level they may want to cut down on the stress at work or go home on time. The person who seeks out both the logical and emotional/human needs will succeed over the person who meets only the logical need. In order to do this, you must learn to present both logical *and* emotional proofs.

For presentations, the formula is easy. First you need to decide what point you want to make. Then you must provide emotional proof, alternating with logical proof. And you can alternate them in any order.

For example:

1 Your point
2 Emotional proof
3 Logical proof

Or it could look like this:

1 Logical proof
2 Your point
3 Emotional proof

Or:

1 Emotional proof
2 Logical proof
3 Your point

How to develop logical proof

Let's look at logical proof first, not because it's more important, but because it's more familiar.

With logical proof you have several options. They include supporting your point as follows.

Three methods of logical proof

1 Numbers and statistics
2 References
3 Quotations from experts

Numbers and statistics have power

Let's look at some examples:

'When we changed to the new machinery, we needed three fewer employees for the same productivity,' the manager said.

'According to research, when children are six years old, 90% of them have an "I can do it" attitude towards learning. By the time they are 12, only 10% still have the "I can do it" attitude,' said the psychologist to the student teachers. As you see, this has much more impact with the statistics, rather than saying, 'We need teachers who encourage children.' People need proof, and statistics make powerful proofs.

When you use statistical proof, be sure that your sentence compares the results. You can compare the results to another method or to the situation that existed prior to the change.

Don't say: 'This orange juice has 20% more vitamin C.' This is a false claim because the '20% more' is compared to nothing. The listener asks '20% more than what?' Do say: 'This orange juice has 20% more vitamin C than Brand X,' or, 'This orange juice from today's crop has 20% more vitamin C than orange juice made from the crop of five days ago.'

Of course, the percentage or number you quote must be true. Now let's look at how to use references to create proof and persuasion.

References for persuasion

Just as you learned how to use personal credibility prefaces in the last chapter, you can use references to another person or group as a credibility preface for your point. Here are some examples:

'George Schmidt from company ABC says that the method I'm going to tell you about saved his business.' (Then make your point.)

'The award winning football team for seven consecutive seasons, always practised the method that we're speaking about today.' (Then make your point.)

Quotations from experts lend credibility

When you want to make personal impact and have your points accepted it's beneficial to use a quote from an expert. Make sure that your audience, be it one or many, know and respect the person you are quoting. The use of quotes by respected authorities adds credibility to your statement.

'John Oppenheimer, the Nobel Prize winner, said, "This method helped me more than anything in my career."'

'Karl Kantor, world expert in fire fighting said, "If you follow the procedure that you see on the film coming up, you'll save your own life and the lives of others."'

Perfecting 'logical proof' impact

1 *Think of a point you want to make.*
2 *Think about the three possible forms of logical proof you could choose from*

   a) *numbers and statistics*
   b) *references to another person or group*
   c) *quotations from experts*

3 *Choose which to use, either actual or hypothetical for now.*
4 *Jot down your choice, with the actual words you would use. Later you can refer to this for ideas.*

How to develop emotional proof

With emotional proof you can use this formula. Develop a true story based on your life experience, if possible, because it's the most effective. Also, no one can refute it as it is your experience and no one else's. Alternatively, you can also use another person's true story if it is powerful.

1 **WHEN** did it happen?
2 **WHERE** did it happen?
3 **WHAT** happened?

Here are some examples:
   When did it happen? You can state it in several ways:
   'Yesterday ...'
   'Last Tuesday ...'
   'When I was 21 ...'
   'In 2011 ...'
   Where did it happen?
   'I was at the world trade conference ...'
   'I was sitting at my desk ...'
   'I stood in the doorway ...'
   'We were walking from the elevator to my office ...'
   What happened?
   'Suddenly the boss walked up and said ...'
   'I saw the most amazing sight in the sky. It looked ...'
   'At that very instant, she slammed the report down on my desk ...'
   'I realized for the first time in my life that ...'
   Now try it for yourself. Here's an example of linking childhood stories to points in management to help spark your ideas:
   'When I was seven, I was playing on a swing with the neighbour's child who was five. She jumped off and the swing hit her on the head. My father thought it was my fault and punished me. That taught me an important lesson. Now, even in management, I try never to blame an employee or colleague for anything until I hear their side of the story.'
   Notice the use the three parts of the formula:
   (When) *'When I was seven ...'*
   (Where) *'I was playing on a swing ...'*
   (What) – now your story.

Create memory value

Compare the impact of the story above to simply lecturing about management with something like this. *'Never blame an employee for anything without hearing their side of the story.'* It holds no 'memory value' because it is missing the emotional content. When you want to make personal impact and have your points remembered, there is hardly anything more powerful than a personal story.

Don't hold yourself back by wondering if you have the 'right' incident or a 'good' incident. The important thing is to practise the when, where, what, until it flows easily.

Perfecting 'emotional proof' impact

1 Think of an incident from your life experience and a lesson it taught you. It could have happened yesterday or years ago.

2 Develop three sentences to make your story. Use the three part formula.

   a. When:

   b. Where:

   c. What:

3 Good. When it starts to flow, it shouldn't take you more than 30 seconds to develop such a story. In the beginning it will take you much longer. Again, don't worry about what's right.

Now let's develop the *point* segment of your impact formula.

Know your point – make your point!

Have you ever listened to anyone – your spouse, your best friend, your doctor, your politician – and wondered, 'What's the point, what are you trying to get at?'

If you want to hold the attention of your listeners, know your point and make your point. You may even need to repeat it more than once.

Remember, *your listener doesn't know where you are heading,* nor does he have all your background and expertise. Don't assume that your point is too obvious to mention. *Never leave your point to chance.* You have to give it to them straight.

There's no rule that says you can't make the point at the beginning and again at the end after your emotional and logical proof. It would look like this:

● Your point
● *Emotional Proof*
● *Logical Proof*
● Your point

For example:

'Thank you, Margaret, for your introduction. Good morning everyone. Today I'm going to make an important point about warning your children about the misuse of drugs in society. (This is your point.)

In 2010, I was travelling from London to New York, when I met an expert who told me ... (This is your emotional proof story.)

Research shows that 83% of all youngsters between the ages of 10 and 16 ... (This is your logical proof statistic.)

The point is that we as parents must warn our children about the misuse of drugs in our society. It is our responsibility. It is not an option. If you don't want your children to succumb to drugs, you must talk with them tonight and not delay.' (This is your point again.)

Or you could start immediately with your emotional proof, then the logical proof, then the point. *'Thank you ... Good morning ... In 2010, I was travelling ...'*

Alternatively, you could start immediately with your logical proof. *'Thank you ... Good morning ... Research shows that 83% of all ...'* then the emotional proof, then the point.

Whichever way you decide to do it, you must know your point and state your point! State it clearly and succinctly, before and/or after your proofs.

Put yourself in the listeners' shoes. They are bombarded by words, words, words, and more words. Their minds are racing, trying to deduce your point. When you say *'The point is ...'* it's a relief to your listener's mind.

Structure your presentation – for high impact

Winston Churchill was once told, 'If you are a Parliamentarian you can make one point. If you are a Minister, you can make two points. If you are the Prime Minister, you can make three points.'

I'm afraid there are many of us – bosses, managers, parents, teachers, experts and presenters of all disciplines – who forget that. The fact is that we can be much more effective if we make one point, and one point only. By that I mean we should have one message. *All points, and their connected proofs, serve to establish and strengthen one message.*

Below you'll find a tool I've created for our Effective Presentation Seminars, called the Circular 'Impact Formula' Chart. You'll find this tool not only effective for presentations, but also for any point you want to prepare for a meeting, a talk with the boss or staff members, or any other time you want to make high impact.

Here's an example of how to use it. One of my favourite messages is about the need to use positivity in our lives and our businesses. That's my message. Then I have several points and connected proofs to show why it's important and how to do it. The structure will look like the chart below, or have similar variations.

As you look at the diagram below, imagine the presentation you might make. In the centre is the main message you want to deliver. Mine, in this case, is 'Use positivity for results in management'.

After you choose your main message, think of five or more points that support your message. In my points below, I have three showing why my message is important, one showing how *not* to do it and one showing how *to* do it, all with supporting proofs.

Note that in my point six, I actually give two logical proofs to support my point along with one emotional proof – a personal story. The two logical proofs might be a statistic along with a reference for persuasion or a quote for credibility.

My final point under point six is a call to action. As in my previous example, a call to action would sound like this: 'If you want X, then you must do Y without delay.' The specific words in that example were: 'If you don't want your children to succumb to drugs, you must talk with them tonight and not delay.'

Circular 'impact formula' chart

The exciting part of this impact formula is the flexibility you have to design it according to your field, your profession and your personality. By adding as many logical and emotional proofs as you like, always remembering to make your point clearly before and/or after the proofs, you have a fool-proof formula. It's a matter of multiplying your points and related proofs: both logical and emotional, making sure they all support your message.

Take a moment now to structure a talk of your own. Pick a topic from your business, your life or your community. Pick something you feel strongly about, perhaps product potential, the economy, the environment, etc. It can be a talk you really need to give, or a hypothetical one. Either one is excellent preparation. Use the questions in the Tip Box below to formulate your thoughts, before creating your own Circular Impact Chart.

 Impact Journal

Structure a talk now, point by point in your impact journal, using the Circular Impact Formula above as a guideline.

1 *What is the main message you want to get across?* _____

2 *Now your 1st supporting point, and proofs in any order*

3 *Now your 2nd supporting point, and proofs in any order*

4 *Now your 3rd supporting point, and proofs in any order*

5 *Continue with as many points and supporting proofs as you wish*

6 *Now your closing point. Restate your main message, and the suggested action that should be taken.*

Congratulations. If you have to get up on your feet tomorrow and give a presentation, you will do a fine job with this structure. You can rest assured that you will be perceived as a professional, and your points will be taken seriously.

Make smooth transitions

After you become proficient at choosing your points and proofs, you'll want to think about 'transitions'. How will you switch from one story or point to another? How will you give your audience a clue that you are changing to a new point? Transitions let the 'computer of their mind' store the new point in a new place in the brain, thus not merging or confusing the two stories.

One way to do it is with a *pause*. You can give your first point and proof, then pause, then start your new point and proof.

For example, the point could be '... *The lesson I learned from that incident is that people are not motivated by money alone.'* PAUSE *'Research proves ...'*. (Make your next proof.)

Another way to do it is with a *linking sentence.* State your incident/story, then say: *'After that incident, I started to research the subject and I discovered that...'*. (This is your transition to the next point, the research finding such as a statistic, which is your logical proof.)

Don't make the mistake of making your transition sentence too long or complicated. If you do, you'll lose your listeners. It's better to have a nice solid pause, than to fill your speech with words that serve no purpose.

Remember the lesson we learn from film producers and script writers who make every word and every scene count. Each has a purpose and leads to the plot. Nothing is extraneous. We must do the same in our presentations.

Social media application

If you are making a video for any purpose including YouTube, or if you are recording for internet radio, there is nothing more powerful for proving your points than the logical and emotional methods of proof contained in this chapter.

Draw upon numbers and statistics to make your point stick in the mind of your viewers. The same is true for readers or listeners. Draw upon your background for stories that you can use to make an emotional/human impact link to your point.

When using quotes or references, make absolutely sure that your quote is accurate. No one wants to be quoted wrongly, and neither do we. The best way to build followers and a positive support base is by giving accurate credit where credit is due. And when deciding on your content, remember to utilize the Circular Impact Formula in this chapter. Decide on your main message, list your points to support your message, and support your points with your high impact stories, stats, numbers, quotes and references.

Summary

This chapter provided you with the Circular Impact Formula – an easy and powerful way to structure your presentations. The key to having a memorable talk is providing proof for the listener – both logical and emotional proofs. Both are essential to high impact. Both are necessary to reach the left and right hemispheres of the listener's brain regardless of the subject.

For logical proofs you learned about three exceptionally powerful sources. Those are statistics, references for persuasion and quotes that lend credibility. For emotional proofs, we need to reach back through our experiences in life and select personal stories that link with our points, our audience, and our profession. Your list of background points from the last chapter can serve as a valuable source for personal stories.

The Circular Impact Formula allows you to combine your main message, points and proofs into a powerful presentation. You also learned two ways to transition from point to point, including a pause or a linking sentence. These transitions give the mind of the listener a clue that your next point is coming. The Circular Impact Formula allows you to get on your feet tomorrow if necessary and deliver a memorable talk with the highest of professionalism.

Fact-check (answers at the back)

1. When we deliver a message, we must provide proof to our listeners. Which of the following is true?
   a) Logical proof is the most important ❏
   b) Emotional proof is the most important ❏
   c) They are equally important ❏
   d) Neither is important ❏

2. When making the proofs for our points, we should
   a) make our logical point first ❏
   b) make our emotional point first ❏
   c) make them in either order ❏
   d) make the logical proof after the point ❏

3. Numbers and statistics have power because they appeal to the logical side of the brain. Which is true below?
   a) These proofs always need a percentage ❏
   b) These proofs always need a number ❏
   c) These proofs can provide either ❏
   d) These proofs don't need to be accurate ❏

4. Another method of logical proof is to refer to a well-known person and show that they
   a) agree with our point ❏
   b) disagree with our point ❏
   c) know you well ❏
   d) know your company well ❏

5. A third way to give logical proof is to
   a) quote a fortune cookie ❏
   b) quote an expert ❏
   c) quote the most attractive person at the meeting ❏
   d) quote a fictitious magazine ❏

6. When giving emotional proof, it's possible to relay a story from what source?
   a) From your personal life experience ❏
   b) From your personal career experience ❏
   c) From either of the above ❏
   d) From none of the above ❏

7. Three points should be used to make a story powerful. They include:
   a) When, where, what ❏
   b) Who, where, when ❏
   c) She, he, they ❏
   d) Why, where, when ❏

8. When making your point, it's important to verbalize it, and not assume that your listener will catch it. The best time to state your point is
   a) before your emotional proof ❏
   b) before your logical proof ❏
   c) at the beginning AND end of your proofs ❏
   d) any of the above ❏

9. Winston Churchill was once given advice we should all follow. He was told that if you are a Parliamentarian, and not a Prime Minister, you should make how many points each time you speak?
a) Three ❑
b) Two ❑
c) One ❑
d) Any of the above ❑

10. If you want to inspire your audience to take a certain action based on your presentation, you should state that action succinctly at what part of your talk?
a) Beginning ❑
b) Middle ❑
c) End ❑
d) Any of the above ❑

CHAPTER 4

Make your point stick using incidents, analogies, and humour

Listen to a small child talking to his parents, 'Tell me a story, tell me a story.'

The love of stories never leaves a person. Stories are listened to. Statements are ignored. Stories are remembered. Statements are forgotten.

'A picture is worth a thousand words.' When you relay an incident, you are painting a mental picture for your listener.

These mental pictures touch the hearts of listeners and help them remember. If you can touch the emotions of people, your message stays indelibly ingrained on them. You make your point stick.

The purpose of this chapter is to lead you away from ineffective presentations and ineffective personal impact. You will learn to drop the notion of using filler words, and go straight to that which is effective – the incident or story, analogies and even humour.

In this chapter you will learn how to:

- Use high impact stories and incidents for maximum results
- Make your messages memorable with analogies
- Use humour to your advantage

Use incidents for high impact

I remember one speaking engagement early in my career in which I was the third speaker. The conference theme was technical, dealing with proposed changes in British legislation. I prepared by studying the government 'white paper' on the subject, and then I developed my stories and proofs.

However, the two people who preceded me gave very traditional talks. They read from their papers, they had all facts, no analogies or stories – nothing to make their points stick. I started to get cold feet. 'Should I change my presentation?' I wondered. 'Perhaps I should just give facts too and drop the stories, analogies and humour.' I remember struggling with myself about what to do, but at last I decided to stick with my plan.

I delivered my speech *with* the stories. Can you guess how the audience reacted? They loved it. And the proof of the success is that the organization invited me back – not once, but three times. My point is this. If you want to have high impact and have your points remembered, don't change your plan. Use stories and incidents no matter what the other presenters do.

Influence decisions

Whether you're speaking to people one to one, in a management meeting, or giving a presentation, your goal should be to formulate incidents or high impact stories, so that you can influence decision making. *That's the essence of personal impact.*

> ## Always remember
> Stories are listened to, but statements are ignored.
> Stories are remembered, but statements are forgotten.

Think of each sentence you create as a brush stroke. You're painting a scene in an animated movie. First you have to set the scene, as you studied in Chapter 3 for emotional proof. In this chapter you'll be applying it to make your point stick. As you remember, it's best to state the when and where before you state what happened.

Think of the WHEN and the WHERE as the container of your WHAT action, just as a tea cup is the container of tea. If you pour tea out without having a container, it will spill in all directions making a mess. It will be useless to the drinkers.

The same is true of your story. If you pour out the action part without the WHEN and WHERE container, there will be no place in the listener's mind for the WHAT action to fall. It will make a mess in the mind rather than being contained in its proper mental compartment.for proper impact.

Show WHEN it was; *'day, night, yesterday, last week, two years ago.'* Second you show WHERE it was; *'inside, outside, in a car, in a building, standing by a desk.'* Now your listener has his mental picture into which he can put the action – the WHAT of our story.

Now you can tell what happened; *'my boss said to me..., or, suddenly I realized..., or, she tripped in front of my eyes...'.*

Magnetic effect of incidents/stories

Think of small children again. They are energetic. When they talk and when they run, they ooze out energy. We adore them, we admire them. It draws us to them like a magnet. The same is true with presenters. Listeners are drawn to energy and vitality. You can have it too when you use high impact stories.

And don't use them sparingly. I remember teaching my trainers about the power of personal incidents and stories. They all learned quickly using the formulas in this chapter. They could stand up and deliver a perfect incident/story, with incredible skill. But when I heard them deliver an entire presentation, I was shocked. I realized that I had made a big mistake. I hadn't told them to start their speech with a story. I hadn't told them to make every point with a story. I hadn't told them to end with a story. I hadn't told them that their speech should be a string of stories with proofs or analogies.

I discovered they thought they should just insert a story here and there to accent it, similar to the way jewellery accents a garment. If we go out without earrings or a tie clip, the world doesn't come to an end. That's how they viewed stories.

I don't want you to make the same mistake. Stories and incidents should not accent your speeches, they should *be* your speech. This is true whether you are addressing a medical convention, educators, business colleagues or Parliament.

Why do I give you this advice? The answer is simple. If you make each point with a story, people will listen. If you don't, they won't. Which do you want?

I know at first this is hard to believe. You may be used to hearing people speak without stories and incidents. But do you remember what they said? Probably not.

I was once interviewed on radio in London. The interviewer was tough and had a worldwide reputation for turning callers and guests into mincemeat if they seemed the slightest bit unprepared or illogical.

I was told that I would have six minutes to present my case on a controversial issue, and then the interviewer and the callers would be turned loose to let me self-destruct. Anyone who was invited to be interviewed on this show was thought to be terribly 'gutsy'.

Here's how I prepared. I drew a line down the centre of my paper. I made a list of points I wanted to make in the left column. In the right column I put a list of high impact stories that made my point. I used credibility prefaces such as: *'When I met Prince Charles I made this point about marketing in Great Britain....'* And *'When I was Chair of the London Chamber of Commerce...'*

When the show was over I had many congratulatory phone calls from people who I hadn't seen for years. It was a wonderful experience, due to preparation and reliance on high impact stories and incidents.

 TIP *No one can argue with personal experience. You own it. It's yours.*

You might be tempted to think you can't use stories in business or in high powered situations. Not true.

As an example, here is how I started my speech to the Parliament of Czechoslovakia after Communism dissolved, in 1990, on the subject of Privatization of Industry: *'Yesterday in Prague, I was training a group of senior managers in the subject* of...' (Note the *WHEN, WHERE* and *WHAT* format. Note also that the *WHERE* part of the story has high impact because it takes place in their country, giving credibility to the story.)

Then I talked about uncertainty, which was the issue at hand for them at this difficult time of transition away from Communism: *'The point of the story is this: When we are working in uncharted waters, we can never be sure of what results we can get. We can do research, we can debate, we can take an educated guess, but in the end, we have to start some place.'*

My 45 minute address consisted of 20 incidents to support my point, which was to speed up the passage of their Privatization Bill. I ended with this story. *'My grandparents left Prague to immigrate to America looking for greener pastures. Today your country has the opportunity to be the greener pasture. There are 16 million people here right now, ready and willing to move forward with you...*

'... In closing, I repeat my point. The country waits for you. The world waits for you. History waits for you. As you leave here today, keep with you the passion to be focused – not on the problems but on the solutions – in order to pass the Privatization Bill without delay.' (Note the use of the words 'in closing' to focus their attention on my final 'call for action' power closing: *'to pass the Privatization Bill without delay.'*)

What's my point? If you want to succeed even in the most formal circumstances, use stories and incidents as the building blocks of your presentation. If every story has a point, and all points support your message, then your presentation is done. You're ready to fly. Make your stories and incidents the meat of your talk, *not* an accessory.

Impact Journal

1 *Think of something you feel strongly about, or some-thing you're likely to talk about in the future.*
2 *Now jot down segments of your talk:*

a) *the opening*
b) *your point*
c) *a couple of incidents or stories*
d) *your power ending, calling for action*

Now you're ready for more embellishments. Let's look at how to make your messages more memorable with analogies and humour.

Analogies – for memorable messages

What is an analogy? It's actually something totally unrelated to your point, yet you draw a comparison to it. Does that sound strange? Well, it is. That's why we remember analogies when we hear them. And that's what you want from your listeners.

It's the same principle that humourists use. They take something ordinary from life and do the unexpected with it. That's why we laugh.

Analogies call on the unexpected too, but they don't provoke humour, they provoke our memory. Analogies can seem odd at first, but after you try it and see the effect it has on your listeners, you'll never turn back.

Now, let's apply analogies to concepts you may want to convey. To create an analogy, you simply need two things:

1 A concept you want to convey
2 An object for comparison

Let's say that John, a new manager, wants to impress this concept upon his employees: *'It's imperative to be here on time each morning.'*

Now he chooses an object for his analogy. He looks around the office and chooses 'carpet'. Now he'll link 'carpet' to being on time each morning.

Speaking to his employees he says: *'I want to draw your attention to our carpet. We know it protects the floor from scratches. In some ways it's like employees when they are on time. Being on time protects the company from losing business because the phones get answered, and customers place orders.*

'This provides work for the company and pay cheques for employees. If we want to protect our floor from scratches, we

need a carpet. If we want to protect customers and employees, we have to be here on time each morning.'

In the example above, John considered the words 'ash tray' and 'window' for his analogy, and finally settled on 'carpet'. *Any* object can be used for a good analogy on any subject. It's just a matter of looking at it from different angles until you find one that fits.

Another time John's message is about good customer service. The object he chooses is 'magnet'. His analogy sounded like this: *'Do you notice how often people choose to go to sunny places for holidays? The sunshine seems to act like a magnet. They feel good and rejuvenated. However, if the sun doesn't shine, that's the first thing they complain about when they come back!*

'It's the same with customer service. If we are polite and helpful to customers, they keep coming back. Our helpfulness acts like a magnet. It makes them feel good. On the other hand if we are discourteous, they complain to everyone and we lose customers. Next time you deal with a customer, remember to be the magnet that keeps pulling them back.'

How often should you use analogies? Use them like accessories. If you have a 45 minute presentation, you might want to make your point with two or three analogies. Use them on the points that need highest impact.

Impact Journal
1 *Now think of a concept you want to communicate.*
2 *Pick an object.*
3 *Turn the object and the concept around in your mind. Where can you find a link? Use the two analogies above from John, the new manager, as an example. Try different objects until you find one you like.*
4 *Then make the link to your concept and write it out. Keep it for future reference.*

Use analogies sparingly for the highest impact. I once heard two men on the radio speak for 15 minutes non-stop using analogy after analogy. They had no stories and no points. Just analogies. By the time they finished, the listeners' minds were in overdrive. My point is this. Definitely use analogies, but use them as a special treat for your listeners, not the main course.

In Chapter 6, you'll find The Presentation Planning Matrix – a great tool to let you plan ahead for a good mix of analogies, stories, proofs and other component parts of good presentations. I've created this for our Effective Presentation Seminars to make presentation planning easier and more effective. With the matrix you can easily decide how many analogies to use and on which points to use them.

For now, let's move on to humour.

Use humour to your advantage

What about humour in the workplace? Have you ever been in a meeting in which tensions grew high? People feel uncomfortable, and no one knows quite what to say. At those moments, humour can save the day. And if you can use humour effectively, it can give you an edge over your competition. More importantly, humour can be used to make your point stick in the mind of your listeners, whether in a meeting or a presentation.

The essential thing to remember in the workplace is always to use humour positively, never at the expense of another person.

Since you've already studied analogies, you'll proceed to humour easily. The basis of humour is the unexpected. With analogies, you are taking two unrelated concepts and finding a comparison. With humour you'll take an incident or a word or phrase and find an unexpected twist. You point out something the others didn't see.

Begin by drawing on your own true life experiences and your success with humour will come easier. Here's a longer list you can also draw upon:

Sources of humour	
True incidents from your life	
Incidents from the life of another person	Names
	News incidents
Childhood incidents	Near-miss incidents
Film incidents/lines	Famous people
TV incidents/lines	Neighbours
Signs	Sports
Song titles	Your occupation
Article titles	Note other options as you think of them:

Humour can be thought of as a form of emotion. When your words or actions make people laugh, they are physically moved, not just mentally touched. This is what makes your message more firmly planted.

Perfecting the impact of humour

Look at the list above. Choose one of the categories and write down any situation as it actually happened, but then add a twist. Perhaps how someone else would have seen it – a stranger, or a Martian or your mother-in-law, or the school head master. Perhaps how it would look 50 years from now, or a hundred years ago.

Don't worry if it takes you some time.

Let your mind work on it, even overnight. The twist will come.

Remember, the twist is what makes people laugh because it is the unexpected.

Take a tip from professional humourists. They all worry about whether their lines will go over the first time. They just put the line out, pause, and hope!

You may find that the reverse is true too. You may deliver a
serious line, which touches people as funny. That's all right.
You can laugh too. Then go home and analyse it. You can even
record your presentations to review later. Perhaps you can
build on the laugh to make it bigger, or circle back to it later in
the presentation for another laugh.

Good. You've worked through a lot of material on creating
power and high impact. When you add stories, analogies, and
humour, you are armed with tremendous power to use in your
profession, in presentations and in leadership.

Social media application

The three tools of story, analogies and humour can be used in
all social media, whether visual or text.

Practise making them short, sharp and crisp. In social
media you will lose people quickly if you don't get to your point
immediately. Don't be misguided by thinking that a story needs
to be long. A story with a powerful point can be merely one
sentence or two. The same is true for analogies and
humour.

You might start like this. Write out your story, analogy or
humour point. Then take an axe to it and cut out each and
every extraneous word.

Like the film producer, make sure each word leads you to
your point. Short and sharp. A two-minute video clip could
contain six segments of 20-second stories, analogies and
humour points. *That* is high impact.

Summary

The three tools of stories/incidents, analogies and humour are captivating ways to have high impact and set you apart from others on your career path. They make your message stick in the minds of your listeners. They can be used for influencing decision making whether you are speaking one to one, in a management meeting, or giving a presentation.

You learned that unlike statements, stories and incidents live long in the memory of our listeners. It's often said that a picture is worth a thousand words. Your story, or the relaying of an incident, is the painting of that picture.

Next you learned how to use analogies for the concepts you want to convey. An analogy, like humour, provides your listener with an unexpected twist. It links something quite unrelated to the concept you want them to remember, in an unexpected way.

Humour can be used in the workplace to take the edge off tension or to make your message stick. However, we must remember to never use humour at the expense of another person in order to avoid negative repercussions.

Fact-check (answers at the back)

1. The three methods of making your point stick are stories/ incidents, analogies and humour. Which of them utilizes 'a twist'?
   a) Story or incident ❏
   b) Analogy ❏
   c) Humour ❏
   d) Both analogy and humour ❏

2. The mental pictures you create through relaying stories or incidents, do what to the listener?
   a) Help them remember ❏
   b) Touch their heart ❏
   c) Keep your message indelibly ingrained ❏
   d) All of the above ❏

3. Which of the following is true?
   a) Stories are listened to ❏
   b) Statements are forgotten ❏
   c) Stories are remembered ❏
   d) All of the above ❏

4. Stories and incidents should be used to make your point with the following groups:
   a) Business colleagues ❏
   b) A medical convention, educators, or Parliament ❏
   c) All of the above ❏
   d) None of the above ❏

5. The mistake I made when training my trainers about the effective use of stories and incidents was that I didn't tell them which of the following?
   a) To start every presentation with a story and proofs ❏
   b) To make every point with a story and a proof or analogy ❏
   c) To end with a story ❏
   d) All of the above ❏

6. An analogy contains which of the following?
   a) Something unrelated to your point, yet you can draw a comparison to it ❏
   b) It takes something ordinary from life and does the unexpected with it ❏
   c) It doesn't usually provoke humour, it provokes memory ❏
   d) All of the above ❏

7. To develop your own analogy, first think of a concept you want to convey. Second you pick an object to draw a comparison to. The object should be:
   a) Something sensible ❏
   b) Something outlandish ❏
   c) Something the listener can relate to ❏
   d) It could be anything ❏

8. Should analogies be like an accessory or the meat of a presentation? For example, in a 45-minute presentation, how many analogies are ideal?
a) One ❏
b) Two/three ❏
c) Five to seven ❏
d) At least 10 ❏

9. Sources for humour can come from where?
a) Life situations ❏
b) TV, articles, books ❏
c) Almost anything ❏
d) All of the above ❏

10. Humour is best used about harmless situations. If used at the expense of another person, it can
a) backfire on you ❏
b) hinder your career ❏
c) cause you to lose friends ❏
d) all of the above ❏

CHAPTER 5

Grasp 13 ways to 'grab and hold' attention

Anyone can address a group, providing they have the courage, but how many can grab and hold the attention of their listeners and have high impact? The answer is, not many.

More often than not, their openings are lacklustre. These include what we call the 'housekeeping' start, the 'apology' start, the 'humble speaker' start, and the 'ho-hum' start. These openings discourage your listeners, put them to sleep and make them wish they hadn't come. Don't let this happen to you. Instead, use dynamic openings and ways to grab attention immediately.

We must continue to hold attention throughout our presentations, whether in meetings at work, or in prestigious conferences of all sizes.

In this chapter you'll learn 13 ways to grab attention in the beginning and hold it throughout the beginning, middle and end. These include:

- Power openings
- The use of questions – with and without answers
- Audience participation
- Using objects to hold the attention
- Creating suspense
- Power closings
- Social media applications

Power openings

How often have you gone to a meeting or conference with high expectations, only to have those expectations dashed by a long or boring kick-off?

Just yesterday I heard this conference opening: 'I was just given this list 30 seconds ago by Jane, so don't blame me if I come across unprepared!' What a derogatory start! Firstly, it reflects badly on the speaker for not taking responsibility for preparing himself, and for blaming a colleague. Secondly, it reflects badly on Jane, his colleague. Thirdly, it reflects badly on his organization for not ensuring better preparation. And last but not least, it leaves the listeners totally discouraged and uninspired about what is to follow! This is a variation of the 'apology opening' which you'll read about soon.

Openings are best without preamble. Our purpose as presenters is to grab the attention of the listener immediately. Personally, I want to be able to hear a pin drop within 10 seconds of my opening words. You should aim for the same, even as a beginning presenter.

How can you do this? Go straight into your story/incident as you learned in the previous chapter. Let's say your subject is education. After thanking your introducer, you might say: 'My first child had tremendous problems at school reading and consequently ... '. By starting this way, you have grabbed your audience. They are now ready to hear more. Don't make the mistake of starting with: 'Tonight I want to speak about education, its advances, and its shortcomings. From the early part of the century ...'. That shouts 'boring, boring.' Today's audiences are used to quick-pace media and they want a quick start. If you feel it's important to state your topic, say it briefly after your personal story, once you have grabbed their attention.

Don't be guided by what is 'average' or 'normal' in other presentations you hear. Your purpose in reading this Part is to be good or great, not average. And you *can* be great by going straight for the grabber opening, either with a personal incident or any one of the 13 'grab and hold' attention techniques listed for you in the box that follows.

13 Ways to 'grab and hold' attention

Start your speech with something exciting. Start with something that engages the listener's mind. A personal incident grabs their attention immediately. A question also gets their attention. There are many ways to start a presentation, whether it's around a meeting table or a conference room. You can draw upon any of these methods in order to create dynamic openings:

The first seven you learned about in previous chapters
  1 Incidents and stories
  2 Statistics and numbers
  3 Expert quotes
  4 Refer to a well-known source – usually a person, company or organization
  5 Refer to a credible journal or research source
  6 A personal credibility point
  7 Humour

The following are covered in this chapter

  8 Power openings
  9 Questions – with or without answers
10 Audience participation
11 Demonstrate or exhibit something
12 Create suspense
13 Power closings

These 13 can be used effectively *throughout* your presentation.

Now let's look at what *won't* get attention. These ways of starting will discourage your listeners, put them to sleep, and make them wish they hadn't come. They may make you chuckle as you read them, but believe me, these lacklustre and demeaning openings are going on every day, in every corner of the earth. Don't let it happen to you.

Don'ts

1 'The Housekeeping Opening'
It may sound like this: *'Good morning. Our first break will be at 10:00. If you need to make a call, try to wait until the break. The ladies' room is around the corner, down the hall on the right, the men's is ...'*

Instead, post the housekeeping details on the notice board or print them on a hand-out. Start immediately by talking about the exciting programme you have scheduled, how happy you are that these people are attending, and what positive results they can expect from the day.

2 'The Apology Opening'

It may sound like this: *'Good morning. Our speaker for today, the award-winning expert on 19th century art, Mr Clement Smith couldn't be here tonight. He had to fly to Italy to see the Pope. He's really a very sought after person as you can tell. We're all really disappointed about it, but Mr Jones said he would come and do his best.'*

Now do you think that we in the audience are really psyched up? No, we wish we had the original speaker after that build up. Instead you should introduce Mr Jones *properly* and mention *in passing* that 'Mr Smith regrets he can't be here but would like to join us another time.'

Find out what Mr Jones's qualifications are and say: *'Good morning. Our speaker for today has had an interest in 19th century art since 2002 when he was lucky enough to live in Italy in his position as Cultural Attaché. In addition, he studies ..., and did ... We are very pleased that he is able to join us today in place of Mr Smith to enlighten us about ... Please help me welcome Arthur Jones.'*

3 'The Humble Speaker Opening'

It may sound like this: *'Good morning. I was quite stunned when Elizabeth invited me to talk to you. I don't quite know why she thought I was qualified, but I'll do my best ... .'*

If you say this, you are discrediting your audience, saying that they are stupid to come and hear you. You might think it's humbling, but in fact it insults your listeners.

Instead, learn to prepare your own introduction in the next chapter and give this to the organizer to present before your talk.

4 'The Ho-Hum Opening'

It may sound like this: *'Good morning. I thought a lot about what I could speak to you about. I could concentrate on X ..., or I could tell you about Y ..., but then I considered Z ... , finally I thought ..., but then again ... .'*

By the time you've finished your first paragraph, the audience is asleep. Instead, start with your incident – story, emotional proof or logical proof, or credibility prefaces as you learned in the previous chapter, or one of the points below.

The question technique

Not all questions need to have answers. Often it's enough to let people internalize their answers. The best questions are ones in which people reflect on life. Or perhaps on the way they do things.

There are three ways to use questions to grab and hold the attention of your listeners in meetings and conferences

1 Reflective questions, in which people internalize their answers
2 The 'show of hands' question
3 The 'verbal answer' question

The reflective question

It might sound like this: *'I'm going to ask you a question. Just reflect on the answer to yourself. How many teachers ... ?'*

This process is good as an opening, or for very thought-provoking issues later in a presentation. Often you don't want to break the emotional feeling you've created within people. If instead, you had people waving their hands around, it would break the focus. By having them internalize the answer, you can move them to a deeper level of thought or prepare them for your message to come.

This method is also good when you want people to think or reflect on what you've covered so far but you don't want to take time out for answers. For example, I use it effectively in workshops. I might say, *'What's the point we're trying to make in this module?'* Pause. Then I answer it. *'The point is ... .'*

In this way, a question can serve as a reflective think period, a mental review. It's important to give your listeners some time for mental review so that they can consolidate your material, before moving to your next plateau of ideas or points.

The reflective question is also good when people could be embarrassed by revealing the answer. It allows them to reflect without committing.

The 'show of hands' question

Questions with 'show of hands' answers serve to get the audience involved. When they have to answer, they have to think. The process helps to focus their minds and helps to get their support.

Examples could be: *'How many of you have ever tried this?'* Or: *'Put your hand up if you ever tried this.'* Be sure to tell the audience *before* your question that they will hold up their hands after the question.

Questions with 'show of hands' answers can also get commitment. For example, *'Put your hand up if you think you COULD use this.'* I sometimes take it further and ask a second question: *'Put your hand up if you WILL use it.'*

I'm always careful to only do this with a group which is already behind an idea. If you were to use it on an issue that people were not supporting, they would feel pressure and not like it. A boss couldn't use it, for example, to get employees to support their own goals with which the employees disagree, without causing resentment.

It's good to use the 'show of hands' question technique to prove a point. *'How many of you have experienced such and such?'* By doing that you involve the audience, you prove your point, and you don't alienate anyone.

The 'verbal answer' question

When soliciting verbal answers from your group, the important thing to remember is that the person is taking a risk by answering. The last thing they want is to look foolish in front of their peers, or in front of strangers, or in front of you. They don't like it when you ask them a question, and then tell them that their answer is *wrong*. I've watched speakers do this. It's the shortest path to sudden death. It's up to you *not* to let this happen.

Instead, handle it like this. Ask questions that don't have wrong and right answers. For example: *'Who will tell us what methods of success they use in this area?'* It's their method. It works for them. You congratulate them. You can also move on until you get the answer you are seeking.

It might sound like this, *'Here's the problem, what do you think causes this problem?'* You can even put answers on display. You can continue to pull answers until you get to the ones you want. In this way you never need to say *'Wrong'*, just *'Thank you, what else?'* Then you or the group can decide on the best answer and the virtues of it.

Impact Journal

Remember that questions can be used to open your talk or to hold attention during your talk. It's a wonderful tool to use.

Questions give diversity to your talks.

Questions can deepen the thinking of your listeners.

Questions can lighten the atmosphere.

Questions can change the pace.

Questions can break the ice.

1 *Imagine a situation in which you could use a question effectively when working with a group.*

2 *Write down when it might be, where it might be, what type of questions you can use. Jot down a note in your journal.*

Good, now let's move on to other aspects of getting the audience involved.

Audience participation

I remember fondly one of our courses on Effective Presentations. Each person was deciding how to use audience participation to fit their topic. Suddenly I saw two people down on their knees, waving their arms around, holding out their trouser legs as though wind was blowing through them. It was an incredible sight. They really looked as though they were flying.

I went over and discovered they were demonstrating the art of parachute jumping! One was the speaker. The other was an audience 'volunteer' who the speaker had chosen to assist in demonstrating the excitement of parachute jumping. We were all captivated by the sight, waiting with bated breath to hear more.

The point is that audiences love participation. They feel that the audience member who goes to the front represents them. It has a uniting affect. They see their 'representative' interacting with you and it creates a bond and closeness between you and the audience. And you don't have to be an experienced speaker to get results with it.

In your presentations, you can bring an audience member up to accentuate any point. For example, during my motivational presentations I might ask an audience member to join me at the front and tell us about what they want to achieve. Perhaps improvements in productivity, or sales or morale building. Then they say what they plan to do to get the required results. I know from experience that my message sticks with my audience ten times more effectively by using audience participation. This will be true for you too.

 Impact Journal
Take a moment now to think about ways you can use audience participation in your next presentation.

Where can you use it?

When can you use it?

How can you use it?

What results would you like to achieve?

Jot this down in your impact journal while it's fresh in your mind. In the future you can refer to it when you need it.

Using an object to hold attention

If you want to make a real impact on your audience, show an object. You might change their lives. In a meeting I attended long ago, the presenter held up a book about property investment.

He said, *'This book changed my life – the principles in here really work.'* I can still see that man in front of our group, holding that book up. It's as clear as if it was yesterday. I was so motivated that I went out and bought that book. And indeed, it changed my life too.

I'll always be grateful to that man. Why is that? It's because he got my attention and my interest. If he hadn't held that book up as an exhibit, his talk would not have been as powerful. My life would not have been affected.

Using objects to make your point is effective, whether you use them at the beginning, the middle or the end of your presentation. It's just as effective at work in a small meeting as it is in a large conference.

Let's look at some objects you can use:

Effective objects to grab and hold attention	
Book	Blank paper you mark on during speech
Map	Enlarged photograph
Chart	Diploma
Graph	Plaque
Report	Object (chair, instrument, machinery, sport item, business item)
Newspaper	
Magazine	Other (list your own ideas)
Computer printout	

Well done. Now let's move on to holding your audience in suspense. It is a very powerful aspect of speech making.

Create suspense

A promise plants the idea that something important is coming later *and* keeps your listener alert for it. It holds attention.

For example you could say: *'Later tonight I'm going to give you the exact secret of success told to me by the world's top sales performers. But first, let's look at ... .'*

Or you could start an intriguing story, but not don't finish it at that moment. You intersperse your other points, then come back to the story later. The listeners know you will come back to it, or at least hope you will, and thus stay in suspense waiting.

You can create the same effect with props and exhibits. For example, you can have something near you and either not mention it, or you can say that you'll come back to it later. That holds suspense too.

For example, I once used a long rope in this way. Two colleagues carried it to the stage, one holding each end. We rolled it up and put a blanket over it. I told the audience we would use it later, I didn't mention it again until a point late in my talk. Then we stretched the rope across the front of the room, horizontally, about 3 feet above the floor and used it as 'the line of demarcation' between negativity and positivity that we must cross in order to bring success into our lives. The audience never forgot it, and were still talking about it months later. Using a promise or suspense to hold attention is an effective way to get your point across and make it memorable.

Think now about how you can use a promise or suspense to hold attention. The list is endless, and no doubt you will think of others that relate to points you intend to convey.

Examples of creating suspense

- An important point you promise to give later
- Part of a story you promise to finish later
- An important quotation, secret, statistic or method you promise to give later
- An exhibit you promise to show later
- A demonstration you promise to do later
- A chance for them to participate later
- A person for them to meet later
- Part of a point, story or any of the above, which you start but don't finish, thus leaving the audience in suspense, knowing you'll come back to it

Now let's move on to one of the most important aspects of your presentation, powerful closings.

Power closings

Closings are best when they call for action and tell the audience what benefit they'll get by carrying out the action. For example, *'Remember that 90% of the people who write their goals down, achieve them. Go home tonight and do it. As the research shows, taking two minutes to write your goals down brings success.'*

You can preface your closing with the words: *'In closing, ...'* if you like the feeling it brings. Some researchers believe that the ears of the audience pick up when they hear the words 'in closing'. However, then you must close, preferably within two to five sentences. If you talk longer, they will feel that you've not delivered on your promise, and your entire talk can be discredited. The simpler your close, the better. They've heard a lot from you. Now is the time to tell them what action to take and what results they can expect. Simple. Clear. Precise. You are telling them what they can do now to achieve the results you have discussed.

Social media application

The concept of powerful openings and closings can be used in both text formats and video formats. The same is true with the methods of grabbing and holding attention. So whether it's Facebook or YouTube or anything in the social media spectrum, use these principles to your advantage.

On YouTube, for example, a tremendous amount can be achieved in two or three minutes. If you prefer longer, that's great too. Remember that your viewers' needs are the same as those at work. They will tune you out if you have fatally boring openings and can't hold their attention throughout.

So make use of the reflective questions in which they can internalize their answers. Make use of audience participation by recruiting a volunteer to be taped with you. Make use of objects and promises to hold attention. When you do, your followers will multiply.

Summary

In this chapter you learned about the difference between a powerful opening and a lacklustre opening to your presentations. One puts people to sleep. The other energizes them. One makes people wish they hadn't come. The other raises their participation and positive results.

On the 'don't' side are trite and outdated openings such as housekeeping points, apologies, discrediting oneself, and the boring unprepared rambler.

Equally important are the 13 methods for grabbing and holding attention. The list of options includes the use of questions – with or without answers, audience participation, exhibits and objects, plus suspense or a promise of something you'll divulge later. All of these can be used quickly and effectively to grab and hold attention at the beginning, end and throughout your presentation for high impact.

Power closings are essential and are best when they call for action from the listener.

Fact-check (answers at the back)

1. In opening your presentation, you want to grab the attention of your listeners immediately. In fact, you should be able to hear a pin drop, within how many minutes or seconds of your opening?
   a) 10 seconds ❏
   b) 30 seconds ❏
   c) one minute ❏
   d) three minutes ❏

2. The best way to grab attention immediately is to
   a) tell a story or incident related to your message ❏
   b) start with the history of your subject ❏
   c) announce the break times ❏
   d) deliver a long preamble ❏

3. An 'excuse opening' has what downfalls?
   a) It reflects badly on the speaker ❏
   b) It reflects badly on the person being blamed ❏
   c) It reflects badly on the organization ❏
   d) All of the above ❏

4. In closing your presentation, you can use words such as 'In closing ... .' This re-engages your listeners to hear your final point. When using this closing, you should come to a close within
   a) the next sentence ❏
   b) one to five sentences ❏
   c) three to five minutes ❏
   d) ten minutes ❏

5. All bad openings have what in common?
   a) They leave your listeners discouraged ❏
   b) They leave your listeners uninspired about what is to follow ❏
   c) They leave your listeners bored ❏
   d) All of the above ❏

6. Using reflective questions is very good for
   a) thought provoking issues ❏
   b) allowing people to reflect on what you've covered ❏
   c) not embarrassing people by requiring a verbal response ❏
   d) all of the above ❏

7. Using questions is an excellent way to grab and hold attention. Why is this true?
   a) Questions break the ice ❏
   b) They bring variety to your talk ❏
   c) They change the pace ❏
   d) All of the above ❏

8. Some of the world's greatest presenters use the technique of audience participation for high impact. By bringing a member of the audience to the front to interact with you, the other audience members feel what?
   a) Represented ❏
   b) Afraid ❏
   c) Resentful ❏
   d) Threatened ❏

9. Using objects in your presentation is a highly effective way to hold attention. It is most effective if used when?
a) At the beginning ❏
b) In the middle ❏
c) At the end ❏
d) Any and all of the above ❏

10. A promise plants the idea that something important is coming later and keeps your listener alert for it. Some examples are:
a) Start an intriguing story, but finish it later ❏
b) Promise to show an exhibit later ❏
c) Pose a question and promise to answer it later ❏
d) All of the above ❏

CHAPTER 6

Build your fool-proof 'Presentation Planning Matrix'

Now we come to the time for the ultimate decision – what points will you include in your meeting or presentation? What points do you want to hammer home? What result do you want for your listeners?

Now it's time to let your creative juices flow. Which of the methods will you use to prove your points? Emotional proof stories, logical proof statistics, analogies, humour – what will you choose?

And how will you open and close your presentation? Will you avoid the typical lacklustre start and go for a power opening? A power close? Which of the 13 methods of grabbing and holding attention will you use? This is the moment to take everything you've learned, and like a puzzle, pull all the pieces together as you like it.

In this chapter you'll be given a magnificent tool, the 'Presentation Planning Matrix', to help you put the puzzle pieces together with both ease and high impact. This matrix allows you to:

- Choose your main message
- Plot the points to support your message
- Time your message appropriately
- Gear your points to your listeners for high impact
- Know what to do when invited to speak
- Use social media applications

Benefits of the 'Presentation Planning Matrix'

No one said it's easy to get your points across effectively. In conferences and meetings, people rarely put their points across well. Instead, they often mumble their thoughts to each other as they leave the room. This is negative for the organization because the best ideas stay hidden from discussion. Thus decisions are made without the best talent and ideas coming forward.

The second thing you'll notice about meetings and conferences is the timing. Rarely does a conference, or even a high level Board of Directors meeting, end on time. Seldom do people know how to time their presentations and still incorporate all their points.

Fortunately, this won't happen to you. Why? Because you'll have our fool-proof Presentation Planning Matrix that you can use to plan your presentation. As you'll see below, it aids you in choosing your main message, plus your points and proofs to support it. It also allows you to add variety to 'grab and hold' attention, thus utilizing all you've learned to do in previous chapters. By utilizing these methods, you'll have a high impact presentation and, best of all, you'll develop it with ease and confidence.

And there's one more important ingredient in the matrix. It's your timing! The brilliance of the matrix is that by choosing your specific points, proofs, etc., you'll be able to time each one so that your finished presentation fits the requirements of the meeting or conference.

Sample of 'The Matrix'

Let's have a look now at a sample of the filled-in 'Presentation Planning Matrix'. This is a sample of one I used myself for a 45-minute motivational conference presentation. Use this as a model. Next you'll have a chance to fill in your own.

PRESENTATION PLANNING MATRIX MY MAIN MESSAGE: YOU CAN DO IT						
Point	Emotional proof Personal Incident Story	Time	Logical Proof Statistic/Quote/ Reference	Time	Analogy Demonstration/ Participation/ Question	Time
Neg/Pos.	Airplane Story	4	Children 6–12	2		
	Lady LA	2			Pebbles in a Pond	6
			Expert Journal	2		
Dolphin method	Management Incident Mercedes	2				
	Home incident Tom	4				
	Management Song	2				
			Pearson Whistle	2		
Catch Self					Self Talk	2
	Woman Entrepreneur	4			Demo Try	4
			Survey %	2		
Power Close	Red jacket Australia	4				
					Call for Action	5
	Time Subtotal	22	·	8		15
Total time = 45						

© *Christine Harvey*

Let's do a walk through. Notice the top line 'Main Message'. This is where you fill in either your title or simply the message you intend to deliver.

Next you'll find a block of headings. The first is 'Point'. Under this heading you'll list the points you would like to use to support your main message. Notice that I have four points to support my main message called 'You Can Do It'. My key words are 'negativity vs positivity', 'dolphin method', 'catch self', and 'power close'. The words you enter on the blank matrix that follows will be key words such as mine which remind you of your points.

The next column is headed 'Emotional Proof/Personal Incident Story'. Here you'll decide which emotional proofs you can deliver to support your point, and next to that you'll enter the time it should take to deliver that point. Notice that mine, the airplane incident, will take four minutes.

Next we look across to the following column, the 'Logical Proof/Stat/Quote/Reference'. This is where you choose a logical proof to support the *same* point. Mine is a statistic about children aged 6 to 12, which supports my point about negativity vs positivity, and it will take two minutes of my presentation.

As we look across further, we see the column 'Analogy/ Demo/Participation/Question.' This is where you draw upon your creativity by using an analogy or another of the 13 'grab and hold' methods to keep our listeners engaged. My analogy is 'pebbles in a pond', and it will take six minutes.

Creating your own fool-proof 'Matrix'

Now start thinking about your message and points. Notice that you *don't* need to restrict yourself to one proof for each point. On my second point, for example, I used three emotional proofs to support my point called 'dolphin method'. These are all key words. Dolphin method brings an entire incident to my mind, just as your key words will bring points, stories, analogies etc., to your mind.

The 'Presentation Planning Matrix' is designed to keep you on track, to give your listeners variety and to help you prove your points. It's a high impact methodology and allows you to customize your presentation or meeting content to your group. For example, if you are addressing a group of aerospace engineers, you may choose to use three of the logical/statistical type proofs for every one emotional proof. Don't be tempted, however, to eliminate the emotional/

story/incident proofs and analogies. Why is that? Because stories, as we stressed before, are remembered whereas statements are forgotten. Stories have impact, statements are ignored.

Now it's time to try your hand at filling in your own matrix. In filling it in below, you'll want to review all the possible options for making your presentation powerful, with lasting impact. Regardless of whether you are giving a presentation at work, giving an after dinner speech, a wedding toast, addressing a sales conference, giving an impromptu answer to your boss, or going for a job interview, you'll want to draw upon many of these aspects of powerful communication.

Options for making your presentation powerful

- Rely upon your background (see Chapter 2) for points and proof
- Remember to prove your point
- Give emotional proofs
- Give logical proofs
- Reiterate your point
- Don't discredit yourself
- Add powerful stories and incidents
- Use analogies
- Start the day professionally
- Use questions in your presentation
- Get audience participation
- Use demonstrations or show an object
- Use suspense or a promise
- Use humour

PRESENTATION PLANNING MATRIX							
YOUR MAIN MESSAGE _____							
Point	Emotional Proof Personal Incident Story	Time	Logical Proof Statistic/Quote/ Reference	Time	Analogy Demonstration/ Participation/ Question	Time
Time Subtotal							
Total Time =							

© *Christine Harvey*

When you are invited to speak

What if someone hears your presentation and asks you to come to speak to their group? How will you prepare for that?

I like to know the composition of the audience. How many women, how many men, how many junior and senior managers, how many salespeople, etc? This gives me a feeling of who will be listening, what level they are, what stories, emotional proof and logical proof I will use.

I also ask another question: *'When the audience leaves the room, what feeling or knowledge do you want them to be left with?'* This question lets me zero in on my main message. Then I start to connect all my points, stories, and proofs to it.

If you are starting out and speaking on a volunteer basis, you may want to simply ask a few questions over the telephone. You will want to know at least:

- The number of people expected
- Their professions
- Percentage male/female
- Their age spread
- The time allocated to you

If you start to speak on a paid basis, you may want to develop a questionnaire and ask questions such as: *'Do they want skill building?'* Or *'Do they want their people to be motivated?'* Or *'Do they want both, and in what balance?'* Other questions could be: *'Are there any sensitive issues you do not want mentioned? If so, what?'* Or, *'Are there any people or groups you want mentioned or acknowledged? If so, who?'* As you gain experience, you'll develop more questions that are important to you and your industry.

Social media application

If you intend to create video, either for incorporation in your presentation or for YouTube or for any other purpose, you'll find this chapter extremely useful. The matrix can be equally effective for a three minute message as for a 45 minute message.

With video it's essential to time your message in advance and to keep the pace fast moving for high impact. Thus a point or proof you might use in a live presentation lasting two minutes, could be cut to 20 seconds for a video. With practice you'll be able to cull the essential words to fit a 20 second segment and have it sound perfectly appropriate on video or YouTube, whereas it would sound clipped and short with a live group in a longer presentation. A promise, or one of the 13 'grab and hold' methods, is as effective here as anywhere else.

Even with Twitter, where your number of characters are so restricted, choose your words carefully to relay the highest possible impact and interest.

In preparing only written text, such as Facebook business or LinkedIn etc, you can draw upon concepts of point – proof – grab and hold, just as effectively as in your verbal presentations.

For maximum effectiveness, keep the needs of your listeners, viewers or readers in mind as you prepare your messages.

Summary

In this chapter you were given a powerfully effective tool – The 'Presentation Planning Matrix'. This tool allows you to plot the points, and then choose options under three headings to support each. The first heading is your emotional proof relayed through a personal incident/story. The second is your logical proof relayed through statistics, quotes, and references. The third heading is that of grabbing and holding attention including analogies, demonstrations, audience participation and questions – with or without answers.

You started with your ultimate goal – the result you want to achieve. You considered whether you want your listeners to take a specific action based on your presentation, or make a specific change, or whether you simply want to relay information. Your goal will determine your main message plus the points and proofs you want to use to hammer that message home.

The matrix also allows you to consider the total time for your presentation and then break it down into the segment times required to deliver each point, proof and analogies within your allocated time. Listeners will grasp your message and either take action or be informed, depending on your intent.

Fact-check (answers at the back)

1. In meetings, people usually don't put their points across as effectively as possible, and discussion moves on to other subjects before the matter is fully discussed. This results in
a) decisions being made without the best ideas coming forward ❏
b) more time for others to speak ❏
c) the most effective use of time ❏
d) none of the above ❏

2. Conferences rarely end on time. This is because
a) breaks are too long ❏
b) speakers don't time their presentations well ❏
c) boring speakers always take longer ❏
d) none of the above ❏

3. As a presenter, you should know how many minutes your proofs and points will take to deliver.
a) True ❏
b) False ❏
c) It doesn't matter ❏
d) None of the above ❏

4. The Presentation Planning Matrix in this chapter is designed to help you in what ways?
a) To keep you on track ❏
b) To give your listeners variety ❏
c) To prove your points ❏
d) All of the above ❏

5. When providing proofs for your points, you don't need to restrict yourself to one proof per point.
a) True ❏
b) False ❏
c) It doesn't matter ❏
d) None of the above ❏

6. It's not good to use both an emotional proof and a logical proof to support the same point.
a) True ❏
b) False ❏
c) It doesn't matter ❏
d) None of the above ❏

7. The Presentation Planning Matrix allows you to
a) customize your presentation to your audience ❏
b) plan the number of points you'll use in advance ❏
c) plan the number of proofs you'll use in advance ❏
d) all of the above ❏

8. The Matrix also allows you to
a) have high impact with your proof ❏
b) deliver with a high degree of professionalism ❏
c) end on time while still including all your points effectively ❏
d) all of the above ❏

9. If you're going to speak at a conference, a good question to ask the organizer in advance is:
a) How long should I speak? ❏
b) What is the composition of the audience? ❏
c) When the audience leaves the room, what feeling or knowledge do you want them to be left with? ❏
d) All of the above ❏

10. If you start to speak on a paid basis, you may want to
a) ask if there are any sensitive issues they don't want mentioned ❏
b) develop a questionnaire so that you can customize your talk to the needs of the group ❏
c) ask if there are people or groups they want acknowledged ❏
d) all of the above ❏

CHAPTER 7

Put icing on the cake of professionalism

Now it's time to put the icing on the cake. You've learned how to plan and deliver your presentation for high impact. But what about the extras that might come up?

For example, the way you handle questions and answers after your presentation, can help you stand above the crowd professionally. Or, how you handle a microphone – you'll want to avoid annoying feedback.

And, what about introducing guest speakers? You'll learn about a 1 – 3 – 6 – 1 formula that makes introductions a breeze. And, you'll have an equally effective guideline for thanking a speaker. And, finally there are awards, wedding toasts and even eulogies. You'll be able to give these with an air of professionalism by using the uniquely helpful formulas included here.

Thus in this chapter you will learn:

- How to breeze through Q & A sessions
- The pros and cons of PowerPoint presentations
- How to handle a microphone
- A powerful formula for introducing a guest speaker
- How to prepare your own introduction
- Formulas for weddings and eulogies
- How to thank a speaker
- How to graciously give and accept awards
- Social media applications

Breeze through Q & A sessions

Your listeners love variety. They don't want just one offering. They've heard your speech. That was the main course and they've had enough. Now they want to participate. They want the surprise element. Your Q & A session is their dessert – the icing on the cake, a smorgasbord of desserts!

There's no need to fear the questions, in fact the Q & A session gives you a chance to expand on your points, and often allows you to restate the credibility of your points.

When answering, give yourself time to think. A good way to do this is to repeat the question. Listeners like this. They can't always hear the question. And while you are repeating the question, ideas will rush to your head. Trust yourself, they will.

In addition there are two methods of generating ideas as you repeat the question. One is to prepare a list of points in advance that you couldn't fit into your presentation. Glance at it as you repeat the question. Choose a point that could link to the question asked. Then start to talk about it and weave your answer in the direction of the question.

The second method is to think of your life experiences even vaguely relating to the question. Let yourself start to talk about those areas, and then more material will come to your mind related to the question as you speak. Try to review your experiences from the exercises in Chapter 2 before your presentation so that your mind will respond more quickly.

Always thank the questioner immediately *before* you give the answer. This makes you feel good, the questioner feel good, and the audience feel good. It sets up rapport between you and them.

Give acknowledgment

You can say one of the following:

'Thank you for that question.'

'That's an excellent question.'

'I'm glad you asked that.'

'Thank you.'

You'll find the 'thank you' that you give to the first questioner will set up a safe environment for others to ask questions. It brings harmony into the room. Don't neglect it.

The pros and cons of PowerPoint presentations

There are definite pros and cons to using PowerPoint slides during your presentation.

The negative side is this. While people are looking at the screen, what do you think they are connecting with – you or the screen? Yes, the screen, of course. Thus you may lose that all important connection.

The positive side is this. Your listeners can take in your points through their visual senses as well as their hearing senses.

If you watch the most powerful company CEOs and professional speakers, you'll notice that they seldom use PowerPoint slides at all, and if so, they use them as an accent. They may put up an important point once or twice in a 20 to 40 minute presentation.

But let's say you like PowerPoint slides or that it's expected in your industry or company. What now? How do you make it the best it can be and still connect with your listeners? The best way is to reduce the number of words. Some professionals think that six words should be the maximum per slide. And of course, pictures are worth a 1000 words. Often a good sketch and a few words make your presentation memorable.

However, as you learned in previous chapters, the picture you paint through your incident/story will have far more lasting impact than a sketch on a slide. Why? Because you create an emotional link with your story, and with your eye contact, that cannot be created between a viewer and a slide.

Remember too, that if you like visual media, there are many other options besides PowerPoint slides. You might consider video clips, clips from YouTube, or even music if the lyrics match your message and suit your audience.

It's your presentation and your group. So experiment and try to move out of the traditional box. Doing so will not only bring you satisfaction it will be a relief to your listeners to have variety and something new.

How to handle a microphone

Perhaps you'll be asked to use a microphone during your presentation. What then? Should you turn it down? If not, why not?

Look at it this way. Without a microphone, people won't hear you well and they'll be annoyed. They've come to hear you and suddenly they're at a disadvantage if you don't use it.

Secondly, you've taken time and great effort to prepare your presentation. Logically, why would you not want it to be heard? The answer is simple. It's fear. And fear comes from lack of practice. The solution is practice. You should practise now because you never know when someone will thrust a microphone into your hand and you'll have to use it. It's true. I've seen it happen to people many, many times.

If you act uncomfortably with a microphone, it will draw more attention to yourself. You probably want just the opposite. My guess is that you want high professionalism.

So let's practise now.

Practise using the microphone now

First, take a piece of ordinary paper and roll it up into a one inch diameter roll. Now hold it up on an angle of 45 degrees from your mouth.

Most neophytes hold it straight up. Don't do that. That's wrong for two reasons. First it doesn't pick up sound properly when it's straight up and down and can set off a ghastly feedback noise. It picks up better sound when facing your mouth. Secondly if you hold it up and down, it tips you off as a neophyte. Someone from the sound department might have to come to your rescue and show you how to do it in front of everyone. That's bound to distress you *and* your listeners. Better to practise it now.

Next is distance. How close, how far from the mouth? The answer is this – fist distance! Practise like this. Hold your 'paper microphone' in one hand. Now make a fist with your other hand and put it up to your lips. Then put the mic on the other side of your fist. That's the right distance. If you put it closer, the sound will really be distorted. Again the system can give off feedback and hurt everyone's ears. If you put it further away, it doesn't pick up your sound.

Lapel or earpiece microphone

Of course if you have a lapel or ear piece mic, and *if* the sound people wire you up and check it in advance, you don't have too much to worry about. Just be sure you don't bang it as you move, and always remember to turn it off at breaks during personal discussions or use of the ladies'/men's rooms. Don't laugh. It happens often!

Powerful formula for introducing a guest speaker

If you've ever had to introduce a speaker, did you consider it a privilege and opportunity that you looked forward to with joy? Or did you anticipate it with shaky knees?

If you are like most people, it was the latter. There are probably two reasons.

1 Lack of professional 'know how' and practice.
2 Not being sure what to say.

In this section you will conquer both roadblocks. Consider this. You have the privilege of setting the meeting tone and mood. You can make it wonderful. You can make the audience feel privileged. You can make the topic important. You can make the speaker important – and indeed they are, or you would not have invited them to address your group.

Look at it this way. If the speaker talks for 45 minutes, and you have 20 people attending, that's 15 man hours being used to listen to that speaker. The same 15 man hours could be used for something else, but they are not. People are there to hear your speaker. Isn't it worth giving them an introduction that sets a positive tone? Of course it is. If you don't, the audience will wish they hadn't come. So set aside your anxieties and dig into the most professional introduction you can create.

Here is a superb introduction formula from our Effective Presentation Seminars. It's professional and gives credit where credit is due. It makes your attendees happy they've come, and it puts you in a good light.

The 1-3-6-1 formula for introductions

A. Subject or Title – Give **1** sentence

B. Why important to group – Give **3** examples

C. Why speaker is qualified – Give **6** reasons

D. Welcome speaker – Give **1** name

When you flesh it out it will sound like this:

A. The subject (or title of our talk) today is ...

B. The subject is important to us because ... (give 3 reasons)

C. Our speaker is extremely qualified because ... (give 6 qualifications)

D. Please help me welcome ... (Name)

Preparing your own introduction

When I first started speaking professionally, I read that speakers should prepare their own introduction. I was quite shocked by this idea. It seemed very arrogant.

The writer went on to say that we are the professionals and it is important to the audience to find out who is speaking to them and why they are qualified. He warned that it is foolhardy not to prepare our own introduction, because without it, the organizers won't know what to say. It is our *obligation* to brief them, for the sake of the audience.

Since then, I've discovered this advice to be sound. I've discovered that the majority of conference organizers welcome introductions prepared by speakers. It takes the worry out of it for them. Why? Because they know that you will be happy with it, that it's accurate and it's professionally prepared. It makes them look good too.

Simply follow the 1-3-6-1 formula for preparing your own introduction.

On the few occasions in which the introduction didn't reach the correct person before the speech, I've found that one of three things can happen. All are detrimental.

First is that the facts are often wrong because the introducer was not briefed properly. The second is that the introducer, often ill at ease with speaking, tries to make a joke as part of the introduction and it fails miserably. Third is that they fail to set up the importance of your speech topic to the audience. This failure to link your topic to the audience's interests or needs, gives your speech a not-so-promising start.

What steps should you take therefore in briefing your introducer? Simply email or fax an introduction which is specifically prepared for each group. Include a cover letter, saying that they may use it in full or in part. Thus you've taken a load off their shoulders and given them permission to shorten it if they wish.

Let's move on to other uses for the 1-3-6-1 formula.

Formula for wedding speeches and toasts

The 1-3-6-1 formula can be used for wedding speeches as well. It looks like this.

A Give 1 sentence about the reason you are all there ... (To honour the bride and groom and families, etc.)

B Give 3 memories you have of the groom and/or bride and why they are important in your life. An incident/story is powerful here.

C Give 6 wishes you have for their future ... (blessings for their health, happiness, prosperity, etc.)

D Propose your toast.

Formula for eulogies

Eulogies follow the same format except that point C should include six of the person's qualities and/or achievements in life and career, as well as their impact on family, friends, community, etc. Point D can be a prayer or a wish from your heart.

Now let's move on to thanking a guest speaker or conference speaker.

How to thank a speaker

If you've been chosen to thank a speaker, start by considering it to be an honour, just as we discussed in introducing a speaker. Here too you have an opportunity to uplift your event, making both the audience and speaker feel honoured. That's important for the morale of the group.

With the formula below, you will *not* have to worry ahead of time. You will use this as a framework and fill in the appropriate points *as the speaker speaks*.

In fact, it's far better not to prepare a thank you in advance because it will not link closely to the speaker's message. This 'canned' approach can be interpreted as superficial to the audience and speaker. It's better to use the formula below and speak from your heart, unless of course you have the speaker's text in advance.

Formula for thanking a speaker

You'll be surprised how easily this formula can be used on the spot.

1 **Thank you**, (Name)
2 **What the person said** that: *(choose one)*

   a) you liked

   b) helped you, or

   c) caught your attention

3 **Group benefit**: What the person said that is likely to help or benefit the group.
4 **How you'll remember** the speaker and their contribution (For example, 'Every time I see a rose in the future, I know I'll think of your helpful suggestions about horticulture.'
5 **Express appreciation** for their time and sharing their expertise. If you are presenting a gift, do that now.
6 **Thank**: Please join me in thanking, (Name of speaker) Start the applause.

Give and accept awards

Now let's look at another aspect of speaking, that of giving and receiving awards. Even if you're not going to give or receive an award now, it will prepare you in developing your professionalism. And who knows – you may receive an award when you least expect it!

Present an award

In giving awards, it's quite suspenseful if you leave the name of the award winner until the end, just as we did in the introduction.

Formula for presenting an award
1 **What** the award is and why the award was created.
2 **Who** chose the winner.
3 **Why** that winner was chosen.
4 **Who** won (Name) Then, applaud.
5 Invite the winner to the front, present the award or plaque, shake hands, and applaud again.

Let's look at an example. It's one we use in our seminars to acknowledge one person who shows exceptional promise:

Example

1 *'It's my pleasure to present to one of you this gold plated pen, with this inscription.* (Hold the pen up and read the inscription.) *This award was created to acknowledge exceptional contribution.*
2 *You, the winner, were chosen by the vote of your fellow delegates.*
3 *You were chosen on the basis of the action plans you devised, which you will carry out when you get back to the office.*
4 *Now, it's with great pleasure that I present this award, on behalf of your fellow delegates to* (Name).'
   (Applaud)
5 *'Please come to the front.'* (Shake hands and give award).
   (Applaud)

How to accept an award

If you are going to accept an award sometime in the future, memorize this simple format. It will be easy to follow as you stand and accept the award. It will be sincere and spontaneous and the group will love your response.

Formula for accepting an award

1 **Thank** those responsible.
2 Tell what the **award means** to you.
3 Tell how you'll **use the award**, or where you'll display it.
4 Tell how you'll **remember the group** fondly.
5 **Thank** them again.

Example

1 *'I want to thank all of you, my fellow delegates, for voting for me. I'm highly honoured. I also want to thank Mrs Leventhal and Mr Brown, our instructors, for their support.*
2 *This award means a lot to me and I commit to you now to put everything into practice as we discussed in this workshop.*
3 *I'm going to keep this pen close to my heart here (shows breast pocket of jacket) and*
4 *Every time I use it, I'll think of our group and your support.*
5 *Thank you very much.'*

When you sit down after your acceptance talk, you'll feel very good about yourself. That's important. Don't give in to a simple *'Thank you'* or worse yet, the humble denial, *'I hardly deserve this... .'* Why? Because these discredit those who chose you. You are a winner. Otherwise you wouldn't be chosen. By visualizing yourself accepting an award calmly and composed, you'll handle it as an everyday event when the time comes.

Have you ever watched people presenting and accepting awards in the film industry on television? If so, you'll notice that the same fundamentals are followed. We discover who gave the award and why. The winner thanks those responsible and says why they appreciate the award.

If your award presentation is going to be televised or filmed on video, you should practise the eye contact exercises in Chapter 1. Don't let yourself be distracted by the lights or the cameras. Ignore them and keep concentrating on the audience. If you act naturally, you'll come across as a professional. If you do need to look directly into the camera, which happens in some interviews, keep concentrating on the fact that there is only one person sitting in their own living room watching you. Think of it like a conversation, and you'll be fine.

Social media application

Let's think about all the points covered in this chapter as they could relate to the various social media outlets. As we said in the beginning, the points in this chapter are the icing on the cake of professionalism.

On YouTube and any use of video, how you handle the microphone is paramount. You won't want to make the mistake of some YouTube presenters who have a stationary mic positioned on their desk, and then proceed to shift their body back and forth away from the mic. This results in the sound level going from high to low, high to low, and high to low, like a yoyo! If you like to move around a lot, then a lapel or an earpiece mic is the best solution. Some presenters like the look and feel of a hand-held mic, or a stationary mic on a table top is fine, but then you must keep your mouth the same distance from the mic at all times, even if you move your hands and arms for emphasis.

What about virtual meetings, teleconferences and web conferencing? There you'll have an opportunity to introduce and thank guest speakers according to the formulas in this chapter.

With teleconferences and video you may find a PowerPoint format to be effective, utilizing a few key words rather than long sentences or jam-packed slides.

Q & A can be effectively utilized in both video/YouTube and text formats, even if you are the sole presenter. Simply use the most common or relevant questions, attributing them to a person if appropriate, and then give your answer.

Be sure to refer to the social media sections near the end of each chapter to maximize your personal impact.

A final word

In closing, I'd like to thank you all for reading this masterclass and preparing to heighten your communication, personal impact and leadership skills. Dale Carnegie, the legendary instructor of public speaking, was once told that the graduates from his course were more powerful speakers than most senators in the United States. This will happen to you as you apply these principles. As I said in the introduction, it's a pity to have a good education but not be able to put a point across with high impact. That's not something we're born with, it's something we must learn and practise.

Now go forward and let your thoughts be known! Your ideas are important to the world.

Summary

In this chapter you learned that listeners love variety and that Q & A sessions are like a smorgasbord of desserts for them. You learned to repeat their question, thus giving your mind time to conceive your answer. You also learned two ways to jog your mind for answers, including a pre-prepared bullet list and reliance on your background strengths.

You learned several high impact formulas to use for specific presentations. These include the 1-3-6-1 formula for introducing a speaker, preparing your own introduction, wedding and eulogy speeches, plus thanking a speaker, and presenting and accepting an award. All of these formulas provide you with a fool-proof way to make your job easy and your professionalism high.

And what if you choose to use PowerPoint slides? You discovered that they can disconnect you from your audience, and that limited use is best, especially with limited number of words per screen. Additionally you had practice using a microphone. Yes, practice, even without the mic! You learned that the 'fist' distance and the 45 degree angle of the mic are all important in avoiding the screeching sound of mic feedback.

Fact-check (answers at the back)

1. There is no need to fear Q & A sessions because they give you the following benefits:
   a) A chance to expand on your points ❏
   b) A chance to restate your credibility, giving validity to your points ❏
   c) None of the above ❏
   d) All of the above ❏

2. In Q & A sessions it's a good idea to repeat the question before you answer because
   a) it gives you time to think ❏
   b) it allows listeners to hear the question well ❏
   c) while you repeat it, answers will come to your mind ❏
   d) all of the above ❏

3. There are two good methods for generating your answers during Q & A. They are:
   a) Refer to a pre-prepared bullet list ❏
   b) Think back over your wide ranging experience ❏
   c) Both of the above ❏
   d) None of the above ❏

4. During Q & A it's always good to thank the person asking the question. Why?
   a) It makes you feel good ❏
   b) It makes the questioner feel good ❏
   c) It makes the audience feel good ❏
   d) All of the above ❏

5. Why do PowerPoint slides often cause you to lose connection with your audience?
   a) You lose eye contact ❏
   b) You lose emotional link ❏
   c) Both of the above ❏
   d) Neither of the above ❏

6. When using microphones, the two most important factors are angle and distance. How far should the mic be from your lips?
   a) two inches ❏
   b) finger distance ❏
   c) fist distance ❏
   d) six inches ❏

7. The introduction formula is called 1 – 3 – 6 – 1. What does the 3 stand for?
   a) 3 minutes before the presentation starts ❏
   b) 3 reasons the message will be important to the group ❏
   c) 3 questions that must be answered ❏
   d) 3 people who would be involved ❏

8. It's okay to prepare your own introduction and pass it on to the conference organizer because
   a) it sets up the right background for your presentation ❏
   b) it takes a load off the organizer ❏
   c) both a and b above ❏
   d) neither a nor b above ❏

9. In thanking a speaker, it is better to
a) prepare your comments in advance ❑
b) prepare your comments as they speak, using the formula ❑
c) pass the job on to someone else ❑
d) none of the above ❑

10. In accepting an award, it's a good idea to ❑
a) thank those responsible ❑
b) tell what the award means to you ❑
c) tell how you'll use or display the award ❑
d) all of the above ❑

7 × 7

1 Seven reasons to develop your skills

- Career advancement happens when you know how to ask for a salary increase and can communicate your vision, knowledge, ideas; when you can make impactful presentations and present yourself confidently.
- Family success happens when you see, hear and speak about the needs of others and merge them with your own, so that all people gain.
- Financial escalation comes as a result of career advancement, goal setting, courage and leadership, which all depend on your ability to develop your power of expression and personal impact.
- Self-development and self-discovery are achieved only when you continue to delve into new areas, explore your own potential, and develop your skills throughout your lifetime. Speaking and communication skills are some of the highest on the list.
- Role modeling: your actions to master these skills will impact your family, your colleagues, employees, and community members. That's true Personal Impact!
- Continual self-fulfillment cancels out self-doubt, fears and negative feelings that are holding you back. It allows you to go from strength to strength and look back at an exciting and successful life.
- Self-confidence can be your ultimate goal. Think about this quote from Mr Morita, founder of the Sony Corporation: 'We have to keep trying new things to keep our confidence up.' He said this when he was asked why he wanted to learn to fly a helicopter.

2 Seven keys to success

- Push yourself to conquer your fear. Remember that the people who move ahead the fastest, and achieve the highest heights are the ones who have conquered the fear of speaking out at meetings and going up to a microphone. Push yourself little by little *daily*. Don't miss any opportunity.
- Eye contact is essential. Know that making eye contact is one of the most impactful things you can do, both one-on-one *and* with an audience.
- Inspire others to take action. Use the Presentation Planning Matrix from Chapter 6 to powerfully impact your audience or listeners. This will motivate your listeners to grasp your message and run with it.
- Trust that you will learn. Learning a totally new sport is difficult. Therefore keep practicing the tools of this book knowing that soon you will do these things subconsciously and effectively.
- Motivate yourself towards continual improvement. Keep a list of your successes after trying each of the tools and techniques. Review the list frequently.
- Know your goal. Keep in mind *why* you want to gain these skills. It's essential to remember why you are giving time and effort to learning these new skills.
- Know that persistence is power. If children were afraid to fall, they would never learn to walk. Take the same attitude of persistence even if you do not seem to succeed as fast as you like.

3 Seven things to do today

- Watch out for social media examples. Think of a person you admire from social media and examine what they do or say to enhance their person credibility. Now decide what *you* can do to create an effect that is equally compelling.

- Explore television examples. Watch television or the internet news and focus on the facial gestures people make. Practise the ones that you feel make the most impact.
- Magnify your message. Remember that gestures with your hands and arms serve to magnify your message. Read the Chapter 1 and then try using gestures yourself as you speak.
- Master logical proof and emotional proof. Chapter 3 will give you these powerful methods.
- Practise analogies. They will give your message extra power. Chapter 4 will make you an expert.
- Practise with every person you encounter. Realize that people don't learn these skills in school. Take today to choose one chapter for focus. Practise these tools at work, home and with every person you encounter.
- Make a list of all your important successes and then determine what lesson was learned from each. Make the lesson short, such as 'Persistence pays.' Keep this list and use these stories for 'personal proof points' when you speak. See Chapter 4 for ideas.

4 Seven questions to ask yourself

- How high do you think your career will progress if you become a world-class expert at putting your point across?
- What is your goal? Is it for confidence, a pay rise, personal growth, a feeling of satisfaction? How strong is your goal? Keep it in mind each time you push yourself to try one of the tools herein.
- What strengths can *you* draw upon to project *your* credibility? See Chapter 2 for ideas and apply them to your own experiences and skills.
- Which stories will make your message stick? What story from your personal life, or that of others, can you use to touch the hearts and minds of listeners and make your message stick?
- Can you overcome your fears of speaking? Surveys show that most people are more afraid of speaking in public than dying! So you're not alone. Let your reason for learning

inspire you as you learn tips from this book each day and watch your success soar.

- Why do you want to improve your personal impact? Envision it. Keeping this in mind daily will motivate you to practise and improve.
- How long will it take for you to become proficient? A surprising statistic is that people can become world experts by studying one subject each day for 10 minutes. Practise the principles from this masterclass each day for 10 minutes. Your success will begin the day you start!

5 Seven things to avoid

- Avoid quoting public figures unless you are *sure* that *all* your listeners approve of the person you are quoting. Instead, use statistics or analogies for persuasion.
- Don't ramble. Instead get to the point using the tools you learn here. Your audience will respect you for not wasting their time.
- Don't start with a joke – it could fall flat. Instead, open with a question or a show of hands. Master openings and closings (see Chapter 5).
- Avoid visualizing negative results. Instead, visualize your success just before you speak.
- Avoid thinking you'll make a fool of yourself. Instead, remember that people who get promoted and are respected are the ones who speak out. Often your ideas will be as good as or better than theirs.
- Avoid listening to people who discourage you from trying these skills. Their doubts could be based on their own fears that have nothing to do with you.
- Avoid the fear of using these new tools when speaking anywhere. Don't go back to your old ways even if other speakers use outdated, ineffective methods. They will not succeed, you *will* succeed.

6 Seven ways to stay motivated

- Consider additional resources for continual improvement and practice – see Chapter 7 for ideas.
- Commit to trying to speak up using these tools suggested in Chapter 7. Then do it again, using a different tool from another chapter.
- Congratulate yourself EACH TIME you push yourself to speak up at a meeting or one on one.
- Start small: if you're afraid to speak up, then make yourself try it. Bask in the glory of small successes. Overcoming fear is a step-by-step process.
- Then take bigger steps next time. Start by simply verbalizing your support for someone else's idea. Then gradually add to it with your own ideas.
- Think about how high your self-esteem will soar if you become highly proficient at putting your point across. You'll discover that your results are limitless as you progress.
- Don't feel dejected after you speak if no one congratulates you. Most people simply don't know how to give you their support.

7 Seven application areas

- Overcome your fear of speaking in meetings and in public
- Enhance your credibility through speaking, social media and leadership
- Structure your presentation to prove your point powerfully
- Grab and hold your audience's attention
- Handle questions and answers fearlessly
- Handle a microphone effectively when accepting and presenting awards
- Introduce and thank guest speakers, give toasts, eulogies & impromptu speeches

PART 2
Your Networking Masterclass

Introduction

Networking is a word that is firmly embedded in our vocabulary. It is not unusual to hear the word used to describe a range of activities and behaviours.

The **activities** of a successful networker are often focussed on outcomes. Our research and observations suggest that successful networkers build their networks by developing close relationships with work colleagues, professional communities and associations and virtually, through social and professional networking sites, referrals and references from friends or colleagues.

The **behaviours** of a successful networker are often social. Successful networkers may be considered to be gregarious; when you observe them, it becomes clear they build relationships through empathic connections, being respectful, purposeful and reciprocal relationships that are founded on principles such as 'do as you would be done by'.

Individuals respond to the word **network** in different ways. While researching the material for this masterclass, we talked to many people and found diametrically opposed views. At one extreme, there were those who were vehemently opposed to networking:

I wouldn't dream of using people in such a manipulative way!

I hate asking for favours!

I dread going when the invitation says it's a networking event!

At the other end of the extreme, we found strong believers in networking who enjoyed the benefits of their well-developed network:

I couldn't exist without it!

Professionally and personally, it's a lifesaver!

I've been given opportunities that I would have missed otherwise!

However you respond to the word, networks can make the difference for you personally and professionally. This masterclass is designed to help you understand, benefit from and develop your network.

CHAPTER 8

Networks and networking

Traditionally, organizations were structured as relatively self-contained units and those who operated within them were assigned clearly defined roles. This level of structure, definition and order meant that most internal processes were routine and the channels of communication were well mapped. Today, organizations are very different. Hierarchy and 'chains of command' have been replaced by fluid, organic arrangements in a global context that can respond rapidly to the needs of the market.

Jobs at all levels of any organization are no longer defined by a set of impersonal and technical tasks. Managers' performance is judged on their ability to deliver, adapt and add value by being creative and 'fleet of foot'. Their success will be dependent upon their understanding of the relationships that exist inside and outside the organization and their ability to invest in them using their networking skills.

Building and managing your network is not only your key to organizational success, it supports and nourishes you personally. However, as a concept, networking is in need of demystifying. Let's look first at the *Webster's Dictionary* definition:

n. 'A fabric or structure of cords or wires that cross at regular intervals and are knotted or secured at the crossings'

v. 'To make connections among people or groups'

What you require from your network will undoubtedly vary. Your networking goals may be formal and structured, such as meeting peers and asking for their advice on how to achieve your career goals. Or they may be informal and unstructured, such as contacting a friend and saying: 'Am I going crazy? You'll never believe what happened to me today!' Or semi-formal and structured, such as the social networking sites that have proliferated on the Internet.

Networking is not a precise science, nor is it an entirely tangible range of activities and behaviours. To help you understand networking, we are going to give you a framework that focuses on the benefits and types of networks. This chapter gives the following overview:

- Networks:
  - Network types
  - Network relationships
  - Networks? What networks?!
- Networking:
  - Networking styles.

Networks

If you were to take a bird's-eye view of your life and focus on your relationships and networks, it would soon become clear that they are both complex and dynamic. Networks spring from different sources; they are established in different environments and serve different purposes.

Network types

Your relationships evolve mainly through associations. These may have developed through a variety of circumstances, such as attending the same school or college, living in the same area or working in the same organization. Or they may have evolved through your interests, your desire to be in regular contact with people you know, or your wish to meet new people.

We have identified four basic types of network:

- personal
- organizational
- professional
- social.

The relationships we establish through these networks are active and reciprocal – and their boundaries are sometimes blurred. For example, relationships initially established through working together (your organizational network) often progress to friendships and, as such, become part of your personal or social network – where your engagement and expectations are different.

Personal networks

These include: friends, family and acquaintances or 'friends' you have made on the social networking sites. Whether they are face-to-face or virtual, personal networks often emerge around a school, college, church, sports club, shared interest or activity. Generally, you choose your personal networks based upon liking, reciprocity, mutual connections or interests. Personal networks tend to be social; they are usually developed outside the working environment and are based upon an exchange of help and support.

Organizational networks

The range of social, cultural and technological processes that have existed in the more traditional, hierarchical, organizations are now breaking down, resulting in devolution of power and responsibility. This promotes sharing information and co-working in order to pursue common objectives, solve problems and satisfy the expectations and needs of internal and external stakeholders.

Team and project work are now common in today's organizations. They don't have the restrictions of departments, divisions, culture, locality or hierarchy. Teams, project groups, committees and councils all provide ideal conditions for networking. When you put together a team or become part of a project, you've assembled a vast and powerful network.

These networks are normally focussed and developed on the basis of who you need to know in order to meet your objective within a particular timescale. They are not necessarily based on status, but on knowledge, skills and influence. A key strategy, when joining a new department, division or organization is to identify the organizational network as soon as possible, and in particular, those with overt and covert power.

Professional networks

Professional networks are normally made up of associates, colleagues, suppliers and clients. Professional networks are built around common work interests and tasks. They can be formal networks to which you affiliate, such as institutes, societies, alumni groups and professional associations. Or they can be more fluid and exploratory, such as those held on LinkedIn®. They can also be less formal, such as a voluntary group that comes together over a set of values or a charitable cause.

Whereas a personal network is determined by whom you like, a professional network is created around knowledge and circumstances. Your professional networks will no doubt change over time. You may, for example, join an organization that reflects your technical speciality at the beginning of your career. As your career develops, you may join other organizations that reflect your changing responsibilities, aspirations and interests. You may also be invited to participate in executive or non-executive roles that place you in a wider professional, and perhaps more diverse, network.

Social networks

The opportunity to make personal connections of global scope is now only one click away. Social networks – now too many to name – have enjoyed exponential growth and many of them count their members by tens, if not hundreds, of millions. The blessing and the curse of this phenomenon is access to people you would probably never have encountered in your everyday life – a blessing because the social and cultural barriers have almost completely dissolved, a curse because it is difficult to manage the myriad 'friends' and the flow of information that stems from them.

Increased exposure and visibility are two of the outcomes of social networking, again, bringing both advantages and disadvantages. If you seek notoriety, it is there for the taking. If you seek privacy, you may be disappointed.

Network relationships

Regardless of the type of network in which you operate, you will be forming relationships for different reasons. The most basic reason is need. We are social creatures by nature and need the approval and feedback provided by those with whom we relate. Not only this, but also we need the more practical assistance and guidance that our network can offer us. You will no doubt benefit from your networks in different ways:

Networks provide:

- information
- development
- support
- influence.

Information
Every manager needs information for gaining new perspectives. Information in the form of data on trends, markets and opportunities facilitate sound planning. Information is not solely about the future; being well-informed means that you can tackle situations before they occur, anticipate problems and manage tricky situations. Our action can also be influenced by information on options, strategies and possible solutions.

Development
Managers are confronted by an ever-changing environment. For this reason, they need to be constantly developing their skills and behaviours. Development can take many forms. Traditionally, training was the route to development but today there are many other forms of development at our disposal. Coaching and mentoring have gained popularity as a time and money efficient approach to targeted development.

Support

Our well-being depends on feeling supported. Perhaps we only recognize its importance when it is removed. Support can be as simple as someone showing an interest, being there or offering guidance or practical help.

Influence

Networks can give you access to resources and political muscle. In the short term, these are clearly important to your success. However, these networks can also be important to your long-term future. Identifying key people, who can open doors, sponsor and be an advocate for you can make a real difference to your career.

Defining these categories of networks should provide you with the framework you require to look objectively at yours and make the necessary judgements about how to build and manage them. The key to successful networking is balance. We have heard managers say:

'All my energy has been concentrated on work. I'm not sure if I still have any friends!'

'I seem to spend all my time supporting others. Who's supporting me?!'

Many people concentrate their efforts on organizational networks to the detriment of their personal networks. Or the relationships in their networks become one-sided. Many networks have evolved rather than been planned and, as a result, they can become unbalanced and demanding. Networks need monitoring and reviewing to ensure that they are still serving their purpose and are beneficial to all members.

Networks? What networks?!

Networks do not exist by magic. They develop as a result of an investment of time and energy. Unfortunately, investment in one area can result in a lack of investment in another. Think about the kind of relationships you have in your networks. Do you currently have restricted access to information, development, support or influence? If so, what adjustments would benefit you?

Networks evolve over time; they change shape and size according to your interests and circumstances. Ask yourself the following questions:

What do I want from my network?
Is my network serving me?
How could my network work better for me?

It is important to ask yourself these key questions regularly. If you are clear about what you want, you can be precise in your networking.

Networking

The benefits of establishing and maintaining effective relationships are well documented. Most people recognize that relationships are vitally important in all areas of life. Your personal happiness, satisfaction and your physical well-being depend on the quality of your relationships. Networking is all about relationships!

Before we move on, try answering the following questions. Do you:

- usually accept opportunities to meet new people?
- have contacts in a wide variety of groups?
- feel that you're generally well informed?
- share information with those around you?
- stay in close contact with your customers or clients?
- regularly attend meetings, training courses and conferences?
- know and talk to peers in other organizations?

If you answered no to any of the above, think about the reasons why. What prevents you?

To be successful at networking, you need to have an interest in building relationships and create opportunities for doing so. This can be achieved by adopting different styles. You may recognize your style from the following model.

Networking styles

When you start on any journey, you have choices. You will choose your means of transportation, your preferred route and your schedule. Networking is like planning a journey. First, you have to be clear about your destination and then you have to make your choices. These will depend upon:

- the time available
- how specific your destination is.

You also have choices regarding your style of networking. The main styles of networking are:

- targeted
- intuitive
- open.

Targeted
Targeted networkers recognize the gaps in their networks. They identify opportunities to exploit and people to fill the gaps. This style is often used by those seeking career development and for creating purposeful alliances.

Intuitive
Intuitive networkers are natural catalysts and enablers. Their relationships are based on mutuality and are prompted by common needs or values. Naturally, they develop strong and wide networks. However, the focus for all their networks tends to be altruistic, and sometimes intuitive networkers have trouble translating their networks into something that can benefit them.

Open
Open networkers tend to travel in a defined direction. They invest in networks for their future potential. They develop new networks to match their interests and careers.

So, what's your natural networking style?

Summary

We began this chapter by proposing that networks and networking could be the key to your personal happiness and professional success. If your continued happiness and success are important to you, we suggest that you take this proposition seriously. Networking is not a miracle cure or a fad. Networks are all around us. It is how we use and benefit from them that can make all the difference to our futures.

Take the time to understand:

Your networks

- Types
  - Personal
  - Organizational
  - Professional
  - Social
- Benefits
  - Information
  - Development
  - Support
  - Influence
- Your networking style
  - Targeted
  - Intuitive
  - Open

Challenge yourself with these questions:
- How has my network developed?
- What does my network look like?
- How comfortable do I feel with networking?
- What is my style?
- What do I want from my network?
- How could I network more effectively?
- What do I need to do differently?

In each chapter, we'll build on your responses to these questions.

Fact-check (answers at the back)

Answer the following questions honestly, reflecting on your approach to networking:

1. **What do you believe is the purpose of networking?**
   a) To build a dynamic community ❏
   b) To assist others get what they want ❏
   c) To get what you want ❏
   d) To give you the upper hand ❏

2. **How do you feel about your networking abilities?**
   a) I use my network when I need assistance ❏
   b) To build 'credit' in my network by helping others ❏
   c) I avoid asking others for help ❏
   d) I think networking is manipulative and I dislike it ❏

3. **What is your preferred style of networking?**
   a) Conscious ❏
   b) Intuitive ❏
   c) Open ❏
   d) I don't network ❏

4. **How often do you access your network?**
   a) 1–2 day ❏
   b) 1–2 week ❏
   c) 1–2 month ❏
   d) Hardly ever ❏

5. **What kind of networks do you build?**
   a) Personal ❏
   b) Organizational ❏
   c) Professional ❏
   d) Social ❏

6. **Primarily, what do you use your networks for?**
   a) Information ❏
   b) Development ❏
   c) Support ❏
   d) Influence ❏

7. **Reflecting on your network, what has been the most useful/helpful outcome?**
   a) A new role or organization ❏
   b) Essential commercial information ❏
   c) I have built some important personal/business relationships ❏
   d) I have had fun ❏

8. **What does your network look like?**
   a) It is diverse ❏
   b) It is focussed on my profession/specialism/role ❏
   c) It is predominantly social ❏
   d) It is based around my interests ❏

9. **How could you network more effectively?**

a) I could be more proactive ❏
b) Being more effective would be challenging ❏
c) I could seek new networks ❏
d) I could regularly communicate with my network ❏

10. **How do you manage your network?**

a) I prune contacts that I no longer need ❏
b) My network manages me ❏
c) I communicate with each person regularly ❏
d) I invite new members to join my network ❏

CHAPTER 9

Personal networks

You are born into a network. Personal networks are central to your early development: supporting, teaching and guiding you. As you grow older, some of these functions are replaced by institutions, organizations or significant others – and the importance of your family network changes.

You never lose your need for personal networks and, as you mature, they remain as important to your well-being as they ever were in your formative years. You may, however, become focussed on other networks. We have often heard managers admit that their personal networks are small compared to their professional networks. Indeed, they may be solely focussed on their nuclear family and a few friends. This happens mainly because they have spent time putting emphasis on their professional networks to the detriment of those in their close circle.

Personal networks are usually based on mutuality and liking. You meet many people throughout your life but only a few of these would be classified as friends and allowed into your personal network. You can gauge eligibility using a number of indicators. Personal networks are made up of those whom you:

● choose to spend time with
● invite to your home
● miss, if deprived of their company.

Think for a moment about your personal network.

Personal networks need investment, development, nurturing and commitment. This is not a simple task. It can be more challenging to develop a personal network than any professional or organizational network because you have to build the structure. It is easy to take the goodwill of those in our personal network for granted. Being as conscious of these people as we are of those in our professional network is very important. We will begin by identifying methods to help you.

This chapter discusses:

● Recognizing personal networks
● Developing networks
● Nurturing networks

Recognizing personal networks

There are many personal networks at your disposal.

Education

When we mention personal networks established through education, we are not only talking about old school friends. Your school ties may have remained strong, but many find they have little in common with school friends beyond their shared experience at school. It is more likely that the personal relationships you established in your later educational career will stand the test of time. The strength of these networks is often based upon an interest in a specific subject, entry into a similar profession or on shared formative memories.

Work

We meet many people through work, including:

- bosses
- colleagues
- peers
- subordinates
- suppliers
- customers.

The proximity of working relationships and the time you spend at work creates an environment in which close friendships and partnerships can develop. Other networks develop through extracurricular activities such as a social club, health club, interest groups, commuting together, or something as informal as a drink after work.

The personal networks established though work can be powerful.

Leisure

As you develop interests, you will build different networks.
Leisure networks could be built around:

- sport and fitness
- interests
- hobbies
- voluntary work
- causes.

Shared interests and a common commitment bring you together with people in leisure networks. The reason for meeting can become less important than the meeting itself as these networks develop. Golf clubs, health clubs, sports teams, volunteering, interests, night school and political or cause-related groups provide excellent opportunities for networking.

Family

It is likely that you will be influenced most strongly by your family network and how it functions. Your perspective on networks and networking will be determined by this experience. Your family networks include the nuclear family, the extended family and family friends.

One of the positive facets of a family network is that members generally have high regard for each other – or at least, loyalty towards each other! For the purposes of its survival, if nothing else, a family tends to have each other's well-being at heart. Referrals from family members can sometimes be the strongest and often result in really valuable opportunities.

Personal networks are not entities that just happen. As with other networks, they can be developed to match your needs at critical points in your life.

All of your existing networks have peripheral networks attached to them. If you are clear about what you want from your personal network, you are likely to be able to access it and its extended network and develop both 'first tier' and 'second tier' relationships to help you meet your life goals.

Think about your personal network:

- *What peripheral networks are attached to your personal networks?*
- *Where are the gaps in your network?*
- *How would you like your personal networks to develop?*
- *How can you develop them?*

What you may be seeking through your personal networks are opportunities to meet with like-minded people in a non-work environment. Be clear about your needs and goals in establishing personal networks. Personal networks can provide opportunities for:

- support
- stimulation
- challenge
- appreciation
- acceptance

- involvement
- enjoyment.

A simple gauge to help you identify your needs is balance. It is as important to have balanced relationships as it is to develop the right personal network to reflect your needs.
So how do you develop these relationships?

Developing networks

Personal networks exist all around you. Although, for many, these remain untapped resources, they can serve many functions and develop in all sorts of ways. You establish personal networks by:

- keeping in touch
- taking initiatives
- building bridges
- communicating proactively
- cultivating contacts
- offering assistance.

This doesn't mean being pushy. First, identify the gap between your network and your needs. Think about who could help you enter other networks that could fill the gaps and bring you value. Then start talking, meeting and building your network.

Nurturing networks

Networks are sensitive. If you feed networks and look after them with care and attention, you will reap the rewards.
In order to nurture networks:

- be open-minded
- keep commitments
- treat others as you would like to be treated
- don't be afraid to ask
- give without exception or expectation
- recognize problems and address them
- say 'thank you' – in word and/or in deed.

Be open-minded

Being open-minded is the golden rule of networking. If you close your mind to the concept or the principle of networking, your efforts are likely to fail. Enter new situations with a degree of optimism about the people you'll meet and their role in your future.

Try to treat those you dislike as respectfully as those you favour. They may have just as much to offer. Often, what you dislike in others is a reflection of what you dislike in yourself. So try not to judge others and be generous and accepting of them.

Keep commitments

When you make a commitment to do something for someone else, you can never be sure of its importance or value to them. People tend to build their hopes around promises and commitments. By cultivating the habit of always keeping commitments and being reliable, you can build relationships on the basis of trust and credibility that can span the gaps in your network and generate warmth, good will and reciprocity.

Treat others as you would like to be treated

Standards and expectations are important in building relationships.

Ask yourself: *How would I like to be treated?*

Be honest in developing relationships. Only nurture those that you are prepared to invest in. Otherwise, it can seem that you discard people callously when they have served their purpose. Personal integrity generates trust.

You will be noticed by others and you will gain a reputation – for good or bad!

Don't be afraid to ask

Dependency is a value-laden term. To be told that you are dependent smacks of an insult in a society like ours that values independence. However, the notion of 'true' independence is misconceived. People are not utterly self-sufficient. We all need relationships to perform our work effectively and to live happy and fulfilled lives – interdependency seems to us a much better description.

Many managers have strong networks but they often lack the ability to benefit from them personally and professionally.

Give without exception or expectation

Anthropologists tell us that exchanges, assistance and giving are the most common functions of friendships in all cultures. Giving is one of the basic rules of networking.

People help each other in different ways for different reasons. This is why it can be difficult to network with those you have little in common with or even dislike. The type of help you offer is not particularly important. The fact that you are prepared to give is what counts.

A level of altruism is required to be a successful networker. You should not give with the expectation that you'll receive something in return. You will benefit at some stage in your relationship but if you make this the only reason for networking, you may be disappointed. Be careful of giving excessively. An effusive networker can be a real turn-off.

Recognize problems

It may seem harsh to speak of relationships, and particularly those within your personal network, as effective or ineffective. However, it is vital to assess your relationships in this way when considering your network.

Personal networks need to stay effective. They often begin this way and it is likely that this is why they formed in the first place. But they can be corrupted by changes in circumstances, such as others coming into the network or the rationale for the existence of your network changing, such as a change in your goals and aspirations.

By investing in some relationships, you can change them from being ineffective to effective. The strength of the tie may determine whether you choose to invest in the relationship or not. You may decide, simply, to distance yourself from ineffective relationships in recognition that they will not change.

Be sure to act when you recognize a problem in your network. By careful and regular monitoring, you can ensure that relationship issues rarely occur.

Say thank you

If someone is helping you, let them know how much you appreciate it. If you take the time to say or do something to show your appreciation, it will create an ongoing dynamic of assistance. Personal networks are often the most sensitive. You can express your appreciation in a variety of ways. Send them a newspaper clipping, an article, details of a seminar, meeting or social event. Very little effort is required to create a feeling of concern and belonging.

Summary

Personal networks are easy to overlook because they are almost like 'second nature' to us.

The pressing needs of our busy lives can create situations where we neglect the relationships that we benefit from the most.

Yet personal networks can deliver immense value if we care to nurture them and use them with care and consideration. Think about how many years of experience is collectively held by the members of your personal network. There will be those who have had successful careers, those who have started new businesses, those who have made a social impact in their local community and those who have a global network that will keep you alert and attuned to different behavioural rhythms.

Take time to review and invest in your personal network. This means thinking about who your personal network contains, the expectations you have of each other and identifying the gaps between your goals and aspirations and what your network can deliver. Ensure that you 'do unto others as you would be done to' and consider what proactive steps would build and maintain the goodwill in your network.

Your personal network contains people who have known you the longest and have seen you in all your personal and career incarnations. As a result of their long-term perspective, the members of your personal network hold valuable insights into your talents and potential. Their words may be challenging, but they are often wise. Overlook your personal network at your peril!

Fact-check (answers at the back)

Answer the following questions honestly, reflecting on the nature of the relationships within your network.

1. How often do you review your personal network?
a) Daily–weekly ❏
b) Monthly–yearly ❏
c) Less than every two years ❏
d) Never ❏

2. What is your attitude when meeting new people?
a) I love to meet new people ❏
b) I'm shy of meeting people ❏
c) I force myself to network when I think it's important ❏
d) I dread meeting new people ❏

3. How often do you use your personal network to make contacts?
a) My personal network is my 'first stop' ❏
b) My personal network is social ❏
c) I rarely look to my personal network ❏
d) I never think of my personal network ❏

4. How effective is your personal network?
a) Members of my personal network deliver value ❏
b) My network contains some valuable relationships ❏
c) My network is very patchy ❏
d) My personal network doesn't serve me at all ❏

5. How could you build your personal network?
a) I need to invest time nurturing relationships ❏
b) I need to be proactive in building my network ❏
c) I need to rid my network of redundant members ❏
d) It serves its purpose ❏

6. What will you do to build and sustain your personal network?
a) I will attend more events at which I can network ❏
b) I will access new networks through the members of my own ❏
c) I am focussing on my professional network ❏
d) I will think about what I can do for others in my network ❏

7. How do you select the members of your personal network?
a) I invite people I like to join my network ❏
b) I see who is active in other people's networks ❏
c) I wait for people to build relationships with me ❏
d) I wait until I have a need ❏

8. **How do you nurture your network?**
a) I make sure I speak to everyone regularly ❏
b) I invite people to come with me to events ❏
c) I regularly send articles, papers or other things of interest ❏
d) I wait to be asked ❏

9. **When you have a particular need, how do you meet it through your network?**
a) I approach people and ask for help directly ❏
b) I find an opportunity to get together ❏
c) I ask what I can do for them ❏
d) I drop hints that I need help and hope that they offer ❏

10. **How do you use your network to leverage your reputation?**
a) I ask to join others at events ❏
b) I ask for feedback on my impact on others ❏
c) I make myself known make myself known to a wider audience ❏
d) I look to my organizational network for my reputation ❏

CHAPTER 10

Organizational networks

Traditionally, organizations were founded on the principles of hierarchy, systems and structures. They were, by character, inflexible and bureaucratic with prescribed ways to approach tasks that now seem time-consuming and clumsy.

This is only part of the picture. On closer inspection, under the formal façade, you would discover an informal power base. People were and are the power holders in organizations. These people are the hubs of your organizational network. You are probably intuitively aware of who they are. You may or may not like them very much.

Who are the hubs within your organization?

Hubs can:

- Inform
  - What's going on?
  - How would this be seen?
- Influence
  - Who should I talk to?
  - How should I present myself and my ideas?
- Get things done
  - What are the shortcuts?
  - Are there 'hidden' rules?

Hubs are not necessarily those people with the longest service, highest status or the outward exhibition of power. They are more likely to be natural networkers.

When you enter any new environment, it is worth identifying the hubs. Don't do this rashly – first impressions can be misleading. Consider carefully where the informal information and power lies. These centres of information and power can be identified by making some of the following observations.

Who:

- eats together and socializes (friends)?
- provides solutions (experts)?
- are the sources of 'sensitive' information (moles)?
- receives the resources (support)?
- is in the right place at the right time (guides)?

The traditional organizations we have discussed are changing. Generally speaking, hierarchies are being replaced by democracies and status is being replaced by relationships as the basis of power.

To be successful within any organizational culture, you need to understand the principles of networking and recognize the power of relationships. It is these organizational networks that we will be focussing upon in this chapter:

- Organizational structures
- The 'network principle'
- Inter-organizational networks

Organizational structures

Just as physical structures are designed for a specific purpose or effect – rockers on rocking chairs enabling them to rock, wheels on wheelbarrows enabling them to roll – organizational structures can be, and are, designed for a specific purpose or effect.

Organizational structures are typically defined by production processes or service provision. They have characteristics that reflect different sectors, people, history, ownership, culture... The list is endless. We have chosen three common, yet different, structures for contrast:

- flat organizations
- hierarchical organizations
- networked organizations.

Flat organizations

As a result of economic difficulties, many organizations have stripped out layers of management. This has been necessary to meet the competitive market challenges and withstand the pressures of the troubled global economy.

As a result, a high value has been placed on managers who not only have a functional speciality, but also have diverse experience and understand the business drivers. To complement this experience, knowledge and understanding, organizations value managers with interpersonal and communications skills. These are people who can demonstrate leadership capabilities on projects and with teams and who have the ability to communicate effectively across various departments and business units.

Hierarchical organizations

These organizations have the traditional, pyramid style of organization. They usually have a chairperson and chief executive officer at the apex of the pyramid and multiple layers of management, which increase in number as they descend to the bottom of the pyramid where the 'real' work is done!

The method of communication in these organizations is strictly controlled. It is usually vertical (up and down the organization) and can become blocked very easily if someone chooses to withhold information or a decision.

Hierarchical structures encourage specialities. Managers tend to focus on the small, rather than the big picture, with limited insights across their functional borders.
It can create an environment of divisions – or silos – which makes it difficult for the organization to advance as an integrated 'whole'.

Networked organizations

The new and emerging organizations of today are often based upon the 'network principle'. They have changed their structure and their styles of communication to enhance their efficiency and performance. Networked (or matrix) organizations aim to combine the best of hierarchical vision and control with a cross-functional, project-based approach.

These three organizational structures are compared in the table below:

	Flat	Hierarchical	Networked
Communication	Horizontal Without boundaries Between peers	Vertical Pre-defined channels Within functional groups	Vertical/ Horizontal Broad communication encouraged Focussed on projects/ outcomes
Innovation	Flourishes Practical problems resolved	Can be lost in the hierarchy Progress can be slow until 'go' decision made	Emergent and supported Implemented through project teams
Information	Fluid Information readily circulated	Through specific/ formal channels Information protected and sometimes withheld	No formal boundaries Focussed on purpose and outcome
Experience	Functionally focussed Specialists, experts	Specialists, experts Silo	Breadth and depth of experience rewarded
Behaviours	Promotes team Communication is key	Formal, traditional Protective	Opportunistic, fleet of foot Copes well with change
Networking	Cross-functional	Status driven	Spans functional and geographic boundaries
Recognition	Team achievements	Personal success and 'time served'	Team achievements and personal network

The 'network principle'

The 'network principle' has some common features:

- essential characteristics
- establishing the culture
- barriers to change
- unblocking organizations.

Essential characteristics

Networked organizations have advantages, not solely because of their internal characteristics, but also because of their ability to compete.

Essential characteristics of networked organizations are that they are:

- innovative
- flexible
- fast-footed.

Innovative

Innovation is the key to survival in the highly competitive environments in which organizations exist today. Truly innovative organizations encourage creativity at all levels.

In hierarchical organizations, ideas tend to be passed from one person to another rather like a baton in a relay race. If there is a weak link in the chain, the idea goes no further and creativity is quashed.

For people in an organization to innovate successfully, it is important that they are free to network between functions and geographies. This type of network is one in which ideas are challenges, encouraged and examined from many different vantage points. If ideas are good, they fan out, get picked up and adopted.

Innovation through networks:

- encourages
- refines
- reinforces
- recreates
- implements new ideas.

The culture and structure to support this innovation is characterized by open channels of communication that encourage and reward an enthusiastic exchange of ideas across functional and geographical boundaries.

Flexible

This style of organization demands new skills of managers and team members. Managers have to broaden their range of competences to become more effective as:

- team members
- catalysts
- communicators
- influencers/negotiators
- enablers
- informers
- project managers.

The traditional styles of management are not helpful in this new and evolving environment and managers, rather than working in a structured environment with a predictable pattern to their week, are much more likely to be faced with managing:

- cross-functional teams
- briefings
- brainstorming groups
- continuous improvement groups
- focus groups.

Managers who thrive in these environments are open to different views and approaches and are not threatened by change or by the unknown.

Fast-footed

Fast-footed organizations are those that are able to respond rapidly to changes in the demands placed upon them from:

- employees
- customers
- suppliers
- the (extended) community in which they exist
- the Political, Economic, Social and Technological environment (PEST).

There is no substitute for keeping your ear close to the ground, hearing and acting upon new ideas and developing trends.

Organizational structures have to be able to withstand the pressures of these new demands. If they are too brittle, or too inflexible, they will shatter. Flatter structures and networked organizations will assist in the process of toughening up and developing the kind of resilience that will enable them to respond to the complexities of the environment. However, the speed and complexity of organizations requires an effective network for managers to survive.

Establishing the culture

Regardless of the dominant style of your organization, there will be aspects of it that you will wish to retain and those that need revising. Unless there is a crisis in your industry or your organization, the adjustments that need to be made in order to become network-oriented need not be dramatic. Indeed, it may take some time to encourage people to change their behaviour. However, with constant reminders, reinforcement and reward, this can be accelerated.

When trying to establish a network culture, employees will need to know exactly what the organization is trying to achieve. Messages coming down from the top should be reinforced time and time again. Senior managers need to be seen to practise what they preach.

If you occupy a secure position in a traditionally hierarchical organization, networking may seem self-defeating. Sharing information may be perceived as giving power away. However, it is a two-way process and can, in the right conditions, enrich everyone.

But first, the conditions in which new behaviours can emerge must be put in place. These will only take root if everyone understands the change and can see its value. The following imperatives will help to fuel the change:

● Recognize individual and team contributions.
● Encourage career paths across functional boundaries.
● Remove functional focus from analysis.
● Instil discipline of broader perspective.

- Encourage cross-functional communication.
- Share organizational information.
- Support change with training and development.
- Monitor and evaluate all of these processes.

By doing this, you are, in essence, capitalizing on the expertise contained within the organization. This involves recognition and action. Try some simple steps such as building project teams across functional boundaries, introducing network mentors, identifying behavioural role models, offering coaching and support. Create opportunities that will naturally encourage networking: continuous improvement groups, quality forums, brainstorming activities, job shadowing and social functions.

Networked organizations are not constrained by the boundaries of the organizational structure. They look outside for examples of good practice, innovation and success. Look beyond your organizations at:

- competitors (benchmarking – as a minimum standard)
- customers
- suppliers
- professional bodies
- conferences
- research
- possibilities for joint projects or joint ventures.

In multinational organizations, additional mechanisms are required to facilitate communication across national borders. Such mechanisms include:

- email
- teleconferencing
- exchange visits
- international training and development
- newsletters
- international conferences
- intranet (and social networking).

Networking should be encouraged between opposite numbers in the organization and these opposite number networks should be tapped too. The exchange of experience in similar roles but dissimilar contexts is bound to be valuable and stimulate new ideas and approaches to the role.

Barriers to change

There are a number of different stumbling blocks that prevent effective and efficient networking. These come in the following forms:

- inertia
- fear
- ignorance.

Inertia

Inertia is often found in organizations that do not place a high importance on networking. These are likely to be the more traditional types of organizational structure that may believe that networking is idle gossip and has no value. These organizations often like to keep the channels of communication distinct and sealed.

Fear

Fear stems from the belief that control will be lost and that those who don't believe in networking will sabotage all efforts to change the culture. Control is an interesting issue. If too much of it is exerted, people identify subversive techniques to get around it. This results in a two-tier culture, the overt and the covert. This sits in direct opposition to the culture of a networked organization. Too little control, on the other hand, results in frustration and a loss of respect for those who occupy the positions where control is expected of them. A firm but receptive approach is generally the most effective.

Fear is exhibited in different ways. It may show itself in retrenchment where ideas, information and power are held possessively. It also may show itself in lack of co-operation and passive/aggressive behaviour. Organizations that contain those who do not want to share information for fear of losing their positional power may hear phrases like:

Mind your own business!
If you need the information, I'll give it to you!
Did you not know!?

Ignorance

Many people do not possess natural networking skills, so these must be developed and encouraged so that the new culture has a good chance of becoming established.

Often people think that the only component of networking is technology. This is merely a tool so we do not view it as a network in its own right. Networking is about human interactions. These interactions can be facilitated through communication technology but never replaced by it.

People in organizations hold a lot of experience and many skills that are not well advertised. Some of them are related to their professional roles, others are personal. It is amazing what talents you can unearth when you spend time networking.

Unblocking organizations

Variety is exciting, creative and dynamic and needs to be celebrated. Recognition of transferable skills and qualities need to be expressed in a way that will mobilize the workforce and motivate people to network and give more of their worth. If a match can be made between individual and organizational objectives, all the activities that take place within the workplace will contribute towards the overall strategic objectives of the organization.

The secret behind a successful shift to a networking culture can be remembered using the '4 Cs':

- Clear goal and commitment from the top
- Communication (four times over!)
- Constant and consistent reinforcement
- Celebration of success

There is hardly ever enough communication. This is pivotal!

Inter-organizational networks

Organizations can benefit greatly from careful strategic positioning in relation to other organizations' products and services. What attracts a customer to another product or service could equally well attract a customer to your own. For years, washing machine manufacturers have struck up beneficial relationships with detergent manufacturers. One carries the recommendation of the other – they go hand in hand – and together, they aim for the same target market with more force and precision than they could do alone.

These synergistic relationships now extend beyond the mere marrying of products and services to the physical positioning of retail outlets. With industrial parks and suburban shopping centres now firmly established in most economic cultures, many such relationships exist. McDonald's or Pizza Hut can often be found on the same sites as certain retail stores or entertainment venues. Customers are much more inclined to visit a shopping centre if many of their consumer objectives can be achieved in one fell swoop.

The same is true of more exclusive retailers. Haute-couture designer shops or exclusive department stores are co-located to bring in larger numbers of shoppers.

Summary

Organizations dominate our lives. It is perhaps more helpful to understand them as communities of people that need to interact rather than treat them as entities that are impermeable to human expression. In this way, we can create pathways to those people that can assist us in our career progression.

Finding supportive coaches or mentors is a good way to use the organizational network. Peers or senior managers are often happy to give back something to those people in the organization who will contribute to its success in the future. They will give you a listening ear, help you to understand the politics and rules of survival, introduce you to those who can offer you new opportunities and give you feedback before you take a wrong turn. It will be your turn to do this for others in the future but for the time being, see yourself as a worthy human asset that will pay dividends in the end.

By understanding the structure and style of your own organization in this way, and by building robust channels of communication, you will put yourself in the driving seat of your own professional life.

Fact-check (answers at the back)

Answer the following questions honestly, reflecting on the network nature of your organization:

1. **How would you describe your organizational structure?**
   a) Flat ❏
   b) Hierarchical ❏
   c) Networked ❏
   d) None of these ❏

2. **What networking do you see in your organization?**
   a) Informal gatherings ❏
   b) Communication/social events taking place ❏
   c) Communication with colleagues ❏
   d) People doing their work, heads down and isolated ❏

3. **Where are the hubs in your organization?**
   a) Senior executives ❏
   b) Line managers ❏
   c) Those whose work crosses functional boundaries ❏
   d) Everyone ❏

4. **What are the most common barriers to networking in your organization?**
   a) There are none ❏
   b) Inertia ❏
   c) Fear ❏
   d) Ignorance ❏

5. **What are the most common forms of communication in your organization?**
   a) Email ❏
   b) Telephone ❏
   c) Meetings ❏
   d) Communication is not encouraged ❏

6. **What exists to cultivate networking in your organization?**
   a) Training and development ❏
   b) Company gatherings ❏
   c) None ❏
   d) Social events ❏

7. **What inter-organizational initiatives exist in your organization?**
   a) Best practice exchanges ❏
   b) Secondments/job sharing ❏
   c) Joint ventures/strategic alliances ❏
   d) None ❏

8. **How often do you network beyond your immediate working environment?**
   a) Daily–weekly ❏
   b) Monthly–yearly ❏
   c) Less than every two years ❏
   d) Never ❏

9. **Which of the '4 Cs' operate in your organization?**
   a) Clear goal and commitment from the top ❏
   b) Communication ❏
   c) Constant reinforcement ❏
   d) Celebration of success ❏

10. **What is the culture of your organization?**
    a) Innovative ❏
    b) Flexible ❏
    c) Fast-footed ❏
    d) Fragmented ❏

CHAPTER 11

Professional networks

Professional networks assist you in your career progression. They can provide information, support, influence and development. Above all, they are a vehicle through which you can identify and create opportunities.

Career progression

- Information
  - What is the best strategy?
  - Who is the expert?
- Support
  - How do you see it?
  - How would you feel?
- Influence
  - Who should I be talking to?
  - Can you introduce me?
- Development
  - How can I get up to speed?
  - What do I need to be aware of?
  - How can I find out what I don't know?

Professional networks are built around common work interests and tasks. Your organizational network is likely to be a subset of your professional network. However, professional networks can consume other networks to which you affiliate such as clubs, professional societies, alumni and trade associations.

Professional networks have no geographical bounds: they extend right around the globe – particularly if they are virtual.

As a professional, you have automatic licence to tap into the network in the course of carrying out your professional duties or on the wing of a business proposition or idea. Indeed, it is an approach such as this that will lead to the creation of profitable alliances and the building of business opportunities. In this chapter, we will cover the following areas of professional networks:

● What are they?
● It's a small world
● Building bridges
● Feed and water regularly

What are they?

For simplicity, we have divided professional networks into different categories: intra- and extra-organizational, professional organizations and virtual networks. The various forms of professional networks have different codes of conduct so it is useful to consider these and try to determine what they may be.

Intra-organizational

These networks consist of:

● colleagues
● peers
● superiors
● bosses
● casual informants (who form the grapevine)
● politically motivated people (those with career aspirations or change agents)
● personal alliances (friends and informal social acquaintances).

The code of conduct for making connections in the working environment is fairly well defined from a professional standpoint. Understanding the undercurrents that create the political flavour, however, is the key to your success in working in an organizational network effectively. These invisible ebbs and flows need to be considered from a safe distance before entering the fray.

Bide your time. Only when you feel sure that you have correctly identified the various allegiances that exist in the organization is it time for you to form your own alliances. Don't rush in where angels fear to tread. Others' perceptions of you will be coloured by those you fraternize with.

Although you are more or less bound to fall into a political minefield at some stage, persevere – you will soon learn to trust your observations and, with your successes, develop faith in your instincts.

Extra-organizational

Extra-organizational networks consist of:

- competitors
- customers
- suppliers
- agencies
- joint venture partners
- strategic alliances
- family and friends
- former colleagues
- college/university networks
- alumni groups.

When engaging with those outside your working environment, you will need to be aware that all your communications and actions will go towards creating an impression of you and your organization. Your personal integrity will be on show so it is important that you manage the perception of others in what is a small world. You will often find that people you connect with outside your organization have a feeder back into it, albeit through a different channel.

People have a need to judge and they will use whatever material is available to them to base their judgements upon. If you make a wrong move in the initial stages of your relationship with someone, usually within the first few seconds of meeting them, it will determine the dominant impression that they have of you. Recreating or altering an impression is disproportionately harder than creating one in the first place!

Professional network organizations

Professional network organizations include:

● Professional websites (for example LinkedIn®)
● Professional groups, associations and clubs (for example Chambers of Commerce, Writers' Guild, Women's Business Network)
● Professional bodies (for example Chartered Management Institute)

Many network organizations now exist. They are designed to facilitate networking among those with similar interests, values and professions. Some of these organizations are welcoming of new members; others are closed.

The vehicles of communication for activating a network are things such as: regular meetings, seminars, workshops, group activities, social events, blogs, webinars and so forth. Although not everyone's cup of tea, they are extremely useful ways of contacting a target group of others who are highly likely to want to connect with you – professionally or personally.

Professional websites

Virtual networks, held on the Internet, have become extremely popular and much value can be gained from them. These hold the technological answer to the rapid and efficient exchange of contacts and information. Indeed, they have become so ubiquitous that a lack of presence on a website, such as LinkedIn®, can disadvantage you by leaving you out of the way of serendipitous contacts – either from those you have known in the past or from potential future colleagues.

Dependency on a virtual network, however, can have its limitations. It cannot replace the face-to-face benefits of building a relationship or tackling mutual business interests. It also prevents the interpretation of non-verbal signals, which form the largest proportion of the messages we convey in our communication.

Being on a professional website allows you to present your credentials to a wide, but select, audience. Accompanied by a photograph and way of communicating your activities

and new connections, there is an element of dynamism
that compensates for the more traditional, face-to-face,
professional network. However, there is nothing to replace the
alchemy of a personal meeting and often, meaningful virtual
connections result in this.

Professional groups, associations and clubs

There are many professional groups and associations that
will be known to you through your specialization (profession),
aspiration (cause) or attribute (gender) that you share uniquely
with others. These can be fruitful environments for support,
information, practical assistance, advice and the comfort of
sharing a common language and common problems.

Often, professional groups and associations host
networking events to bring members together regularly.
Although membership can be used as a shortcut to convey
credibility, it also provides more practical support in
progressing your career.

Professional bodies

A professional body upholds the standards of your work, through
a Charter, which has been awarded by an academic institution,
legislative or sovereign power. Coaching associations or
management institutes are examples of this kind of professional
body. Members must adhere to the standards of practice, and
honour the code of conduct, that is set out in the Charter – or
their membership may be at risk.

These professional bodies make a statement about the
level of your professionalism and often obviate the need for
proof through other, lengthier, means. Membership of some
organizations and even to a particular standard, level or grade
may be a condition of employment.

It's a small world

A good professional network can support you in your:

- role
- career
- personal life.

Your role

Everyone requires the means for professional enhancement to stay relevant, ahead and successful. Networks can provide you with this in a variety of ways:

- feedback
- know-how
- benchmarking
- management information
- problem-solving
- development.

Your professional network can act as your safety net, providing opportunities to share best practice, thoughts and opinions in a confidential environment that is not constrained by the boundaries of your organization.

Professional networks ensure that you keep up to date and informed of the latest developments in your arena. They provide a mechanism through which you can access knowledge and exchange advice, ideas and insights of professional significance. They also provide an environment in which you can learn from others who have already encountered situations that are new to you.

Some form of self and role evaluation is essential for all professionals. Professional networks provide the professional standards, levels of competence and goals against which you can judge yourself and through which you can identify your development needs. Every professional should take responsibility for their own continuous professional development (CPD) and professional networks give you access to people who enable you to benchmark yourself.

Your career

Your professional responsibility extends beyond the need for CPD in your role, to responsibility for your career.

Career benefits include:

- feedback
- assistance

- exposure
- early warning system.

Professional networks are unique in that they can provide the means of receiving open and objective feedback. Although not always comfortable, you can develop an understanding of how you are perceived by others who know your career path. Not only can they give you candid and valuable feedback, but also visibility and exposure to new people and opportunities. In Chapter 12, we will give you more insights into networking for career development.

Your personal life

Professional networks can support you in a variety of other ways. Personal benefits can include:

- new social circles
- recommendations
- referrals.

Social circles are often created as a result of networking in the professional arena. These will transcend the professional networks from which they came. If this happens, it is a bonus. However, be alert to the confusion that can arise around the liberties friends can take as compared to those professional colleagues can take. It would be hard for your boss – and perhaps for you – if you asked for a babysitting favour, for example!

Building bridges

Networks can emerge and disappear like a mirage. They can be created in order to meet a specific goal and dissolved once this goal has been met.

When a temporary network is required, it needs to be mapped, monitored and evaluated carefully. After its dissolution, some of the good contacts that you have made may be preserved and positioned in another of your networks.

In order to make the most of the potential a network holds, it is important to be clear about what you want from it.
What do you want from your network?

- A new position?
- News of job opportunities?
- Entry to an 'inner circle'?

By identifying what you want from your network, you will be clear about selecting its members.

Feed and water regularly

A network is only as good as the care and attention you give it. This is not necessarily an arduous activity – it can become almost instinctive over time. Nevertheless, your networks will need general maintenance on a regular basis.
Maintain your network by:

- pruning
- growing
- investing
- rewarding.

Pruning

It is likely that you have relationships in your network that no longer serve or benefit you. These relationships can sap your energy and divert your focus unless they are pruned and discarded.

Growing

Consciously and consistently add to your network. Be very clear of your goals and be sure of the key players and their potential to assist you. It is very easy to waste the potential of a good contact.

Investing

Keeping a network alive and active requires an investment of time and energy. Take care to be sensitive and courteous.

It would be a shame to milk the network too much and lose your credibility and the goodwill others have for you. Think about what you can do for others and make the effort to pro-act.

Rewarding

Don't forget to thank those who have assisted you. Showing appreciation is as important as maintenance. Is there anything tangible you can do to exchange the favour you have received?

Summary

Professional networks can be powerful mechanisms if you are clear about:

- what you want from them
- how to make them work for your benefit.

To demonstrate the breadth and potential of your professional network, try the following:

1 Select a high profile name – such as Barack Obama, Oprah Winfrey or Richard Branson – and try to identify how many 'handshakes' you would need to contact that person. (We would be surprised if you were more than four or five handshakes away from these people!)

2 You may already have some superb contacts in your network but try thinking about your network from a different vantage point and see whether you can identify where these contacts could lead you.

3 In relation to your future career aspirations, ask yourself who would be the most valuable people you could connect with. Map out the route to meeting these people and initiate some meetings.

Professional networks checklist:

- Identify your networks
  - Intra-organizational
  - Extra-organizational
  - Professional

- Clarify your goals
- Build relationships
- Monitor, manage and review your network
- Networking is never one-way. To support the existence of your professional networks you need to play your part in serving them.

Fact-check (answers at the back)

Answer the following questions honestly, reflecting on your professional network.

1. **How do you use your professional network?**
   a) For information ☐
   b) For support ☐
   c) For influence ☐
   d) For feedback and development ☐

2. **To which professional network organizations do you belong?**
   a) Professional websites ☐
   b) Professional associations ☐
   c) Professional bodies ☐
   d) None of the above ☐

3. **How do you maintain your professional network?**
   a) Prune ☐
   b) Grow ☐
   c) Invest ☐
   d) I don't. It takes care of itself ☐

4. **How has your professional network assisted you?**
   a) New job ☐
   b) Introductions ☐
   c) Business opportunities ☐
   d) It hasn't ☐

5. **How have you helped those in your professional network?**
   a) Bringing people together ☐
   b) As a carrier of information ☐
   c) Sending articles, papers, conference details ☐
   d) I don't engage with my professional network ☐

6. **Looking over the map of your professional network:**
   a) Who's missing? ☐
   b) Who's no longer actively assisting you? ☐
   c) What professional network? ☐
   d) Is there anyone who can link you to another network? ☐

7. **How much time do you spend managing your professional network?**
   a) I give it daily attention ☐
   b) I think about my network when I have a need ☐
   c) I only notice it when someone wants something from me ☐
   d) I rarely give my attention to my network ☐

8. **How many professional websites are you active on?**
   a) I am active on more than 3 ☐
   b) I am active on 2-3 ☐
   c) I am active on 1-2 ☐
   d) I am not on a professional website ☐

9. **How often do you update your profile?**
   a) I review it weekly ❏
   b) When I receive notifications about my contacts ❏
   c) I am active on my site when I have a specific need ❏
   d) My original profile remains unaltered ❏

10. **How do you feel about professional networking?**
   a) I enjoy meeting people of like mind ❏
   b) I find it useful when I need to achieve something ❏
   c) It feels 'manipulative' to me so I network rarely ❏
   d) I am never proactive ❏

CHAPTER 12

Networking for career development

The concept of networking has its origins in the context of careers. Most people at some stage in their career will have used their network to aid their advancement. Your first job, Saturday job, or summer jobs may have come about because of a contact your parents, family or friends had. When older, you develop a more sophisticated version of this as your network extends beyond your personal networks.

Think about your career:

How did you hear about the jobs?

How did the recruiter hear about you?

This traditional and well-tested means of developing and advancing your career is even more important now that organizations are flatter, allowing fewer opportunities for upward promotion. In these new organizations, the way people group together is far more fluid. This has consequences for the traditional management career and the expectations that many managers hold about their futures.

Traditionally, managers had certain expectations about their careers, which were based on the pyramid structure of organizations. When you entered an organization, your career was pretty much mapped out and you could be clear about your end point, the route between now and then, and the timescales involved.

These days, successful careers are based on networking, not on a traditional career path carved in stone. Knowing how to network to advance your career is an essential survival skill. To survive means using your career networks responsibly and ethically.

You should take responsibility for your career and invest time, energy and money to ensure that your career goal in the short, medium and long term is achievable. This responsibility is as important if you intend to stay with one organization as it is if you intend to move. To place the responsibility for your career onto any organization is to neglect it.

You need to think about your career and how to develop your network to benefit you professionally.

In this chapter we will cover the following:

- Begin with the end in mind!
- It's who you know
- What to say after you've said 'Hello'

Begin with the end in mind!

If we were to pose a simple question to you such as 'Who are you?', we would not be surprised if you hesitated and began by answering 'I'm an operations manager' or 'I'm a training manager'. We tend to think of ourselves as what we do rather than who we are. This can have its dangers. In the past, as a result of the changing needs of the organizations in which we worked, we probably became what was demanded of us with little thought or reflection about what we enjoyed or what we did best.

A successful career is made up of many components: job types, styles and content, development, fulfilment and fit.

Getting this right depends on understanding yourself. What are your:

- skills?
- strengths?
- limitations?
- values?
- interests?
- pleasures?
- achievements?

Do not focus only on your education, skills and experience to formulate your next move. Focus on what makes you unique and how you could contribute to an organization. Also, focus on what you enjoy. Natural enthusiasm is easily conveyed and extremely contagious – and opportunities are in short supply. Communicating your value with enthusiasm is important if you are to outshine the competition and distinguish yourself as the best candidate for the job.

Where do you want to go?

Having taken an honest and thorough look at yourself, how clear are you about where you want to go – your destination? While your future may seem hazy, some idea of where you're going helps you to plan your moves and to gauge your progress.

Where you want to go can have many stages: perhaps the simplest way to think of these stages is as your short, medium and long-term goals.

Some people have goals that are not work related but do have an impact their work. One manager we met had the goal of retiring at 50 so that he could concentrate on his interests. This affected his career and his career choices directly because he needed to achieve a level of income to support him in his ambition. Others have goals such as embarking on a second career. In this case, they will need to invest in the appropriate networks to ensure that this is realized.

In the short to medium term, your goals may be related to more tangible things such as:

- location
- function
- field
- rewards
- work style
- colleagues
- organization.

Goals need reviewing regularly as they might be unrealistic and under- or over-ambitious. The rapidly changing business environment and the high level of uncertainty can significantly affect our goals, and over time goals can change as we develop.

Your end point

Your end point, aspiration or goal can then be built into your daily life so that you can manage yourself each day to be and to do what really matters to you most. Every decision you make will be in the context of your goal so by definition, you will be moving towards it steadily and certainly. This helps you to target your network. Your targets could be triggered by:

- contacts in your preferred locality
- role models
- functional experts
- network 'hubs' in your specialist field.

It's who you know

Your current contacts are the raw material for your career development. They, in turn, have contacts of their own. What you have at your disposal now is an enormous network – and made even larger (and more accessible) if you add yourself to a professional networking website.

Who do you know?

As a start, organize this raw material into a database of contacts – or examine your contacts on your professional website. Think about the following information for each person:

- title/position
- organization
- contact details
- address/location
- how you know this person
- when you met this person
- what kind of relationship do you enjoy with this person
- who else they are connected to in your network
- what networks they are able to access on your behalf.

Keep note of your contact with each person in your network. Include:

- the date of your contact
- a brief outline of the conversation or meeting you had
- any memorable information to refer back to
- the outcome of your meeting
- the date of any follow-up.

Even if you love your job and have no intention of moving at the moment, it would be good to start managing your network now. The perfect time to organize and develop your network is when you don't need it!

The networking process is gradual and requires investment. Building relationships with professional or personal contacts that have the potential to move you towards your long-term career goal is never wasted. The first step in targeted networking of this nature is to identify 'black holes' in your network. Are there gaps in your network between your current job and your desired job?

Maybe you already have contacts in the department, division, organization or industry that you wish to be part of. If not, see whether you can find a point of entry.

Your aim, in doing this, is to establish a network that is made up of contacts that serve you in one of the following ways.

Your contact:

- sees a job advertisement and draws your attention to it
- receives information about a local organization and passes it to you

- knows a recruiter who specializes in your function and introduces you to him or her
- knows someone with influence or information and orchestrates a meeting
- identifies a vacancy in his or her organizations and informs you of it
- offers you a position in his or her organization.

A quality contact could be someone in a position to offer you a job or arrange an interview. However, anyone who has a pair of relevant ears or eyes is a valuable contact.

You cannot always be in the right place at the right time but by developing your network, you have more of a chance of hearing about, seeing or recognizing the right opportunities.

With your goal in mind, it is important to think about who can offer you help. It is often the people you have the weakest links with – your old contacts that have been dormant for years and have almost been forgotten – who can be the most effective in your career progression. Weak links can provide you with new information and essential bridges to other groups and networks. Your strongest links will tend to be functioning well already so they will only need reminding of your aspirations and needs.

Who can you get to know?

You may also need to extend your network and you can do this through using:

- professional websites
- college alumni
- conferences
- committees and project teams
- professional or trade associations
- sponsors who will introduce you to other networks.

Career visibility

Mobility is the key to network building because it can lead to visibility. Make and take every opportunity to move into new networks. Explore new:

- places
- people
- opportunities.

Volunteer to take temporary assignments with another group, division or subsidiary. Join new committees and teams, especially those with representatives from other departments in your organization. Attend and participate in business and social events.

Build networks through:

- outside meetings
- conferences
- seminars
- professional events
- exhibitions.

Remember, the point of this visibility exercise is to meet different people who bridge different business and social circles. You may also want to try local events such as a village or town meeting, parent-teacher association, lectures or any other event where you can naturally meet other people from diverse backgrounds. It is amazing how often you come across someone who is connected to your world in one way or another.

Suggested activity:
Make notes of all the people you meet during the course of each day. Indicate the networking potential of each contact and identify the point of convergence in your respective lives.

What to say after you've said 'Hello'

Be aware of the people you need in your network. Always remember this and plan your networks thoughtfully. You need to ask yourself repeatedly, 'How can I meet the people I need to?'

It is one thing meeting these people, but quite another being able to benefit from the meeting. This is often the point at which many people fall; they have extensive networks but are not skilled at using them.

Think carefully about how you build productive relationships and how to establish rapport.

Building blocks
● Mentor's recommendation
● Your reputation or that of the organization
● Your accomplishments
● Position in the community
● Mutuality
  - An issue you share
  - An organization you both belong to
  - Work or life experience
  - Interests

Prove you are worth talking to: prepare a short summary of your career. Make it positive and base it on recent and relevant achievements. Be succinct and deliver it with energy and enthusiasm. Also, state your career goal.

How can they help?

It is important to communicate how they can help. Their support could be invaluable and information is always useful.

Information
Is the business expanding or shrinking?
What organizations are doing well?
What developments are current or planned?
Who are the key people who make recruitment decisions?
What opportunities are available?
What are the salary levels?

Support
Seek comments on your résumé.
Get advice on your approach.
Ask for some doors to be opened for you.
Get advice/feedback on an interview presentation.

Some people will simply be too busy to spend time with you. But they may know others who can help. Always end with the question: *Who else should I be talking to?*

This is the point at which you are building the bridges between different circles or networks.

If you are asking for an introduction, be aware of what the other person thinks of you. If he or she has any doubts about your abilities, you may be better to talk to someone else.

Script and rehearse what you intend to say. Practice makes perfect. You don't get a second chance to make a first impression!

If someone has taken the time to meet with you and given you valuable information, keep him or her up to date. If you have followed their lead, tell them of your progress. If they haven't heard from you for some time, they may assume that you have been successful in your quest but they may also be slightly fed up that you haven't 'closed the loop' with some feedback and a 'thank you'.

Summary

On first appearance, success may appear to have come easily to some. While they may, indeed, be blessed with advantage, they are much more likely to have developed their skills over many years and built a valuable network that delivers a return on their investment.

To use your network to develop your career, you need to have a good understanding of your skills, competences and strengths. Once you understand yourself to this extent, you can focus on where you want to get to and begin with an end in mind. This will enable you to articulate your career goals clearly to those who are best placed to help you.

The value of networking is that you are constantly advertising yourself. You are shaping the future by:

- being in the right place at the right time
- knowing the right people
- presenting yourself credibly
- sending the right messages.

Of course, this is not a one-way street. Those who are able to help you will only do so if they feel that you reciprocate in kind.

Networking for career development checklist:

- Know yourself and your aspirations
- Communicate your career goals
- Nurture your contacts
- Follow up with feedback and a 'thank you'.

Fact-check (answers at the back)

Answer the following questions honestly, reflecting on your network for career development.

1. How do you describe your short-, medium- and long-term career goals?

a) I am very clear about what I want to achieve ❑

b) I know what I want to do next ❑

c) I like to remain open to opportunities ❑

d) I have no idea what I want to do in my career ❑

2. How do you manage your network for career advancement?

a) I am present – but relatively inactive – on a professional website ❑

b) I am present – and active – on a professional website ❑

c) I make sure that I network regularly ❑

d) I don't manage my network at all ❑

3. When building your professional website, what do you feel is important?

a) That my information is up to date ❑

b) I make connections with those identified by the system to be relevant ❑

c) I put my photo and my CV on the site and accept invitations to join other networks ❑

d) The fact that I'm there is enough ❑

4. How have you benefitted, career-wise, from your network in the past?

a) I have been sent helpful information ❑

b) I have had doors opened for me ❑

c) I have been offered at least one job ❑

d) My network ❑

5. Where could you build your network for career advancement?

a) College and university alumni ❑

b) Former colleagues ❑

c) Professional associations ❑

d) By attending conferences ❑

6. How do you respond when someone asks you for career help?

a) I take time to listen to their needs and give advice ❑

b) I think about who's in my network and contact them ❑

c) I arrange and host a meeting if there is mutual interest ❑

d) I'm too busy managing my own career to assist with anyone else's! ❑

7. What extracurricular activities are you involved in?

a) I am a volunteer ❑

b) I sit on a local committee ❑

c) I socialize with people in my community ❑

d) I don't have any extracurricular activities ❑

8. **How prepared are you to ask for career help?**
a) I contact members of my network readily ❏
b) I think about what I can do to encourage others' assistance ❏
c) I find it hard to ask for help but do ❏
d) I tend not to ask for career help ❏

9. **How do you build your reputation and visibility?**
a) I am an active networker ❏
b) I write articles ❏
c) I give presentations at conferences ❏
d) I like to be invisible! ❏

10. **How do you keep up to date with what's going on in your professional world?**
a) I have a mentor who makes sure that I am plugged in ❏
b) I read the business sections of the newspaper ❏
c) I attend events and seminars ❏
d) I rely on what is circulated around the organization ❏

CHAPTER 13

Social
networking

So far, we have looked at networks from different vantage points: personal, organizational, professional and those that facilitate career advancement. Social networking is something else again. A phenomenon that has swept the world along with the advent of the Internet, social networks have become the face, eyes and ears of individuals on the world – for good and for bad!

Social networking sites are proliferating in many different arenas, spanning both professional and personal settings. They allow people to create or join web-based communities that resonate with them for one reason or another – which may be for career advancement or just for fun. It is a way of reaching out, making contact, disclosing personal information, accessing new information, sharing experiences, building relationships, finding opportunities and offering support.

In this chapter, we're going to look at several aspects of social networking. However, we are not going to do a review of all social networking sites, nor are we going to guide you through building your own site. Rather, we will be raising general issues suggesting how you could use social networking to your advantage.

In this chapter we will focus on:

- What's new about networking on a social networking site?
- What does joining a social network entail?
- Is social networking addictive?
- What level of privacy can you expect?
- What are the pros and cons of social networking?
- What are the dos and don'ts of social networking?
- Using social networks in work time
- Social networking vs professional websites
- What is Twitter®?
- What does Twitter® do for businesses?

What's new about networking on a social networking site?

Although sites enable new acquaintances to be made, by far the most common connection is made with people who are already in your near and 'once removed' network. They may be people whom you have known in the past or people known to those with whom you are already in close contact, either physically or virtually. Social networking sites are successful in making these extended networks tangible and allowing you to build relationships that you might not otherwise have built.

In addition, social networking allows you to reach out to those you probably would never have met in the normal course of your life. Profiles of individuals held on such sites contain all the information others need to decide whether to enter into a correspondence. In this way, new relationships begin their life. Sometimes these are fleeting. Sometimes they are robust and lead to long-term friendships. Sometimes they lead to love and marriage. And, sadly, sometimes they are exploitive.

What does joining a social network entail?

To join a social networking site, you will usually be asked to disclose some personal information about yourself. This may include:

- a photograph – you have an option to omit the photograph but on a professional network such as LinkedIn®, it may be a good idea to include one. On a social networking site, such as Facebook®, people are often tempted to submit an image that is a caricature or symbol that they feel conveys something about them, whether it be humorous, idiosyncratic or oblique!
- work and educational achievements
- personal/professional aims and aspirations
- email address and website links.

And on a more personally orientated social networking site

- your gender
- your birthday
- your relationship status
- interests, hobbies, group membership and causes being pursued
- photographs/videos.

On most sites, you can select which bits of this information enter the public domain and can set levels of access that screen out those people you'd rather not be in contact with. You will be asked to make connections with those you know to build your network of 'friends'. ('Friend' is a term used whether or not you know the person you're in contact with.) Once this has been done, you will be offered the names of those you may know through your emerging network. These are the 'friends' of those you know. These close acquaintances will form the hub of your network.

Activity on the site can take many different forms. You can share photographs, videos, links to other sites, messages, jokes, games... all these create the kaleidoscopic joy of a social networking site!

On professional networking sites, the material you share is work orientated and the purpose of sharing it is to build your reputation or further your career. Instead of 'friends', your network will be comprised of 'connections'.

If you are building a professional network, make sure you have a clear purpose and understand the route by which your invitations have arrived. If you wish to accept an invitation from someone you think will be able to assist you in some way, consider what you can do for them that will incentivize them to do so. This will enable you to start building a reciprocal relationship that will enable you to reach your career goals.

On one professional networking site, this note pops up on joining: 'Welcome to ... – The world's largest business referral network'. As an added bonus, if 20 of your colleagues accept your invite, you'll unlock the 'social networker' badge and be showcased throughout the entire site, putting you in front of thousands of potential clients and referral sources.

Some sites rely upon 'old' acquaintances or shared educational experiences to form a network. 'Ever wondered what happened to so-and-so?' they ask. Or 'Find old school friends', they promise. It is amazing how people from the past become accessible through such sites, even those you'd all but forgotten.

Is social networking addictive?

In 2005, research suggested that young people were spending, on average, at least 1 hour 22 minutes on a variety of sites every day. As an average, this suggests that some people will be spending many more hours than this on their site. Indeed, it is thought possible to become addicted to social networking sites and there have been cases where people neglect their 'real' lives in order to live their 'virtual' lives.

Technology also allows you to access sites on the move, sites and alerts can be put on mobile phones as applications so that you're never more than a click away from your network and able to interact with your 'friends' in real time. You can also leave messages for those who are not logged on and enjoy the advantages of asynchronous communication.

What level of privacy can you expect?

At a time when digital communication can sweep the world in seconds, the question of whether or not there is any privacy is a good one.

It has been found that some young people, who spend a great deal of time on social networking sites, are willing to give personal information quite freely, with a false sense of security about its destination and use. Parents may set rules to control how their children use sites, such as how much time they can spend on a site or the level of parental involvement in selecting 'friends'.

However, it is possible, through various sites, to convey a message, whether it is benign or malign, to hundreds and thousands of people at one time. In several clicks, parties can be planned, flash mobs can be organized – where many people come together to perform in the street and riots can be incited.

Those who post messages on sites have no ultimate control over who reads and circulates the message. Messages can be hijacked and spread beyond the wishes of the messenger to find their way into groups or communities that the messenger would not intend. Once on the Internet, there is no way of retrieving and discarding the message. It is always there, somewhere. Recently, one young person, wishing to celebrate her exam success, announced a party at her parent's house and gave the address. Thousands of people turned up and the police had to be called to break up the party. Needless to say the house was trashed.

It is only recently, too, that Facebook®, Twitter® and BBM® (BlackBerry Messenger) have been used to bring people together to riot in the streets of major cities in the United Kingdom. The ease with which messages can be passed to large groups of people means that it is not only private networks but also extended networks that can be mobilized. This can happen in seconds to bring people together, to organize events or, in this case, a series of riots. Interestingly, the same approach was used to mobilize the cleaning up operation. 'What's sauce for the goose, is sauce for the gander!' Even more recently, two of the rioters who used Facebook® to incite people to destroy their local towns have received extensive prison terms.

There is no country or technology barrier that cannot be crossed using digital communication and there is virtually no control over the content or purpose of the messages. This casts new light on the notion of a 'free press', the consequences of which were inconceivable when it was first mooted in the 17th century.

What are the pros and cons of social networking?

On the one hand, sites allow you to make connections with others from around the world who you would otherwise not encounter. This creates a rare opportunity to build culturally diverse relationships and learn about others' work, lives and cultures.

On the other hand, you have limited control over the information others receive, and you cannot validate (with certainty) the invitations you receive to become 'friends' in their network. Sometimes people pose as 'friends' in order to gain access to your network. If you aren't aware of these 'scams', you could be vulnerable to their effects.

Particularly in the case of young people, anxious parents and bystanders should encourage prudence when inviting or accepting friendships and care in developing information and messages before making these public.

What are the dos and don'ts of social networking?

Do: Think about what would be the 'worst possible outcome' of putting your information on the web. This will help you censor and protect yourself.

Do: Think about what you wish to get from your social networking and choose your 'friends' and connections carefully – you can add or block people if you wish.

Do: Set your levels of privacy so that your site can't be accessed freely.

Do: Manage the time you spend on sites. It is easy to get lost in a virtual world and forget your other priorities!

Do: Think twice about your invitations. If you haven't stayed in touch over the years, why do you think you'll want to be in touch now?

Don't: Enter a stream of consciousness that may get you into difficulty later. You may think your message is innocent or funny but others may not think so!

Don't: Put up contentious photographs of yourself. They could be viewed by those you wouldn't wish to see them, such as parents or potential employers.

Don't: Accept all the invitations you receive. Validate the integrity of the person who is inviting you to become a friend and block those that you know to be untrustworthy or unpleasant.

Don't: Assume your intentions will protect you! To ensure that you don't find yourself on the world stage with a damning message, try thinking about what would be the worst destination for your message and the consequences of it arriving there. By thinking twice, you may decide not to send it or write it in such a way that it won't do any damage – to either the sender or the recipient!

Using social networks in work time

Social networking has become so prolific that some organizations have banned the use of it in the working environment. It is too tempting, they feel, for people to spend their working hours socialising with their 'friends' and not engaging in productive activities. These are some of the reasons:

- They fear confidential material leaking through the social networks.
- Social networking can take up a large proportion of the corporate bandwidth.
- Research finds that huge financial losses occur as productivity dips in favour of social networking.
- There is a threat of web-borne viruses contaminating the organization's IT system.
- People are less likely to be available to their colleagues.

Yet other organizations encourage social networking, for the following reasons:

- It provides a 'snowballing' opportunity for marketing products and services – and brand.
- It provides a possible means of conducting market research.
- Social networking can be a modern means of facilitating the free exchange of information (and gossip) that takes place in all organizations anyway.
- It is a valuable conduit for disseminating organizational information and reinforcing the culture.

Some organizations may strike a balance. This may include:

- restricting access to certain social networking sites
- developing employees' awareness of the benefits and problems
- setting security levels
- creating policies to control what it is allowable to say and how to use the site
- establishing a corporate social networking site.

Social networking vs professional websites

Professional networking is a sub-set of the social networking phenomenon. Professional networking sites share the same technological platform as social networking sites, upon which you can build your professional network. In the same way, they help you do this by making connections with people in your professional field – and beyond. These may be former/current colleagues, bosses, prospective or actual clients, suppliers, friends in the same role or industry... and they help you access extended networks through your list of contacts.

Professional networks are more targeted than social networks and the 'terms of engagement' are more formal. For this reason, it is easier to stay in control of personal information, although there are no real safeguards to circulating information on the Internet.

Every time you are active on your site, your contacts will be notified of this. This underlines the importance of managing your site attentively so that you can be sure that your information is always up to date and relevant to your purposes.

What is Twitter®?

Twitter® is a way of sharing succinct pieces of information with millions of people. Using Twitter®, businesses are able to discover new information and share it widely.

The messages that are shared are restricted to 140 characters so that they are short and sweet – or not so sweet! The messages are public and anyone can read them. This 'rapid fire', 'sound bite' way of communicating has captured the imagination of many people, from celebrities to politicians to 'normal' folk. The audience for receiving specific 'tweets' can be thousands strong; you elect to follow tweets from certain people who interest you and the messages are sent in 'real time'.

What does Twitter® do for businesses?

Businesses use Twitter® to share information rapidly, to gather opinions and insights from the market and to build relationships with people who are interested in their business activities.

Because 'tweets' are restricted in size, they tend to be used for 'chatter' and keeping people connected. However, they can also be used for sending out announcements and key bits of information.

Summary

Never before has 'real time' communication been so available to such a vast number of people. This comes with the advantages and disadvantages of open access and unrestricted content.

The advantages of social networking bring visibility, an easy exchange of information, an instant channel for communication and access to people and events that might otherwise be off your radar. We could list the disadvantages in exactly the same way, but the quality and impression of the messages you send will determine people's perception of you, not only those in your close circle but those who hold the key to your future success as an employee or member of other networks that you might value.

Young people have known nothing different. The gateway to the globe is open by way of information and virtual connections.

Social networking, still in its infancy, needs to be used thoughtfully with attention being given to its management and control. Don't forget, it's not just about how YOU use social networking sites; it's about how OTHERS use them too.

With many routes in, you cannot guarantee that your confidences will be kept. They can just as easily be propelled around the globe.

Professional websites have emerged alongside social networking sites. Using the same underlying technology, these sites allow people to build their professional networks and advance their careers, but the same rules and considerations apply.

Fact-check (answers at the back)

Answer the following questions honestly, reflecting on your social and professional networks.

1. **How many social networking sites are you present on?**
   a) 4–5 (or more) ❑
   b) 3–4 ❑
   c) 1–3 ❑
   d) None ❑

2. **How often do you access your social network?**
   a) Multiple times every day ❑
   b) Once every day ❑
   c) Every week/month ❑
   d) Hardly ever ❑

3. **What do you use your social networking site for?**
   a) To build contacts ❑
   b) To communicate with an extended network ❑
   c) Solely for social purposes ❑
   d) To find work ❑

4. **Where are you when you access your site?**
   a) Anywhere – mobile ❑
   b) With friends ❑
   c) Home ❑
   d) Work ❑

5. **How many contacts do you have on your social networking sites?**
   a) 1–20 ❑
   b) 21–100 ❑
   c) 101–500 ❑
   d) More than 500 ❑

6. **What is the nature of your contacts?**
   a) A mix of personal and professional contacts ❑
   b) Colleagues and professional acquaintances ❑
   c) An extended network of family and friends ❑
   d) Personal friends and family ❑

7. **What is the main purpose of your social network?**
   a) To collect as many 'friends' as possible ❑
   b) To keep in touch with friends ❑
   c) To meet new people ❑
   d) To further my career ❑

8. **How private/secure do you think your site is?**
   a) Entirely confidential ❑
   b) Confidential and safe within my network ❑
   c) Accessible by those who are 'friends' of 'friends' ❑
   d) Entirely open to people I don't know ❑

9. **Has your life been enhanced by your social network?**
a) Without doubt ❑
b) To some extent ❑
c) Hardly at all ❑
d) Not at all ❑

10. **How often to you accept connecting invitations?**
a) Always ❑
b) Sometimes – depending on whether I know them ❑
c) Infrequently – I keep my social network exclusive ❑
d) Never ❑

CHAPTER 14

Simple steps to networking success

Throughout this Part, we have given you a framework for understanding networks and networking. We began by looking at definitions and identifying themes. All commentators agree that networks are built on contacts; contacts at all levels: personal, professional, within organizations and between organizations – virtual as well as real. Whatever the level of the contact and the aim in establishing it, the overriding goal of networking is to build and manage productive relationships.

The primary responsibility for your network lies with you!

In this chapter, we will help you take on this responsibility by summarizing the activities we have covered here, reiterating some of the most important aspects of good networking and suggesting some good habits to form.

For this chapter, we have broken this down into five simple steps, which we cover in this chapter:

- Step one: Map your network
- Step two: Identify your style
- Step three: Clarify your goals
- Step four: Develop networking behaviours
- Step five: Benefit

Step one: Map your network

We live and work within networks, yet most people are unaware of them. If this lack of awareness persists, it will undermine the full effectiveness of managers in the future. Working with, through and in harmony with networks is a necessary skill if managers are to become successful and fulfil their potential. The first step to success requires that you understand who is in your network and where its strengths and weaknesses lie.

Network? What network?

You need to own and recognize your network. The most powerful way to understand your network is to see it. If you are on a professional website, you will be able to do this easily by clicking on your list of connections. Having done this, you will see a long list of people you are connected to and the type of relationship they have with you. You will also be able to see the latest activity on your site. However, you may prefer to map out your network to examine the different aspects and dynamics of it. Here's one method of doing so:

1 Take a piece of flipchart paper (anything smaller will be too small) and an ordinary pen (anything larger will be too large) and draw a circle in the middle of the paper with your name in it.
2 Draw a line to this circle. It will look like a lollipop.
3 At the end of this line, draw another circle. It will now look like a set of dumbbells.
4 Put the name of one of your primary networks in it – professional, personal, organizational, family...

5 Add more such lines until you have what looks like a daisy.
6 For each circle in your network tree, add more 'lollipops', into which you put the name and access information for your contact.
7 If one of your contacts was given to you by another member of your network and you haven't integrated them fully through building a personal relationship with them, connect them with a dotted line. Indicate the strength of your other relationships by thickening the lines between you and them.
8 Note the overlaps and gaps in your different networks and examine these in respect of your networking goals.

Don't be too fussy about how your map develops. Nobody else needs to understand it.

When you have completed your map with as many names as you can, stand back and look at it. Who have you forgotten? In Chapter 1, we gave you a list of potential network contacts. Have you included friends and acquaintances; family; school friends and teachers; college friends and academics; community leaders; church, parish and religious leaders; doctors and dentists; sports leisure or social club members; members of civic associations; former employers; colleagues and bosses from previous organizations; customers, suppliers, contractors, competitors, agents and distributors? Add any of these omissions to your map.

Your map will be constantly changing in accordance with your needs, goals, exposure and experiences.

Support your map with information. There are a number of computer packages that help you to organize the information you hold on people. Customer Relationship Management systems allow you to follow the trail of your communications with prospective clients and customers and record the content of your communication and prompts for the future. They will also remind you to make further contact at specific times. It is helpful to keep snippets of informal information on your records too. It is such an advantage to be able to open your conversation with a question such as:

How's your daughter doing at university?
Was your trip to Europe a success?
How did the bid presentation go?

or some other uncontentious question. Always keep your records up to date and in a format that enables you to update them easily.

Step two: Identify your style

Your map is a tangible illustration of where you have made your investment. To balance this picture, you need to reflect on your style. Attempt to answer the following question honestly:

What is your networking style?

You may need to look to the past to give yourself an indication of your style. *Do you:*

● like meeting new people?
● feel happiest focussed on a task or in a group?
● take opportunities to move in new circles?
● create opportunities to enhance your visibility or reputation?
● develop contacts in a wide variety of groups?
● stay in close contact with your customers or clients?
● enjoy meetings, training courses and conferences?
● know and talk to peers in other organizations?

Your answers to these questions will give you clues about your preferred style.

Remember from Chapter 1, there are three networking styles: conscious, intuitive and open.

● Conscious networkers have clear goals; they recognize the gaps in their network and identify opportunities to explore and find the people to fill the gaps.
● Intuitive networkers feel happiest when they are surrounded by people. They find themselves networking with everyone from their postman to other parents at the school gates.
● Open networkers invest in networks for their future potential. Translating such a network into something that is focussed and can deliver the goods may be a stumbling block for open networkers.

Networking isn't something that everyone feels comfortable with immediately. If the thought of being surrounded by people brings you out in a cold sweat, fills you with dread or immediately raises your anxiety level, you need to develop your skills consciously through scripting, rehearsing and practising. It is not necessarily true that you don't have the ability to network. You have probably never had the chance to practise and develop your skills.

Step three: Clarify your goals

The planning is now complete for your journey. However, to be a successful networker you need to have a destination in mind. Once you have established your destination, it is easier to monitor your progress as you journey along your route. This requires action: establishing, maintaining, nurturing and pruning your network.

What is your destination?

We introduced models in Chapter 1, which we have referred to throughout this masterclass. Networks are for:

- information
- development
- support
- influence.

Information

Managers need to keep up to date. To do this, a large amount of personal commitment, time and energy is required. To help you in this process, you need access to hubs and informers:

- Hubs:
  - are influential sources of information
  - suggest helpful connections.
- Informers:
  - provide new approaches and perspectives
  - recognize problems and opportunities
  - understand market trends and developments.

Be sure to choose your people well. Ensure that you consult with a variety of sources to get a balanced picture.

Development

A manager who isn't developing isn't performing. Continuous professional development (CPD) is now a pursuit expected of all professionals, based on the assumption that development isn't solely gained through initial training. You develop in many other ways: meetings, new projects, visits, seminars and reviews. The key to learning is reflecting on your experiences and making yourself conscious of the value you've taken from them and the skills you've developed as a result of them. It is important to keep asking yourself 'How could I improve?' You should also ask this of others who will be able to give you valuable feedback. Approach:

- Experts
  - those who are respected and valued
  - the people you would recommend to others.
- Challengers
  - cause you to look at your chosen direction
  - ask key questions about your life.

Seeking and receiving feedback openly and regularly creates a natural environment for development.

Support

No manger is an island! You need people to support you and to sponsor your entry into new networks. This will enable you to maintain and develop your networks. Ask yourself, 'Who should I surround myself with?'

- Foundations
  - on whom we depend.
- Sounding boards
  - hold you in the highest esteem
  - give you time.
- Guides
  - help you achieve your objectives
  - offer practical help and support.

Never underestimate the value of support. It can often go unrecognized until it's removed.

Influence

All managers need help along the way – people who can make things happen, endorse a project, open doors and offer you career guidance. Don't restrict yourself to just one person. Seek influential people within your organization or your profession. Ask yourself, 'Who could help me in the short and long term?'

● Resourcers
  – support you with resources
  – believe in your ideas.
● Mentors
  – guide your career
  – teach you the ropes.
● Promoters
  – advise you of opportunities
  – assist in enhancing your visibility.

Don't be afraid to ask. It can be flattering to be asked to fulfil an influencing role. People can always say no!

Planning your route

In planning your route, you first have to refer to your map. Are there any roadblocks? Do you have restricted access to information, development, support or influence?

Asking yourself this question will give you an indication of where you need to:

● invest
● hold
● prune.

Invest
Which relationships warrant investment currently? Which networks have you neglected recently?

- Personal
- Organizational
- Professional
- Social and professional websites

Which network could help you achieve your goals? If you have already decided what you want to achieve, you can probably identify the person who can help or support you in your endeavours. If this person is not immediately identifiable, think of how you might write a job advertisement specifying the type of person who could do it. You may recognize them as being inside one of your networks already.

You may decide to invest in the networks that you want to maintain or you may have identified gaps in your network that are critical. Think about the areas that require investment and who could bridge the gap.

Hold

You may have networks that, while important, require little special attention or effort. These are the networks that you can access at any point and personal investment is not always necessary. It could be that they are well developed or that others within them maintain them on your behalf – the family is a good example of this.

Prune

Which networks aren't so critical or important? You could choose to spend less time and energy on these. Decisions to prune networks are always difficult and can seem callous and calculating.

To have the energy to invest in new networks, you need to be realistic about those that are not serving you well and, where necessary, withdraw from them. You may need to prune people who are leaning too heavily on your good will and unable to repay you in a like manner.

Too many plans fail because the goal is not clear. Be clear in your goals and plan your route towards them. Always remember that plans may need to change as your circumstances change.

Regularly review your progress by asking yourself:

What do I want from my network?
What am I prepared to contribute to those in my network?

Your answers will keep you on the road to success.

Telling somebody about your plan is a good way of making your plan into a contract and ensuring that you stick to it. Also, hearing yourself saying things out loud and seeing others' reactions to what you're saying brings a new understanding and clarity. Choose your sounding boards with care. You could do so on the basis of their experience, skills and the quality of your relationship. This is a great way to start developing your networking skills and behaviours.

Step four: Develop networking behaviours

There is an unwritten code of ethics that ensures good networking practice.

Networking behaviours include the following:

- Be open-minded.
- Keep commitments.
- Treat others as you would like to be treated.
- Don't be afraid to ask.
- Give without expectation of a return.
- Say thank you.

Many people are cynical about networking as an activity. They see it as taking advantage of people's goodwill for personal gain. This is not the case. We all have a natural sense of justice. Try to gauge what this is for each person you contact. People will not co-operate if they feel that there is nothing in it for them – or not for very long, anyway. They very quickly get tired of giving and will soon stop. Networking, therefore, contains its own control system.

The best approach is 'treat others as you would like to be treated'. In this way, you can put yourself in the other person's shoes and ask whether your demands are reasonable. If you think you are stretching your credibility a bit, you might like to think of what incentives or rewards would balance the books.

Remember you are part of others' networks too so:

- Keep your eyes and ears open.
- Open doors for others.
- Refer and recommend people.
- Publicize others' achievements.
- Suggest projects or opportunities that will enhance their standing.

Step five: Benefit

Networking is here to stay. So, if you want to:

- ensure balance
- create visibility
- increase employability

understand and invest in your networks.

Ensure balance

Balance is hard to maintain. This is particularly true in current times because of the complex dynamics of life and the overlaps in our activities that we experience – such as the blurring of work and home. Nevertheless, networks can help you strike a balance between opposing forces in the following ways:

Balance
Support – Challenge
Doing – Thinking
Personal – Professional

By constantly monitoring and managing your networks, you can ensure that you reach a state of equilibrium.

Create visibility

Many large organizations today (especially flat or networked organizations) can be very impersonal. It is easy to get lost in the crowd. If you know how to network and how to identify the hubs and sponsors, people will get to know you.

Outside your organization, networks are fascinating. Once you begin networking, you will realize what a small world it is.

Increase employability

You can ensure your continued employability by:

● building networks with integrity
● bridging the gaps.

Building networks with integrity

Prospective employers may be interested in you solely because of your network. Professionals such as brokers, advertisers, salespeople, editors and consultants generally have key contacts with whom they have developed strong relationships. Often these contacts offer their allegiance to the individual rather than the organization. Employers may judge you on the quality and loyalty of your network. But be aware of contractual restrictions on using your network after leaving your organization.

Bridging the gaps

Successful people know that the way to good opportunities and advancement can come from a network that is carefully maintained. Make sure that you keep your network watertight by plugging the gaps with good 'bridging' relationships.

Summary

To do anything well requires focussed attention and effort. Networking is no exception. Throughout this masterclass, we have been your companion in looking at how best to create and develop your network to advantage. We've encouraged you to think strategically about the purpose of your network, the people in it and your style of networking. Importantly, too, we asked you to think about the reciprocal nature of good networking practice. Small favours demonstrate that you're attentive to others and really do build goodwill.

Developing your network is not something to be done haphazardly. Your time is far too valuable to be wasted that way.

Know, develop and mobilize your network.

You will then be able to enjoy the rewards.

Networking is a highly valuable activity. It holds rewards for all parties if managed conscientiously. Have fun with your networks but use them wisely. With your 'networking eyes', you will see life's possibilities in a new light.

Fact-check (answers at the back)

Answer the following questions honestly, reflecting on your networking skills.

1. **What is your natural networking environment?**
   a) I feel happiest in organizational groups ❏
   b) I look for opportunities to move into new circles ❏
   c) I network when my work depends on it ❏
   d) I don't seek or enjoy networking environments ❏

2. **If others were to describe your main networking characteristic, what would it be?**
   a) I tend to be the hub of others' networks ❏
   b) I am generally approached for the information I hold ❏
   c) I am known as a mentor or sponsor for others ❏
   d) I am not visible in others' networks ❏

3. **How do you use your networks?**
   a) For gathering information ❏
   b) For my personal development ❏
   c) For gaining support for my ideas and career ❏
   d) To access those who can influence on my behalf ❏

4. **If you were to describe your networking style, what would it be?**
   a) I think about and plan my networks ❏
   b) I build relationships naturally ❏
   c) I am conscious about my future needs and seed relationships early ❏
   d) I don't have a dominant style ❏

5. **How do you manage your networks?**
   a) I hold on to those who are important to me ❏
   b) I prune those contacts that are no longer valuable ❏
   c) I invest in those that I feel will bring me value ❏
   d) I don't manage my networks at all ❏

6. **Who do your networks contain?**
   a) No one obviously of benefit ❏
   b) Those who mentor and guide you ❏
   c) Those who promote and sponsor you ❏
   d) Those who build your reputation and visibility ❏

7. **In terms of support, does your network contain:**
a) A foundation – a touchstone on whom you can depend? ❏
b) A sounding board – for bouncing ideas off? ❏
c) A guide – to counsel you? ❏
d) A practitioner – who gives you practical assistance? ❏

8. **Which is the dominant function your network serves?**
a) Being supportive while acting as a challenge ❏
b) Giving you feedback on what you do ❏
c) Maintaining a healthy work/life balance ❏
d) My network doesn't assist me in finding balance ❏

9. **If you were to seek a new position, how ready is your network to assist you?**
a) I have the right people in my network and they are ready to assist me ❏
b) I have key contacts but need to build stronger relationships ❏
c) I need to plug a few gaps before I can use my network in this way ❏
d) My network cannot assist me in finding a new position ❏

10. **Looking forward, how equipped do you feel as a networker?**
a) I feel well equipped as a networker ❏
b) I now know what I need to do ❏
c) I need to build relationships with some key people as a minimum ❏
d) I still dread networking and will continue to avoid it! ❏

7 × 7

1 Seven key ideas

- Networking is not a one-way street. It is a reciprocal activity where valuable information, introductions and good will is exchanged equally.
- Regularly review your network. By their nature networks are dynamic, so keep reviewing them. Think about which parts of your network are rewarding and which are draining and then how best to manage this going forward.
- Most people like to feel important to another person – as long as they're not exploited. Don't feel shy of asking for a favour.
- Develop networking behaviours and the confidence to grow your network. If you are not comfortable with networking then you need to start by giving yourself challenges. Identify someone you want to connect with and think about how you would do this, how you would link with them, what you might say. Then practise (use different methods – face to face, email, telephone and social networks).
- Map your existing network and continue to refresh your map. The first step to networking success is to understand your network: who is in it, how it has grown and how you can develop it to benefit you.
- Be authentic in the way you engage with those in your network. Don't try to act as you think you 'should', act as you are.
- Look for opportunities to be generous to others and do so without expectation of a return favour – you never know what benefits this will bring.

2 Seven best resources

- *Brilliant Networking: What the Best Networkers Know, Say and Do* by Steven D'Souza (Pearson Education, 2011). Contains useful tools, anecdotes and examples of people who have used networking to secure their dream jobs, make career moves, grow their business and find their life partner.
- *Networking for People Who Hate Networking: A Field Guide for Introverts, the Overwhelmed, and the Underconnected* by Devora Zack (Berrett-Koehler, 2010). This book shatters stereotypes about people who dislike networking. They're not shy or misanthropic. Rather, they tend to be reflective and think before they talk.
- *The Financial Times Guide to Business Networking: How to Use the Power of Online and Offline Networking for Business and Personal Success* by Heather Townsend (FT Publishing International, 2014). This is a great, practical guide to all aspects of networking – packed with lots of quick and easy tips to help leverage the power of any network.
- How to Build your LinkedIn Network: http://cdn2.hubspot. net/hub/53/blog/docs/ebooks/learning_linkedin_from_the_ experts.pdf LinkedIn have useful hints and tips about how to build your network which are found in their Help Centre.
- *Never Eat Alone: and other secrets to success, one relationship at a time* by Keith Ferrazzi and Tahl Raz (Portfolio Penguin, 2014). This book focuses on the important element of relationship building; the foundation stone of networking.
- http://www.ted.com/talks/nicholas_christakis_the_hidden_ influence_of_social_networks?language=en We're all embedded in vast social networks. Nicholas Christakis tracks how a wide variety of traits can spread from person to person, showing how your location in the network might impact your life in ways you don't even know!

3 Seven things to avoid

- Lack of support for others – seek 'reciprocity' or 'do as you would be done by'. If you invest in others, they are equally likely to invest in you.
- Don't interpret silence as disinterest. Give people a second chance to respond to you. It may not be personal. They may just be busy or distracted.
- Poor preparation – when you meet new people, be prepared. Do your research: their interests; their role; their organization – and think about how you will approach them and with what message.
- Dropping people in it! Try to avoid introducing people to others who haven't agreed to be introduced.
- Not reviewing – take time to review and think about what you want from your network and how it's meeting your needs. For instance, is your network inclined towards your goal? Are you over-dependent upon a few people? Are people being proactive in contacting you?
- Try not to speak badly of anyone in your network. It's a small world and you may find connections exist that you didn't even think were possible.
- Stagnation – to be successful, networks need to grow. Keep asking people you meet: 'Who else should I be talking to?'

4 Seven inspiring people

- Her Majesty the Queen must be one of the most networked people in the world. You too could be part of her network! You can write to Her Majesty at: Buckingham Palace, London, SW1A 1AA.
- Jimmy Carter, 39th President of the United States of America has been involved in a variety of national and international public policy, conflict resolution, human rights and charitable causes.
- Graham Norton's face is beamed into 3 million homes every Friday night, with *The Graham Norton Show* now in its 13th

series on BBC One. On his red sofa sit the world's most notable people.

- Arianna Huffington, editor-in-chief of The Huffington Post, who has been dubbed 'the world's best networker'.
- His Holiness the 14th Dalai Lama. His Holiness is the spiritual leader of the Tibetan people. He frequently states that his life is guided by three major commitments: the promotion of basic human values or secular ethics in the interest of human happiness, the fostering of inter-religious harmony and the preservation of Tibet. He is known almost everywhere and connects lovingly with everyone he meets.
- Oprah Winfrey is an American media proprietor, talk show host, actress, producer and philanthropist. She is best known for her talk show *The Oprah Winfrey Show*. Dubbed the 'Queen of All Media' she is, according to some assessments, the most influential woman in the world. In 2013, she was awarded the Presidential Medal of Freedom by President Barack Obama.
- Bob Geldof is widely known for his activism having co-founded 'Band Aid' with Midge Ure. Together they tapped into a global musical network to put on the 'Live Aid' concert (1985) in service of famine relief in Ethiopia. The influence of this movement has entered the political arena and Bob Geldof is now seen alongside political heavyweights and his face is known around the world.

5 Seven great quotes

- 'The currency of real networking is not greed but generosity.' Keith Ferrazzi
- 'I've learned that people will forget what you said, people will forget what you did, but people will never forget how you made them feel.' Maya Angelou
- 'You can make more friends in two months by becoming interested in other people than you can in two years by trying to get other people interested in you.' Dale Carnegie
- 'The way of the world is meeting people through other people.' Robert Kerrigan

- 'Position yourself as a centre of influence – the one who knows the movers and shakers. People will respond to that – and you'll soon become what you project.' Bob Burg
- 'It's not what you know but WHO you know that makes the difference.' Anonymous
- 'Giving connects two people; the giver and the receiver, and this connection gives birth to a new sense of belonging.' Deepak Chopra

6 Seven things to do today

- Map your network. With you as a hub, trace outwards towards all the other hubs in your network. Focus on those who may be able to help you reach your networking goal.
- Make one contact, perhaps with someone that you have been delaying getting in touch with – email them, pick up the telephone or have a meeting.
- Think about how you can help someone that you value in your network.
- Imagine something you'd like from your network to see if it's in good enough condition to bring it to you.
- Ask someone to introduce you to someone you want to make contact with.
- Start talking to people about what you want to achieve. When you say it out loud, it becomes 'real' – and that's just the first step to it being 'realized'!
- Put networking time in your diary every week.

7 Seven trends for tomorrow

- The Covid pandemic has had an impact on how people meet, connect and build relationships. However, according to the Global Web Index (GWI) report on the latest trends in social media, between 2019 and 2021, the global use of social media has maintained an average of 2.26 hours per day. www.gwi.com/reports

- TikTok will become bigger. In September 2021, TikTok reported more than 1 billion active monthly users and is still growing. www.techtarget.com/whatis/feature/9-social-media-trends
- With roughly 2.93 billion monthly active users in the first quarter of 2022, Facebook is still the most used online social network worldwide. Nevertheless, its use is declining. Half a million users stopped using it towards the end of the year 2021. www.statista.com/statistics/264810/number-of-monthly-active-facebook-users-worldwide
- LinkedIn key statistics
  - LinkedIn generated $11.5 billion revenue in 2021, an increase of 43.7 per cent year-on-year
  - LinkedIn has 822 million members
  - Over 57 million business and 120,000 schools have LinkedIn accounts
  - The 25–34-year-old age bracket accounts for 60.1 per cent of Linked-In users
  - According to LinkedIn, over 100 million job applications are sent each month. www.businessofapps.com/data/linkedin-statistics
- In 2021, 323 million people worldwide used dating apps or dating sites to meet new people. www.cloudwards.net/online-dating-statistics
- LinkedIn is probably the most powerful tool in your job-hunting arsenal. The majority – 87 per cent – of recruiters and hiring managers use LinkedIn to find job candidates (August 2021). www.forbes.com/sites/forbescoachescouncil/2021/08/12/how-to-land-a-job-through-networking/?sh=f6d960937a5e
- Your network will be an important venue for information, influence, development and support. The old adage 'it's not what you know, it's who you know' still holds true. www.forbes.com/sites/forbescoachescouncil/2021/08/12/how-to-land-a-job-through-networking/?sh=f6d960937a5e

PART 3

Your Assertiveness Masterclass

Introduction

Much has been spoken about the assertive communication style, not all of it complimentary! Many people confuse it with being aggressive, bamboozling others into submission and getting what *you* want, despite what *they* want. However, assertive communication is not domineering; it's just a means of saying what you mean, meaning what you say and allowing others to do the same.

Taking the decision to adopt *assertive* behaviour will mark the beginning of a new way of life: a way of life where you make your own decisions and choices without feeling guilty, and where *you* are in control, not those around you.

By working through some simple steps, and by testing the techniques out in a 'safe' environment, you will soon become confident in your new-found powers of assertion. You will be able to command the respect of others, achieve your personal and professional goals and raise your self-esteem.

The steps to assertive behaviour are:

- Understand the different styles of communication and the effect they have.
- Identify your own style(s) of communication.
- Know your own worth *and* the worth of others.
- Be clear about your goals.
- Be prepared to learn from your successes *and* failures.
- Be flexible, and don't expect too much.
- Learn to listen.

CHAPTER 15

Preparing the foundations

In this chapter we will prepare the foundations for developing assertive behaviour and learn the different styles of communication: passive, passive/aggressive, aggressive and assertive.

This is the beginning of a long journey but it will be one that you'll not regret as it puts you in the driving seat of your own life. This is the point – it is you who drives your life, not others, nor circumstances. You may make mistakes from time to time but, as your assertiveness skills advance, you'll develop the understanding and the resources to pick yourself up, brush yourself down, and start all over again!

There are two main tasks here. The first is to identify your own style of communication:

- passive
- passive/aggressive
- aggressive
- assertive.

Your second task is to know your worth:

- understand yourself
- accept yourself for the way you are
- decide to change – *if you want to*
- give yourself permission to succeed – *and fail.*

Communication styles

In order to understand ourselves, and why we don't behave assertively, we must first examine our current **pattern of behaviour**. We will not dwell on our failures; we will merely use them for information – and for our motivation to change.

Note your behavioural pattern in both your personal and professional life. It is these behaviours that determine the way people respond to you and it is these behaviours that determine the outcome of all your communication.

If you have difficulty identifying these patterns in yourself, ask a friend to help – but remember, they are doing you a favour so try not to get defensive.

For instance: are you very aggressive, uncompromising, fixed in your views, intolerant or impatient? Are you sarcastic, manipulative, dismissive, arrogant or superior? Are you acquiescent, apologetic, deferring, self-effacing or inferior?

It is interesting to note that most people who want to develop assertive behaviour fit into the last category – that of 'victim'.

What's your message?

People always treat you the way you 'ask' to be treated. Understanding what you are 'asking for' is half the battle. You may think you are using assertive language but the way in which you convey your message and the demeanour you adopt when you do so can counteract any intention to be assertive and can undermine your success in doing so. Try 'sitting on your own shoulder' and observing yourself in action. What are you doing? What are people's reactions to you? Are you getting your message across unambiguously? By observing yourself carefully, and honestly, you can identify the changes you'd like to make and make the changes that *will* make a difference.

Try not to feel hopeless at this point: from now on, everything is a positive step.

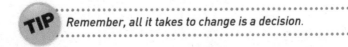

TIP *Remember, all it takes to change is a decision.*

Most people's behaviour patterns will demonstrate some characteristics from each of the four categories noted above – **passive**, **passive/aggressive**, **aggressive** and **assertive** – depending on the circumstances of the communication. However, one category will most likely dominate your style. Read through the descriptions below and see which one holds true for you most of the time.

Passive

Passive behaviour is usually associated with the 'loser': one who is always backing down, giving in and being submissive. Apologies are rife in this mode of communication, as are reluctant agreements and negative statements about oneself. Passive behaviour conveys the message 'You're OK, I'm not OK.'

Passive/aggressive

Passive/aggressive behaviour is usually associated with the 'saboteur'. It is by no means overt, but the aggressive motivation is obvious nonetheless. The distinguishing features of this mode of communication are sarcastic comments, comments with double meanings and non-verbal signals such as mockingly gazing heavenwards. The underlying message is 'I'm not OK, you're not OK.'

Aggressive

Aggressive behaviour takes no account of the rights of others. Although this person may be perceived to be a 'go-getter' or one of life's 'winners', they are usually feared and their style encourages deceitful behaviour from others who would rather not face up to their wrath. The message conveyed by this person is 'I'm OK, you're not OK.'

Assertive

Assertive communication does not diminish or 'put down' another human being, it does not trespass on any human rights and it does not shy away from important issues. Rather, it encourages satisfactory communication where everyone's needs are met in the best way. The identifying characteristic of assertive behaviour is the use of 'I' statements. This indicates that the person communicating is taking responsibility for the message that is being conveyed. For example, 'I am not happy with this decision, I would like to discuss it further.' This form of communication is based on respect for oneself and others. It is driven by the belief that 'I'm OK, you're OK.' There are no losers.

A word of caution. Assertive behaviour does not necessarily mean that you get your way all the time. It does mean that the chances of getting to the best solution, with everyone's self-esteem intact, are significantly enhanced.

What's your communication style?

If you are unsure of your dominant style of communicating behaviour, work through the following simple questionnaire. Do not worry if your responses fall into all the different categories; identify with the strongest trend. The mix of responses will help you focus on the specific areas in your style that you may wish to change.

Broadly speaking, if most of your responses fall into the 'Sometimes' category, you may tend to be aggressive or passive/aggressive. If they fall into the 'Never' category, you are certainly passive. If you find that your responses are predominantly in the 'Often' column, you are well on the way to being assertive.

Communication style questionnaire

	Sometimes	Often	Never
1 I feel that I represent myself well in all communications and am respectful of others.	☐	☐	☐
2 My ideas are considered valuable and are often adopted.	☐	☐	☐
3 I am able to say no without feeling guilty.	☐	☐	☐
4 I am able to make complaints without losing my temper.	☐	☐	☐
5 I am able to give feedback to another without causing offence.	☐	☐	☐
6 I can communicate effectively in a group, allowing each member to be heard.	☐	☐	☐
7 I am able to ask for help.	☐	☐	☐
8 I am able to meet my own and others' needs.	☐	☐	☐
9 I can control my temper.	☐	☐	☐
10 People find that I am good at talking through ideas and problems.	☐	☐	☐
11 I am free from disabling stress.	☐	☐	☐
12 I am comfortable with who I am.	☐	☐	☐

Know your worth

We all have basic human rights:

- the right to choose
- the right to 'be'
- the right to be respected
- the right to make mistakes
- the right to say 'no'
- the right to ask for what we want
- the right to ask for what we need.

Understand your fears

It is often our fears that prevent us from developing assertive behaviour. What are yours? For example, they might be: 'I will lose my friends', 'I will make a fool of myself', 'No one will like me any more', 'I will become irritating', or
'.. ' (fill in your own).

Our fears are usually much larger than reality. Face them; they have a habit of shrinking.

Accept yourself for the way you are

It is very easy to put yourself down. We are our own worst critics. In the main, we are:

- **what** we are supposed to be
- **where** we are supposed to be
- **doing** what we are supposed to be doing.

Release all your disappointments and guilty feelings – forgive yourself. Everything that you have done and experienced has brought you to this point of change. *Everything is to play for.*

Decide to change – if you want to

In making the decision to change your behaviour, you may find it helpful to project forward in time and imagine how it would look, and feel, if you were in control of your communication. Compare this to how you feel now.

The power of 'imaging' or 'visualizing' cannot be over-stressed. It is a very useful tool for achieving your objectives, whatever they are.

By 'bringing to mind' or 'picturing in your mind's eye' your desired state, you are actually putting images into your subconscious that, ultimately, determine your behaviour. Your subconscious mind can work only in images; it does not understand timescales or conditions. Imagine yourself as you would like to be and your subconscious will work tirelessly to make this a reality. It cannot fail. Keep reinforcing the images time after time, using positive affirmations if this helps (see Chapter 16 for more on this) and the old patterns will soon be obliterated and replaced with the new ones that you have chosen.

Old habits die hard, but they do die, with persistence and determination.

 If you continue to behave as you have always behaved, people will continue to treat you as they have always treated you.

Give yourself permission to succeed – and fail

You are embarking on a journey of transformation.

Sometimes you will succeed on your terms; sometimes you will fail. Try to regard these occurrences with dispassion. They are merely learning experiences. It will not always be easy but it will be rewarding.

By now you should have identified your dominant style of communication and decided whether or not you are completely happy to continue in this vein.

If not, you may have come up with a conditional 'maybe' in response to the desire to change. This is good enough. It will drive your awareness and allow you to choose how to respond in different situations. There may be times when you want to submit, for instance. And there may be times when you feel the need to dominate. Being assertive is about the choice to communicate in the way you feel is most appropriate at the time. Being free to flex your communication style at will is part of being assertive.

If you decide to make changes in the way you communicate and in the way you are perceived by your colleagues, then proceed with enthusiasm; there is much you can gain from the following chapters.

Summary

To recap, the different communication styles are broadly divided into the following categories:

- passive
- assertive
- passive/aggressive
- aggressive.

These may sound pejorative descriptors but they do convey the underlying motivations of the person using this form of communication.

They are loosely associated with the following characteristics:

- victim
- achiever
- manipulator
- dictator.

Think about how these terms resonate with you. If you have a strong reaction to one or other of them, it may be worth exploring why this is so. Is it something you find distasteful because you feel it is a 'bit close to the truth'?! Try to objectify the way you analyse your own style and try to prevent yourself from judging or criticizing yourself.

Fact-check (answers at the back)

Think about the following questions and use them to build self-awareness and challenge yourself.

1. My dominant style of communication is...
   a) Aggressive ❑
   b) Passive/aggressive ❑
   c) Passive ❑
   d) Assertive ❑

2. I am able to be assertive...
   a) At will ❑
   b) Sometimes ❑
   c) Occasionally ❑
   d) Never ❑

3. I can flex between communication styles...
   a) When I feel it's appropriate ❑
   b) With preparation and effort ❑
   c) When I want to get something for myself ❑
   d) I can't change my style at all ❑

4. I think the assertive style of communication is...
   a) Dominating and imposing ❑
   b) Manipulative ❑
   c) Highly effective ❑
   d) For wimps! ❑

5. I believe the advantages of assertiveness is...
   a) You can always get what you want ❑
   b) You can establish good rapport ❑
   c) You can make others feel like losers ❑
   d) There are no advantages! ❑

6. When I need to make a customer complaint, I...
   a) Apologize profusely for being a nuisance ❑
   b) Get angry so that I can fire my complaint boldly ❑
   c) Establish the context, the concern and discuss a solution ❑
   d) Leave with the product I'm complaining about! ❑

7. When someone comes to me and asks me for advice, I...
   a) Give it freely and tell them what to do ❑
   b) End up taking on their battle ❑
   c) Encourage them to think about how they're going to deal with the situation ❑
   d) Avoid getting involved in the first place! ❑

8. There are situations when assertive behaviour is definitely not called for!
   a) This statement is true ❑
   b) Assertiveness is always called for ❑
   c) Communication styles are driven by external situations ❑
   d) Communication styles are not dependent upon situations ❑

9. I believe that my personality drives my communication style and...
a) I'm stuck with the communication style that matches my personality ❏
b) I'm an 'introvert' and can never be assertive! ❏
c) I can learn different communication styles regardless of my personality ❏
d) I have to change my personality before I can change my communication style ❏

10. If I could develop more assertiveness, I would benefit by...
a) Getting people to do as they're told by me! ❏
b) Being in charge of my own life ❏
c) Making sure I was in situations that call for assertiveness ❏
d) There would be no benefit to me ❏

CHAPTER 16

Creating winning scenarios

Creating winning scenarios is the foundation stone for being assertive and being in charge of your own life. This does not mean that you always get your own way, but it does mean that you will be satisfied that you have represented yourself assertively and can live happily (or acceptingly!) with the outcome.

The agenda in this chapter is to bring you that little bit closer to being in control of your own life – asserting yourself in the way you choose. In order to achieve this, we will look at:

- 'winning' language
- positive affirmations
- creative visualization
- building self-esteem.

Those who are adept at turning on assertive behaviour are also quite able to observe their actions, talk themselves through their learning and test the effect of new behaviours. Self-knowledge is the key to taking control of our lives.

Observing, questioning and asking for feedback are vital if we are to succeed.

'Winning' language

'Winning' language is the language of assertive behaviour. It speaks more than mere words to those you communicate with and tells them that you are in control.

Those who recognize this quality in you will nonetheless be hard pressed to say exactly what it is that you are doing to give them this impression. Actually, it is a subtle combination of body language, mental attitude and verbal language.

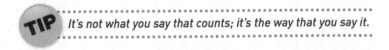

TIP *It's not what you say that counts; it's the way that you say it.*

The 'winning' qualities of an assertive communicator are:

- the use of 'I' statements
- direct, clear language
- an ability to demonstrate understanding and to empathize ('active listening skills')
- an ability to build rapport and maintain relationships
- good posture, voice and eye contact
- confidence in what they say – no self-effacing comments or profuse apologies!

Direct, clear language

Language can be a very inadequate and clumsy tool for communication. It can also be beautifully simple and, combined with reinforcing messages through the various physical channels of communication (body language), it can be extremely effective and evocative.

Here are some simple rules to help you practise assertive, 'winning', language:

- **Set the scene** by describing – very briefly – what you are referring to: 'When you called a meeting last Friday, I...'
- **Simplicity, clarity and brevity** are key to assertive communication. Do not ramble; you will lose the attention of your audience. Make your point quickly.

- **Take responsibility** for what you are saying. This is done by using the first person. Here are two examples, one negative and one positive: 'I am unhappy about the way this project is proceeding'; 'I'm delighted with the outcome of this meeting.'
- **Use repetition** if you feel that your message isn't getting across, but restructure your statement the second time.
- **Use silence appropriately** – it can say more than words. Don't be afraid of it; try it out.

Active listening skills

Active listening ranks highly in the league table of communication skills. It enables you to empathize with your audience and build successful relationships. Stated simply, active listening is listening with curiosity; or listening as if you've never heard the other person speak before. When you do this, you will be able to meter your own communication more precisely because you will have homed in on what others are saying without making premature judgements, assumptions or jumping to conclusions.

Good listeners do several things. They...

- **paraphrase** – briefly summarize what has just been said
- **ask 'open' questions** to elicit good information – 'how?' and 'what?' ('why?' can sound whiney or inquisitorial)
- **show an interest** – maintain good eye contact and prompt more communication by nodding from time to time, using encouraging words like 'Yes', 'Ah-ha' and 'Mmm'.
- **give feedback** – reflect back what they believe is being said.

Building rapport and maintaining relationships

Everybody needs to feel liked and valued. Others are likely to be generous in their dealings with you if you manage to develop a healthy rapport. It is a good investment *if done genuinely and generously.* If you do this as a manipulative technique, your motivation will almost certainly be exposed.

Developing good rapport is based on taking an interest in the other party, understanding and remembering what they have said and remembering to acknowledge significant events or achievements.

Body language also plays a part in developing rapport (more of this in Chapter 20).

It sometimes helps to write down others' activities as well as your own if you are forgetful. However, you will soon find that if you manage to develop active listening skills, you will start to remember things more reliably. This is because you will have been concentrating on what the other person has been saying, and you will have heard yourself summarize the main points.

Hearing yourself say something really does help you to remember. Talking to yourself is not a sign of madness; it is a valuable aide-memoire.

Good posture, voice and eye contact

It is somewhat galling to note that only about 7 per cent of what you say (the words you use) contributes towards the message you are trying to convey.

Much more of the message – 38 per cent – is carried in your voice. This includes tone, pitch, speed and the quality of your voice.

The remainder, some 55 per cent, is conveyed by your body – mostly the eyes. This is why communicating on the telephone or via email can be so misleading. Messages through these media have a tendency to take on a life of their own. Meaning can become distorted when the visual channel of communication is removed. Without the visual cues, it is sometimes difficult to interpret messages accurately and misunderstandings can occur. If read without the visible signals that accompany humour, for instance, messages can sound aggressive or sarcastic. It is important, therefore, to remember this and forestall any likely misinterpretation by signposting or symbolizing humorous remarks.

Good posture and an upright walk look good and convey confidence. Slouching or shuffling along gives completely the opposite impression. Try walking towards yourself in front of a mirror or catch a glimpse of yourself in a shop window. Notice the difference when you try to improve the way you move.

Assertive body language will be covered more fully in Chapter 20.There are several simple rules to consider for the time being:

- **Stand or sit proud** – taking up as little space as possible conveys lack of confidence or weakness
- **Gesture appropriately** – gestures can help to convey a message when used sensibly. Try not to overdo it, however; a lot of extravagant gesturing can be very distracting
- **Don't fidget** – this will make you appear nervous, as no doubt you are if you are fidgeting!

The use and quality of your voice will affect the other person's perception of what you are saying.

A high-pitched, whiney voice, for example, conveys a 'victim' message: 'I'm really rather weak and pathetic and I'm throwing myself on your mercy!' This style of voice can also sound spoilt and petulant.

By contrast, a loud, deep voice delivering words like machine-gun fire sounds incredibly aggressive.

Notice your own style of vocalization. Would you like to change it?

The optimum style – if there really is such a thing – is a calm pace, pitched mid-range with good intonation and clearly enunciated words. It's not always appropriate, of course, but it does for most eventualities.

To communicate assertively, you must maintain good *eye* contact. Aim to maintain almost constant eye contact while you are listening to another person. It is not so easy, indeed it can be actively disconcerting, to maintain constant eye contact while you are talking, so strike a comfortable balance between looking into and away from the other's eyes.

Your eyes will help in the expression of your message and they will no doubt be on the move much of the time. However you decided to use them, return your glance regularly to the other person's eyes throughout the delivery of your message to pick up how they are feeling about what you are saying.

It is worth noting that, if your body language is out of phase with your words, any hidden agenda will immediately become apparent – if not precisely what it is, at least the fact that you have one!

Confidence in what you say

Confidence is fine if you have it, but most unassertive people are sadly lacking in this department. However, here are some useful tips that you can learn to incorporate in your repertoire very easily.

- **Say what you mean and mean what you say** – be succinct and to the point.
- **Never apologize** – unless you sincerely mean it, then do it only once. (Notice how politicians and business leaders almost never apologize. Are we really convinced that they never make mistakes?)
- **Don't claim to be a fool to compensate for feeling a fool.** We often do this to prompt a contradiction. One of the dangers of this strategy is that you will be believed!

Positive affirmations

Used in the right way, positive affirmations can be enormously helpful. They are designed to retrain the brain to think about ourselves differently.

If we have a poor self-opinion (usually as a result of a series of childhood experiences), then as soon as we suffer a loss of confidence, we will return to these experiences and the feelings they engendered. It will take repeated effort to overcome this tendency and to replace it with something more positive.

For some people, positive affirmations can be very helpful in this process.

Positive affirmations are constant repetitions of a belief we wish to install in our brains to replace the less healthy beliefs we have grown up with.

Positive affirmations must be constantly repeated: if you think how long you have lived with your own negativity, just think how often you will have to repeat a desired belief before it will outweigh, and triumph over, the negative belief that is so firmly lodged in your brain.

How to reprogram your brain

Every time we have a thought, an electrical impulse sets off along a particular route through the brain. After this same thought has been through the mind many times, a physical path becomes etched in the brain. This will deepen with every thinking of the thought. If this happens to be a negative or undermining thought, it will colour what you believe about yourself and project to others. A new path must be created, therefore, that is even deeper, and easier, for the thought to follow – the path of least resistance. This can be achieved through positive affirmations.

Say your positive affirmations every day, like a mantra, and eventually you will find that you have reprogrammed your brain and installed a healthier belief.

There are several rules for designing positive affirmations.

- They must be in the present – 'I am...'
- They must *not* be conditional – 'When I... then I will...'
- They must *not* be undermined – hidden message: 'Who am I trying to fool with all this stuff anyway?!'
- They must be about *you*; nobody else.
- They must be spoken out loud – in private if you wish, but it is important to *hear* yourself say them.

Examples of good affirmations are:

- 'I can handle it.'
- 'I am professionally competent.'
- 'I am a valuable and capable member of the team.'

Creative visualization

Creative visualization is an extremely powerful technique for 'seeing' and 'fixing' your far-distant goals in your mind's eye and for planning and rehearsing the execution of the tasks that lead to the achievement of your goals.

As we have already said, the subconscious mind works in images, and when these are clear, it will work tirelessly to turn these images into reality.

What you need for effective creative visualization is a starting point, and an end point. That is to say, you need to understand your current situation completely and notice how far away you are from reaching your goal.

This is not a negative exercise; it is an unemotional and non-judgemental appraisal to enable you to take realistic, positive action and to measure your progress.

Picture your goal

Once you have isolated and fully understood your current situation, you must then form a very clear image of your goal and 'see', 'feel' or 'sense' it. Imagine it from a detached point of view, as if you were watching a film of yourself. Imagine it every way you can until you have a precise picture. Do not dismantle this picture; hold it clearly in your mind. Return to it regularly so that it becomes reinforced, time and again.

Set some time aside for this visualization so that you can build its strength over time. Do not try to hurry the achievement of your goal. Your subconscious will take the strain between your current situation and your desired state and will work to transform the first image into the second.

This method of achieving what you desire is infallible when done diligently. Indeed, you will probably have some personal experience of a time when you did this instinctively; when you desired something so badly, and so clearly, that you managed to bring it to reality.

Try it with big desires and small, but make sure that they are yours and no one else's. You will not be able to use this technique to manipulate others to do what you want!

Seven steps to creative visualization

In summary, here are the basic steps to effective creative visualization – a method that assertive people adopt without even thinking about it:

1 Notice your current situation and your distance from the goal.
2 Develop a clear image of your goal.
3 Breathe it, feel it, smell it, examine it from all angles.
4 Plan and execute your first and second steps only.
5 Do something else and leave your subconscious to work on the next stage undisturbed. Do not interfere, and do not undermine your images. The next steps will come to you in their own time.
6 Return to reinforce the image of your goal and observe your current position regularly – but not too often; the process needs time to work undisturbed.
7 Finally, trust the process; it will work.

Planning and rehearsing the tasks that have to be performed before reaching your goal are like 'mini' creative visualizations. Each step can be treated in the same way as those listed above for a major goal. Never plan more than two steps ahead, however, as the path your subconscious mind leads you down may be different from the one you expect. Follow it though: it will probably be more creative and more effective than your conscious mind.

If you have no clear idea of the tasks, don't worry; they will pop into your mind when the moment is right.

When you have executed the tasks in your mind's eye, you will find that the ease with which you perform them in reality will be truly remarkable.

Once you have a clear idea of your goal, everything you do and every decision you make will bring you closer to this goal.

Building self-esteem

Self-esteem, as opposed to ego, is very difficult to recapture once it is lost. Self-esteem is a measure of how you value yourself, and it is built up from your first breath – or, as in many cases, it is destroyed by damaging experiences or relationships. It is one of the most helpful personal qualities that you can possess because from it stems the belief that you are worthy and able to succeed.

Sometimes people try to camouflage their low self-esteem by portraying excessive confidence. This is just 'noise' used to drown out their feelings of vulnerability and inadequacy. Don't be fooled or intimidated by this. Recognize it as a human solution to intolerable emotional discomfort. In this way, the threat of what appears to be a very confident person will disappear and you will be able to meet them on an equal footing.

Using some of the techniques described above can help to build self-esteem and confidence, but there is no substitute for knowing yourself and knowing the areas in which you are most likely to excel. There is nothing so powerful as a series of successes to lead you towards the establishment of a healthy self-esteem, so plan for them.

Here are some thoughts for you to consider when trying to raise the level of your self-esteem:

- **Let go of being responsible for those around you** – take responsibility for your own choices and feelings.
- **Don't take yourself too seriously** – once you lose your sense of humour, you have lost control.
- **Let go of your 'mad' self-perceptions** – in your rational mind you will know what these are.
- **Know yourself** – understand what is blocking your progress, usually fear of failure, or guilt that you are not good enough.
- **Nurture yourself** – give yourself treats.

Summary

In this chapter you were offered some tips and techniques to enable you to be assertive and to be seen to be in charge of your own thinking and actions. Don't diminish the importance of these tools. If you practise them often, they will become second nature to you and you will soon reap the rewards of your efforts.

Soon your colleagues will notice that you are more decisive, effective and confident. This is excellent news for those who are managing or leading a team.

Remember the following. Project a positive image by:
- adopting 'winning language'
- using body language to reinforce your messages
- developing a positive mental attitude
- listening actively
- building rapport through empathy.

All this will lead to a healthy self-esteem.

Please note, there is no danger of losing your personality by doing these exercises. Your personal style will continue to distinguish you among your colleagues – even if they too are successful at being assertive. Indeed, you will feel freer to express your individuality as you become more comfortable with your powers of assertion.

Fact-check (answers at the back)

Think about the following questions and use them to build self-awareness and challenge yourself.

1. Winning language is the hallmark of assertive communication. When I use winning language, I should...
   a) Use lots of 'I' statements ❏
   b) Tell people of all my successes ❏
   c) Ensure I come out on top ❏
   d) Find ways to undermine others' efforts ❏

2. Active listening is a powerful tool for communication. When I listen actively I should...
   a) Look down and stay quiet ❏
   b) Get involved and anticipate what's about to be said ❏
   c) Ask open questions and remain curious about the answers ❏
   d) Remain actively involved in my own tasks or thoughts while listening to the other person speak ❏

3. I know I have built good rapport when...
   a) I have succeeded in getting my message across ❏
   b) The person I am talking to leaves with lots of tasks ❏
   c) I have convinced the other person of my point of view ❏
   d) I have learned something new about the person I'm communicating with and have shown empathy ❏

4. Good body language involves...
   a) Lots of gestures to underline the message I'm delivering ❏
   b) Sitting on the edge of my seat to show enthusiasm and interest ❏
   c) Gazing into the other person's eyes for the duration of the conversation ❏
   d) Alignment between the physical and the verbal message ❏

5. I use the technique of creative visualization when...
   a) I want to convince others of my good idea ❏
   b) I'm bored in a meeting and need entertainment ❏
   c) I want to define my own goals ❏
   d) I'm designing my PowerPoint presentations ❏

6. I use positive affirmations when...
   a) I want to reward someone for their good performance ❏
   b) I'm trying to convince myself that I have confidence ❏
   c) I'm wanting to transform the negative beliefs I hold about myself ❏
   d) I want to get my own way, no matter what else is going on ❏

7. Positive affirmations...
a) Work whether I believe in
   them or not ❑
b) Work when I put them far
   enough in the future to give
   them time to come true ❑
c) Work when I speak of them
   as if they are true now ❑
d) Don't really work – they're
   just a gimmick! ❑

8. Being assertive demands
   that I...
a) Take full responsibility for
   my decisions ❑
b) Get my own way ❑
c) Am never aggressive or
   passive ❑
d) Can be relied upon to fight
   others' battles ❑

9. Assertive people are...
a) Extraverted ❑
b) Loud and gregarious ❑
c) Bullies ❑
d) People with a a healthy
   self-esteem ❑

10. The ability to be assertive is
    dependent upon...
a) My personality ❑
b) My levels of confidence ❑
c) A desire to dominate ❑
d) A belief in myself ❑

CHAPTER 17

Dealing with the 'negative'

We are constantly challenged by the stresses and strains of life. Finding strategies to manage these in a balanced way may well be the key to feeling happy, healthy and in control. Not only are these stresses and strains to do with the mechanics of living, but also they are to do with the people and situations we encounter. This could be anything from an overcrowded train of tired commuters on a hot day to a curmudgeonly shopkeeper who won't listen to our complaint. It is hard to recover from getting off on the 'wrong foot' but, with awareness and determination, it is possible to turn these events around and protect ourselves from getting swept up in other people's negativity.

In this chapter you will learn some techniques for negotiating your way through this most difficult of territories. To do this, we are going to look at:

- handling anger – yours and others'
- resolving conflict
- giving and receiving critical feedback
- saying no
- handling rejection and failure.

Handling anger – yours and others'

Most of us have an innate fear of anger. This may be a throwback to our childhood years when we felt powerless and vulnerable, or to our more primitive state when we perceived the threat of marauders or predators. When we encounter anger, therefore, our bodies tend to react by preparing us for 'fight or flight' – rapid heartbeat, rapid breathing, an increased supply of blood to the muscles – all as a result of the release of adrenalin into the bloodstream. This is the natural defence mechanism that 'kicks in' when we are threatened, and, at the right time, it is a life-saver. Sometimes, the same set of physiological responses results in a 'freeze' response when we stay stock-still, full of nervous tension, in the hope that the danger will disappear without it noticing us.

In most modern situations, however (on the road or at work, for example), these reactions are inappropriate and unhelpful, and it would benefit us if we learned to override them by reducing our fear and increasing self-understanding and self-control.

What is anger?

Anger is just energy. It will be directed by an angry person indiscriminately at objects or at people. It is like a heat-seeking missile looking for a target and it needs to be deflected, damped or avoided.

The thing to remember when *you* are at the receiving end of someone's anger is that it is not you that has precipitated the anger, but some action or stance that you have taken which has struck an unhappy chord with them. You are still an acceptable human being with rights. The anger you are fielding has risen as a result of the other person's conditioning – sometimes unreasonable conditioning. The same is true of your own anger, of course.

One method for dealing with another's anger – in all but pathological cases – is to remove your personal investment from the situation. View it dispassionately and observe its nature while letting it burn itself out. Don't fuel it.

Try to identify the source of the anger by listening carefully to what is being said – or SHOUTED. You may find that the angry person feels criticized, unimportant, thwarted, hurt – any number of emotions. This will give you a clue as to how to proceed.

If you are still struggling, ask questions to clarify your understanding but try not to be patronizing.

If you are in a public place and you feel embarrassed, just remember that you are the one in control at the moment and that it is the other party that is drawing attention to themselves – and they will, of course; we are a sensation-seeking society.

Once the heat has died down, communicate your understanding of the situation from the other's point of view and negotiate a way forward or a resolution.

If you feel that it is important to douse the anger rapidly, a useful technique to adopt is to match the energy being expended. This is done by making a loud proclamation such as 'I UNDERSTAND WHY YOU ARE SO UPSET and I would feel exactly the same if I were you, but...' As you proceed with your comment, you can drop the pitch of your voice and start to take control.

As an observer, you can often hear when the heat is rising in a situation because voices tend to increase in volume and pitch and words are delivered like bullets.

Try not to be tempted to use 'reason'. The purpose of reasoning is to get the other to agree that their behaviour is unreasonable, and nobody wants to do that when they are at fever pitch. This will obviously build resentment. Reasoning can be a passive/aggressive stance as it attempts to lure the other into a submissive position.

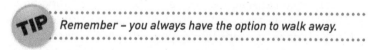

Remember – you always have the option to walk away.

When you feel angry yourself, try the distancing technique. (Deep breathing or counting to ten helps some people.) You can observe your own behaviour quite dispassionately with practice. The observations you make of yourself will contribute enormously to your self-knowledge if you can do it honestly. You will reap untold rewards in your ability to communicate assertively if you can develop the presence of mind to lower your energetic response to a situation and ask yourself 'Are things going to be resolved if I get angry?' If the answer is no, try calming yourself and think of something else.

Here is a checklist for helping you to cope with anger:

- Distance yourself – don't take others' anger personally.
- Understand the cause of the anger by listening and observing carefully.
- Say little or nothing until the anger has died down.
- Respect yourself and the other party; you still both have rights.
- Once a certain degree of tranquillity has been achieved, demonstrate understanding by acknowledging the other's viewpoint – not the same thing as agreeing with it (don't use reason).
- Negotiate a way forward.
- If all else fails, walk away. This is another way of respecting yourself.

Resolving conflict

For the purposes of clarity, conflict is separated from anger, although one can sometimes lead to the other.

Conflict can be invisible, insidious and elusive, particularly with those of the *passive/aggressive* persuasion. It can lead to an impasse, a block which is extremely difficult to move. We have seen many such conflicts in the industrial quarter with unresolved disputes leading to the destruction of organizations or an entire industry.

Conflict can also be clear, reasonable and helpful. Used positively, it can sharpen the mind, increase understanding and lead towards a very satisfying and creative solution.

Many of the techniques for dealing with conflict are similar to those used for dealing with anger. The issues may be more complex because the two opposing positions are often well thought out and rehearsed in advance. The goals of the two parties may at first appear totally different and incompatible. This is rarely the case in reality, however.

Here is a checklist for resolving conflict:

- Establish the desired outcome and priorities for both parties.
- Acknowledge and appreciate the other's position.

- Discuss the points of mutual agreement to establish rapport.
- Compromise on issues that are not central to the desired outcome.
- Identify and clarify those points that are left unresolved.
- Delve for deeper understanding by questioning thoroughly and listening carefully.
- Negotiate a resolution or agree a plan for the next step.

Giving and receiving critical feedback

This is always difficult territory. We usually give critical feedback badly because we are not very good at receiving it.

Giving critical feedback

Giving early critical feedback prevents a bad situation developing into dreadful one.

Here is a guide to giving feedback which may be helpful:

- Be considerate and, above all, be private.
- Don't 'pussyfoot' around – have confidence in what you want to say.
- Take responsibility for the feedback; don't do it because you have been cajoled into doing so and don't base it on rumour or hearsay.
- Make sure that the feedback is based on the behaviour you would like to see changed, not on the personality of the individual.
- Use positive body language (see Chapter 20).

Critical feedback may be given on the back of what is called a 'positive stroke'. For instance: 'I liked the way you handled that call and it might portray better customer service if you used their name.' This is often called the 'feedback sandwich' and, because it is so well known, people often wait for the 'kick' after they've received praise. Try to be sensitive to the individual you're giving feedback to and avoid being formulaic.

Receiving critical feedback

None of us enjoys receiving critical feedback. Indeed, most of us are looking for a confirmation that we are liked and accepted the way we are. However, if we put our vulnerabilities behind us for a moment, it really can be very helpful to hear how others perceive our behaviour or our work. We are then in a better position to make the desired adjustments – if we feel that they are valid.

Sometimes we may feel that the feedback is unfair. If this is the case, try to retain your dignity, state your disagreement and move on. Try not to argue for yourself; you will not convince anybody and you will hand your power straight to the person giving the feedback.

Here is a quick checklist for receiving critical feedback:

● Attend carefully to what is being said.
● Judge for yourself if it is valid; if not, disregard it and move on.
● Do not argue; you will only draw attention to your vulnerabilities.

If you are unfortunate enough to be criticized in public, a dignified reaction will elicit a disproportionate amount of respect from observers while the standing of the person giving the feedback will be severely diminished.

Saying no

We are rewarded with masses of praise when we acquiesce to another's request. This is not surprising as, in doing so, we have taken responsibility for somebody else's task or burden. By comparison, the emotional reward for saying no is somewhat barren.

We are often made to feel guilty and mean when we say no. This is a form of manipulation, a last-ditch attempt to make us change our mind and co-operate after all.

Dealing with this requires a particular kind of resilience. It helps if you really do believe that it is perfectly acceptable to make choices according to your own set of priorities, values and beliefs. This does not mean to say that you need always say no just to prove that you are in control of your own decisions. What it does mean is that you *can* say no.

Here is a list of useful tips that you can use when wishing to say no:

- Really mean it – if you don't, it will probably show and the person making the request will probe and prise until you change your mind. You do not have to give reasons for saying no.
- If you want to think about your response, say 'I will get back to you,' or 'I need some time to think about this.' This is your right – who is doing whom the favour?
- Don't milk the apology, wring your hands anxiously or overplay the excuses.
- You may be able to offer a compromise solution.

Handling rejection and failure

It is very difficult to separate rejection and failure because they are so intrinsically linked. They can bring despair and dejection, a feeling of foolishness, of being unworthy and so many other negative emotions.

Accepting that this is the case for so many of us, the healthy thing to do is to learn from these emotions, work with them and view them from a more positive perspective. This may sound trite and unhelpful, but with a bit of determination your perceived failures and consequent feelings of rejection will disappear into humorous anecdotes: 'Did I tell you about the time when I asked the Chairman if he was authorized to be in the building?!'

Try not to confuse your self-worth with one fleeting, albeit negative, experience. To be too harsh on yourself is unhelpful and, at a time like this, you need all the forgiveness and understanding you can get – even if it has to come from you.

One useful tactic you may like to employ to avoid the feeling of total defeat is to make a series of contingency plans. In thinking through possible, probable or even improbable scenarios that are likely to tarnish your reputation, you can spend some useful time preparing coping strategies. In this way, you can redeem yourself rapidly and divert the destructive feelings of rejection and failure into a more positive arena.

Don't dwell for too long on the negative; you may find you have creatively visualized something you would rather not come true.

These tips may be helpful as part of your survival package:

- Try not to link your own worth to negative experiences.
- Never be short of alternatives – develop contingency plans.
- Know that the significance of negative experiences changes with time.
- Try to distil some learning from the experience – it will protect you next time.
- Be kind to yourself.

The whole gamut of negative experiences and emotions are uncomfortable at best but, having conquered your fear and having successfully dealt with a few difficult situations, you will soon re-educate your reflex reactions to co-operate with the way you would rather be.

Developing a balanced view on these matters will make you much stronger because you won't be trying to avoid issues; instead, you will be making choices and following them through confidently.

You are not invincible, so try not to get over-zealous in your enthusiasm to tackle negativity. There definitely are situations that are best avoided because there can be no victor in their resolution. Anger that turns to physical violence is an irrational act and therefore cannot be approached in a rational way. In these circumstances, self-preservation is the key and, if your body prepares you for flight – do it!

Summary

In summary, what we have been dealing with in this chapter is 'negative energy'. When this is understood, fear can evaporate, and this energy can be transformed into a positive outcome for everyone. Negative energy is frightening and difficult because it 'pings' us back into a vulnerable position and gives rise to fears of survival. These primitive responses are hard-wired into our brains and still operate, whether the trigger is imaginary or real.

Being able to identify with another human being caught in the grip of fury may enable us to empathize with their plight, and in so doing enable us to behave generously.

It is worth noting that behaving assertively, as you would be if you managed to control an angry exchange without destruction to either party's, or your own, esteem, is not always the 'right' solution. Being passive may be the best response if, for instance, you're being mugged. Or dominating aggressively might suit an emergency situation, where people need direction from someone in charge.

Being assertive means that you can make choices about how and what you communicate. It puts you in the driving seat of your own relationships and allows you to remain robust and confident – yet not insensitive. You can achieve this 'healthy self-esteem' if you're prepared to be conscious and make some disciplined changes to your behaviours.

Fact-check (answers at the back)

Think about the following questions and use them to develop your skills in managing negative energy.

1. When someone is angry, it's best to...
a) Reason with them ❑
b) Shout back with equal ferocity ❑
c) Submit to their power and escape at the earliest opportunity ❑
d) Stand firm and try to understand what's going on for them ❑

2. When someone is angry with me, I should...
a) Freeze and submit to their request ❑
b) Fight and endeavour to win the battle ❑
c) Flee from the situation in the hope that they'll calm down ❑
d) Sum up the situation and respond in a way that will lead to a win/win ❑

3. Here is a checklist for resolving conflict. Which is the *incorrect* item on the list?
a) Acknowledge and appreciate the other's position ❑
b) Compromise or relinquish issues that are not central to the desired outcome ❑
c) Seek deeper understanding by questioning and listening thoroughly ❑
d) Ensure that you retain the 'upper hand' by withholding your trump card ❑

4. When you wish to give critical feedback, how should you back up your comments?
a) Canvas others' opinions and add these to your feedback ❑
b) Remind people of their ingrained and persistent personality faults ❑
c) Wait until the situation becomes intolerable and then launch your arsenal ❑
d) Base it on your observations only and focus it on the person's behaviour ❑

5. When you say no, what should you be aiming to feel?
a) Guilty ❑
b) That you're being unreasonable ❑
c) That people will dislike you ❑
d) Fine saying no ❑

6. When you go into a situation that you feel may be 'negative', how should you prepare yourself?
a) Just go in and hope for the best ❑
b) Go in guns blazing to ensure that no one gets the better of you ❑
c) Think about the tensions and tell yourself that they are not personal ❑
d) Try to keep as quiet as possible in the hope that no one notices you ❑

7. When you receive challenging or negative feedback, how should you respond?
a) Tell the person who's giving you feedback to mind their own business ❑
b) Thank the person and tell them you'll think about what they've said ❑
c) Argue your case. No one is going to criticize you and get away with it! ❑
d) Say sorry and that you'll not do it again ❑

8. When handling someone's anger, it is best to...
a) Shout at them to calm them down ❑
b) Reason with them and get them to see they're wrong ❑
c) Appraise the situation and see if you can discover what's causing the problem ❑
d) Leave them to it until their anger burns out ❑

9. When you feel rejected, you should...
a) Blame yourself for being 'wrong' ❑
b) Tell yourself the other person doesn't know what they're doing ❑
c) Try to retain your self-esteem and recognize this is not to do with 'you' ❑
d) Tell them you don't want to be included anyway! ❑

10. Active listening can be done while...
a) Texting friends ❑
b) Emailing work colleagues ❑
c) Being curious about the other person's situation ❑
d) Interrupting enthusiastically to build the conversation ❑

CHAPTER 18

Creating a positive impression

There are many possibilities for making the best of yourself and creating a positive first impression. In this chapter we will be examining some of the techniques that can be adopted to achieve this. They include:

- creating a positive first impression
- developing assertive interviewing skills
- building confidence.

In order to create a good first impression, you will need to manage the perceptions of others. These will be formed through the persona you project – which may, of course, be light years from the one you revert to in private.

It is worth remembering that when people form a perception of us they act as if this is the truth. Once formed, this 'truth' is seldom revisited and reviewed. Rather, it is taken on board as fact and the 'impression-holder' orientates their behaviour towards us accordingly. If we have inadvertently created an unhelpful or misleading first impression, this can give us a long-term problem as people are often reluctant to discuss their initial thoughts about us.

If we attempt to 'manipulate' the perceptions people have of us, it may be hard to sustain – and we may feel alien to ourselves as we are not being authentic. We will explore this phenomenon further in this chapter.

Creating a positive first impression

The first opportunity we have to create a good impression is at an initial meeting or during an interview for a job.

It is undoubtedly true that human beings are judgemental. We generally look for similarities in those we are meeting for the first time because this reinforces us as individuals and gives us common ground to explore. We are less tolerant of those who take diametrically opposed views to our own or who live by a different set of values.

When meeting someone for the first time, you can be absolutely sure that they have this lightning ability, as you do, to sum you up in something under ten seconds and be utterly convinced that their powers of perception are completely accurate! You have only these very few seconds, therefore, to create the impression of your choice.

Very often our first impressions are proven wrong in the long run. However, it does take a huge amount of time and effort to dismantle a first impression and substitute it for a more accurate one.

Let us now examine the many factors that go in to creating a first impression:

- appearance
- size, mobility and national origin
- handshake
- gait, body language
- voice, accent, speech pattern, speech impediment, tone, etc.

Judgements will be made on a combination of some or all of the above factors before we start saying anything of consequence.

We will look at these factors one by one.

Appearance

In order to decide how to make your impact, you must first determine what impression you wish to create. An obvious point, perhaps, but often neglected.

Here are some factors to consider when planning your impact at a job interview:

- the culture of the target organization
- the nature of the job
- the note you wish to strike with your clothes:
  - a large amount of bright **colour** can be overpowering
  - **style** can be appropriate/conventional/unconventional
  - **accessories** – shoes, ties, scarves, hairstyle, hair colour, jewellery, bags, belts and briefcases all contribute to the overall impression.

If you decide to create the image of a non-conformist – beware. Although this gives you greater freedom and enormous scope for painting a very individualistic picture, it is a high-risk strategy, especially in a conventional environment. The question to ask yourself is: How seriously do I want this job?

Size, mobility and national origin

There is very little most of us can do about our size, degree of mobility or origin. Unfortunately, it is undeniable that these factors strongly influence a first impression, so be aware of them and quickly remove any concern that the interviewer may have.

If you think that you may encounter some form of prejudice, be proud and be direct. This is very disarming and will soon put the issue (if any) into the background, leaving you with the upper hand. It will also create a relaxed atmosphere for further discussion. This is an essential step to take if there is any possibility that the interviewer will perceive a physical barrier to your suitability for the job, so deal with likely issues honestly and without apology, then move on.

Here are some examples that illustrate how an interviewee can remove prejudice at the outset:

- 'Although you can see I am very large, I would like to reassure you that this does not hinder my performance.'
- 'I would like you to know that my physical restrictions have enabled me to develop other skills to an extremely high level.'

Handshake

Within a split second of meeting someone for the first time, we are there, proffering our hand as the best etiquette has taught us. There are many varieties of handshake, some desperately disconcerting, others businesslike and almost unremarkable. The conclusions we draw from a handshake are out of all proportion to its significance. However, getting it wrong puts a large obstacle in the way of creating a good impression.

We have all experienced the limp handshake... the 'tip of fingers' handshake... the ferocious 'bone-breaker'... the sweaty handshake... and the 'won't let go' handshake...

The model way to shake someone's hand is to:

- offer an open hand, your palm facing towards theirs
- look the other party in the eye and smile
- take a firm hold of their hand and shake it up and down once or twice (no more)
- release.

Gait, body positioning

Body language will be dealt with in much greater detail in Chapter 20, but as we are on the subject of first impressions, it is necessary to touch on the matter here.

How you enter a room, move towards a greeting, walk or sit, all go towards forming an early impression.

Assertive behaviour can also be demonstrated non-verbally in the following three ways:

1 moving assertively (including the handshake)
2 sitting assertively
3 use of the voice (yes, it is considered to be a non-verbal mode of communication).

Moving assertively: when preparing to enter a room, knock firmly on the door and wait for a response. Once you have been asked to 'come in', open the door fully, step in and close the door behind you. Walk confidently into the room towards the greeting, hand at the ready.

Don't be timid. If you tap lightly on the door, no one will hear and you won't be asked to 'come in'. Then you will probably be anxious and uncertain – you have sabotaged yourself.

If you creep round the door, hug the wall and shuffle hesitantly towards the greeting, you will appear insipid and lacking in confidence. This is typical passive behaviour. However, if you stride in, throw your briefcase down and sit without being invited to do so, it will not appear confident, as you might hope, but aggressive.

Sitting assertively: sit straight and tend to lean slightly forward. This gives the impression of meeting someone part way on their territory and looks interested and enthusiastic.

If you slouch or lean back on your shoulder blades with your bottom pivoting on the edge of the chair, you will appear uninterested and disrespectful.

Contrarily, if you sit huddled and small with your toes pointing together and your hands gripped firmly between your knees, you will look childlike and helpless.

Voice: there are many dimensions to your voice, most of which are difficult to control, such as a national or regional accent, a speech impediment or the quality of your vocal cords.

Some of the vocal properties that you can control are the clarity of your speech, the pitch, the tone and the speed of delivery.

The words that you use, the grammatical patterns you favour when constructing your sentences, and the way you reinforce what you are saying with your hands all have a direct bearing on how you will be perceived, albeit unconsciously. More of this later.

Creating a positive first impression – invisibly

Our first contact with a person may be through email, by letter or on the telephone.

Because these modes of communication are stripped of the normally abundant visible information such as appearance, style, movement and, in the case of the written word, voice, it becomes all the more important to make the most of what is left. 'Remote' modes of communication are still filled with opportunities for creating a good first impression.

We will look at the potential of three forms of 'remote' communication.

Email

Email is quite an informal mode of communication with a tradition for grammatical shortcuts and abbreviations. However, most people now offer their email address and invite contact electronically. If you use this channel of communication to create a first impression, ensure that you do so through a high-quality message. Use the attachment facility to carry properly formatted documents that can be printed by the recipient.

Letter

There are significant advantages to making your first impression by letter. When initial contact is made through the written word, you have the luxury of time to plan the impression you wish to create.

Listed below are some useful tips on how to create a good impression by letter:

- Ensure that the quality of the paper and the appearance of the writing are excellent: no spelling mistakes, daubs of correction fluid, colloquialisms or bad grammar.
- Handwritten letters are fine if you possess a 'good hand' that is attractive and legible. Many bad characteristics are associated with poor handwriting. Word-processed letters look very professional, so do use this method if you can.
- Make sure that what you have to say is succinct and to the point. Any information that you give in addition to what is necessary should be carefully chosen.

The telephone

When communicating by telephone, you have the benefit of being invisible so you can get really comfortable with yourself and what you plan to say.

Here are some helpful tips on making a good first impression using the telephone:

- Do not use a mobile.
- Smile when your call is answered; this can be heard in your voice.
- Use a pleasant greeting and state your name and purpose clearly.
- Plan what you are going to say (writing down key words will ensure you cover all the essential points).
- If you are trying to get your thoughts together, pace about if it helps and use gestures.
- If you are interrupted during your call, explain what has happened so that your distraction does not appear rude or offhand.
- Summarize and confirm all agreements verbally so that you can be sure you have understood accurately.
- Establish who will initiate the next contact; if you are anxious, it is as well to take the responsibility for this yourself.
- It is often useful to follow up a telephone conversation with a letter of confirmation.
- If you seem to be listening for a long time, acknowledge what is being said by using terms like 'Ah-ha', 'Mmm' and 'Yes'. Long silences can sound as if you are no longer there or have stopped paying attention
- If you find you need to be assertive, stand up while talking on the telephone; it really does help to convey a feeling of strength.

Assertive interviewing skills

Many specialist books have been written on the subject of 'the interview'. However, this chapter would not be complete without some reference to 'the interview' and how you can manage this assertively.

During a professionally conducted interview, the interviewer should talk for 5–10 per cent of the time only. Ideally, therefore, you will have the remainder of the time to give as much relevant information about yourself as possible.

Your curriculum vitae will have conveyed all the professional, technical and experiential information necessary to determine your suitability for the post. The interview is primarily geared towards finding out whether you will fit in to the culture of the organization and work effectively with the rest of the team.

You will be prompted to give information about yourself through 'open questions'. Listen out for these because they provide you with the opportunity to show yourself in a good light. Examples of open questions are:

- 'What made you decide to...?'
- 'How would you tackle...?'
- 'Explain more about how you...'

They are 'open' because you determine the content and limits of the answer; there are no bounds to them. They give you masses of scope to talk about your approach and your achievements.

'Closed' questions, for comparison, are those such as:

- 'How long did you work for...?'
- 'How many staff were you responsible for at...?'
- 'When did you pass your driving test?'

These questions prompt short, defined responses and, as a consequence, the interviewer has to work extremely hard to extract sufficient information from you to reach a decision.

If you happen to be at an interview where the interviewer asks you 'closed' questions, take the initiative and open them up yourself, saying something like:

- 'Yes, I enjoyed being an apprentice because it gave me an opportunity to...'
- 'I worked for Hobson's Choice for ten years and thoroughly enjoyed it because it developed my ability to...'

Remember, undertake some basic research on the organization and the nature of its business before you attend an interview. Interviewers often ask 'What do you know about this organization?' You can impress easily with a knowledgeable response to this question.

Summary

To close the learning for this chapter, let us look at what creating a positive image is all about – *confidence*.

By adopting some of the techniques and attitudes given to you in this chapter, you will soon begin to trust that you are capable of forming and maintaining an image that pleases you. Initially, one small success is all you can ask of yourself. Having this safely behind you will be the beginning of building confidence. Start with something you find relatively easy, and move on to greater things from there.

Good habits, firmly established, are soon drawn into the subconscious where they form the bedrock of your behaviour. When you have progressed this far, you will find that your confidence level has increased significantly and you will be able to draw upon it quite naturally. Once you reach this stage, all your positive experiences will go towards reinforcing this new-found quality in yourself. You will have established a virtuous cycle! Confidence and a healthy self-esteem are priceless assets and, if you are not fortunate enough to possess them naturally, they are well worth working for.

A positive mental attitude is key. Many managers have learned this from the experience of athletes who develop their minds as well as their bodies. Belief in yourself, coupled with professional expertise, will ensure your success.

Fact-check (answers at the back)

Think about the following questions and use them to develop your skills in creating a positive impression.

1. What do you need to do to create a positive first impression?
   a) Tell people what you want them to believe of you ❏
   b) Behave authentically, taking account of the context and situation ❏
   c) Act out the person you want to be seen as ❏
   d) Adopt a 'what you see is what you get' approach and leave it to chance ❏

2. Which one of the options below is *incorrect* as a way of making a first impression?
   a) Considering my appearance – appropriate dress and grooming ❏
   b) Building rapport and being congruent with the situation ❏
   c) Demonstrating authenticity and confidence in myself ❏
   d) Acting as if I was the person I want to be ❏

3. Handshakes are very important in creating a first impression. How should you shake someone's hand?
   a) Offer little resistance so that they can determine the strength of the handshake ❏
   b) I dislike shaking hands so try to avoid it ❏
   c) Take the 'firm' approach so that they know you're confident in yourself ❏
   d) My hands are sweaty so I try to minimize contact ❏

4. When entering a room for the first time, perhaps to meet a prospective employer, how can you command the space?
   a) I knock and enter without being invited to show my confidence ❏
   b) I comment on the (good, bad, indifferent) weather immediately to show I'm friendly ❏
   c) I respond confidently to the requests made of me to sit, speak and ask questions ❏
   d) I stand quietly and wait for instructions before I make a move ❏

5. Which one of the statements below is likely to create a *poor* impression when there are no visible channels of communication?
   a) I make sure my written communications are grammatically correct and high quality ❏
   b) I smile on the telephone, knowing that this will be conveyed in my voice ❏
   c) I use texting because it's quick and easy ❏
   d) I make sure my CV is succinct and points towards my capabilities and achievements ❏

6. Interviews that use open questions are designed to check the 'chemistry' between you and your prospective employers. Which statement *incorrectly* defines open questions?

a) They are designed to get you to talk more about yourself ❑

b) They begin with 'Who?', 'What?', 'Where?', 'When?' and 'How?' ❑

c) They are traps that encourage you to say things you don't want to! ❑

d) They are exploratory and encourage you to expand upon your points ❑

7. If you feel that you may possess a barrier to being considered for a new job, how would you diminish it to equal your chances?

a) I'd hope that the interviewer hadn't noticed and say nothing ❑

b) If they mentioned it, I'd deny it was a problem ❑

c) I'd be candid about the perceived barrier and explain why it would not be an obstacle to my suitability ❑

d) I'd point out that it was politically incorrect or illegal to focus on this issue ❑

8. Which statement is incorrect in describing how to communicate assertive behaviour non-verbally?

a) Through posture and well-defined movement ❑

b) By taking every opportunity to stand up and create a physical hierarchy in my favour ❑

c) By sitting slightly forward in the chair to convey engagement ❑

d) By speaking clearly and fluently ❑

9. If you were being interviewed and the interviewer was not asking you the questions you'd like to answer, how would you deal with it?

a) I'd give them a list of questions I'd like them to ask me ❑

b) I'd give feedback to the interviewer that they're not giving me the opportunity to sell myself properly ❑

c) I'd ask if I could outline a project that illustrates my suitability for the role ❑

d) I'd feel disappointed and wish they'd been better at their job! ❑

10. Which statement could endanger my growth in confidence?

a) I could be positive about my capabilities and achievements ❑

b) I could try not taking things too personally ❑

c) I could try envisaging my future successes ❑

d) I could over-act to convey that I really was confident ❑

CHAPTER 19

Being assertive in public

In the previous chapter we looked at ways of creating a positive impression in one-to-one situations: at a job interview, on the telephone and through the written word.

In this chapter we are going to look at how to develop this transient first impression into a durable professional image. You may like to think of this as your 'brand' image. This will be an amalgam of the characteristics, traits and behaviours that you show to the outside world. If you are to transmit your 'brand' effectively, you will need to be consistent in the way your portray yourself. If you try out new things too often, it will fragment your brand and undermine the progress you've made and the reputation you've established.

To assist you, we will concentrate on your ability to communicate assertively in public, among work colleagues and customers. As you grow in professional stature, you will increasingly find yourself in situations where many pairs of eyes will be watching you. You will be visible to a wider audience.

Much of the assertive behaviour about to be described will be applicable to more than one arena. Here we will focus on three of the most frequently met situations in which your ability to communicate assertively will reap great rewards:

- meetings
- negotiations
- presentations.

Meetings

Meetings are often dominated by the most aggressive members of the group. In these circumstances, passive attendees can feel completely overtaken by events because they feel unable to interject and make their points. Passive types will often revert to passive/aggressive behaviour on such occasions – deafeningly 'loud' body language and more than a few sighs – or they will become silent and resign themselves to the decisions made without their input.

A good chairperson will ensure that the meeting is properly orchestrated and that everyone is given the opportunity to contribute. Often, however, this leadership is sadly lacking and meetings either take on the air of a battlefield or wander off the point and waste a lot of time.

For the purposes of illustrating how to handle meetings assertively, we will look at the worst scenario: that of a disorganized gathering dominated by one or two aggressive types. We will pepper this image with a few passive and passive/aggressive characters who are nursing 'hidden agendas'.

After a few words on how to prepare for a meeting, we will pull the above scenario apart and look at each component individually:

- assertive versus aggressive
- assertive versus passive/aggressive
- assertive versus passive
- assertive versus hidden agenda.

Preparing for a meeting

Before attending a meeting, make sure that you have a copy of the agenda and that you fully understand why the meeting has been called.

Take with you all the supporting information you are likely to need. If you are not clear why a particular item has been included on the agenda, ask beforehand.

Make sure you know where the meeting is being held and get there on time. You will lose credibility if you turn up late, confused or ill poorly prepared, and it will then be much harder to make an assertive and constructive contribution.

Assertive versus aggressive

Let's start by dealing with the aggressive component of the meeting. Aggressive behaviour often works in the short term. It intimidates and controls those who fear it, and many do. However, it is not worth adopting aggressive behaviour as a long-term strategy. Eventually colleagues will get angry.

The demonstrable lack of regard and respect that the aggressive person exhibits will eventually lead to unco-operative and undermining responses. Once commitment has been lost, there is no way forward for the aggressor.

The use of assertive behaviour in these circumstances can, however, draw the aggressor towards a healthier realm of communication. Here's how.

When faced with aggressive behaviour, be calm, breathe deeply and know that others at the meeting will be gunning for you. One word of caution, however: assertive behaviour is about taking responsibility for yourself, not for others; so don't speak for the group, speak for yourself. Use 'I' language.

You may have to field anger, criticism and insults before you can start influencing the communication. Remember, though, that aggressive behaviour is weak behaviour. Be confident; you can handle it.

Here is a checklist for dealing with aggressive behaviour:

- Be calm; listen carefully.
- Take a deep breath and look for an opportunity to speak. If you need to interrupt, try to catch the speaker's eye and indicate your wish to contribute. If the speaker is hell-bent on avoiding eye contact, call their name politely and state your intention to contribute.
- Match the volume of your interruption to the volume of the speaker's voice.
- Once you have successfully entered the dialogue, acknowledge what has just been said, then lead off with a statement such as 'I understand the point you are making, but I feel we could achieve more by...'

- If you are dismissed, repeat your comment in a different way. Repeat yourself assertively until you have been heard.
- Once you have the floor you may find you need to halt a 'return play' interruption. In this case, raise your hand to signal 'stop'. Using the person's name increases the power of your gesture.
- Summarize and confirm your understanding of a point or agreement before moving on.
- If you have not succeeded in making your point, register the fact. For example: 'I know that you are keen to cover a lot of ground in this meeting, but I still feel...'
- Maintain dignity even if you are frustrated, and reassert yourself on a later occasion. Persistence really does win out in the end and you will become more effective each time you attempt assertive behaviour.

Assertive versus passive/aggressive

Passive/aggressive behaviour is 'reluctant victim' behaviour. It attempts to be manipulative. A person may be angry with themselves for giving away their power so they do it with bad grace. This type of behaviour causes bad atmospheres, resentment, embarrassment and confusion. Often, one thing is said but the message is completely different. For instance:

Manager: 'Our best customer has just placed an urgent order; would you mind processing it immediately?'

Sales assistant (sarcastically): 'No, that's fine. I have all the time in the world!'

Passive/aggressive behaviour is thinly disguised. In a meeting it may exhibit itself through overt body language – rolling the eyes heavenward, exaggerated shifting in the chair, or impatient tapping with a pen.

Here are some ideas for dealing with passive/aggressive behaviour:

- Expose the 'hidden' message, whether verbal or non-verbal. For example: 'I see that you are feeling negatively about this. Would you mind discussing your objection openly?'
- Ask for their thoughts on the topic of obvious dispute.
- Listen actively and respond.

The passive/aggressive person has several options when their behaviour is exposed. They can rise to the challenge and redeem themselves; deny sending the message in the first place, claiming that you are paranoid; or get defensive. The first option is obviously the best strategy; the latter two will without fail diminish their standing in others' eyes.

Assertive versus passive

Passive behaviour attempts to engender feelings of sympathy in others. It is as manipulative as passive/aggressive behaviour but it pretends to be virtuous. Passive people have very little self-respect, they do not stand up for themselves and tend to get 'put upon' because they are frightened to say no and be rejected.

A distinguishing characteristic of a passive person is the use of silence. This can sometimes go on for a very long time and usually covers up a running dialogue in their mind which is 'victim' based ('Why are you picking on me?' or 'I wish you would shut up and leave me out of this!').

Dealing with passive behaviour

Dealing with a passive person is not dissimilar to handling someone who is passive/aggressive. First, expose their abdication: 'I am not clear where you stand on this issue; would you tell me what your feelings are?' (Note the use of the 'I' statement and the 'open' question, 'what?')

Match silence with silence. It takes an extremely passive person to remain mute in the teeth of a silent and expectant gaze, especially if everyone at the meeting is engaged in the same tactic. Once they start to talk, use your active listening skills to encourage the flow.

However, if you lose patience with their silence, repeat your comment or try a different approach if you think this will help. If you get to a point of exasperation, inform the passive person that you will have to deduce their feelings if they are not prepared to share them and that you will have to proceed according to your deductions. Invite them to support you in your course of action.

Assertive versus hidden agenda

You will inevitably come across people who play their cards very close to their chest, especially in organizations where internal politics are prominent. In these cultures, people are always on the defensive, protecting themselves from exploitation or disadvantage. Sometimes this fear is imaginary, sometimes it is real, but, whatever the cause, you will need common techniques to deal with it.

Identifying hidden agendas

You will probably be able to identify the 'political animals' among your colleagues because their behaviour will appear inconsistent. They will apparently change their opinion or approach without reason, leaving a trail of confusion and uncertainty behind them. Once this erratic style has caught your attention, look at the interplay of circumstances and try to identify the likely political, and usually personal, gain that is being sought. You may then be close to the real motivation of that person.

Significant coincidences that benefit one individual do not usually occur without some help. Look for coincidences, therefore, and identify the beneficiaries. Coupled with hindsight, the hidden agenda may suddenly be revealed to you and past, previously confusing behaviours will fall into context. This knowledge is useful; it is power. Do not try to tackle the individual. Hidden agendas, by their very nature, can always be denied and you will end up looking paranoid or foolish.

It is probably worth testing your theory by predicting the likely reaction of your colleagues in certain circumstances. If, when these circumstances occur, your prediction proves correct, the hidden agenda is likely to be what you suspected. If not, think again; maybe you *are* paranoid!

Planning your approach

Having understood a colleague's private motivation, you will have a clear picture of where you fit into the pattern of things. This will enable you to plan your own approach. This could be one of avoidance, of course, if you choose not to get caught up in the politics of the organization; or it may be a strategic option – the choice, as always, is yours.

Hidden agendas: checklist

Here is a checklist for identifying a hidden agenda:

- Examine coincidences that benefit one person, or a specific group of people.
- Look out for inconsistent behaviour – this may take the form of an unlikely relationship, non-verbal messages or a sudden and inexplicable abdication of responsibility.
- Put your observations into context using hindsight; this may help you identify the 'hidden agenda' specifically.
- Test your theory as innocuously and as anonymously as possible.
- It is probably best to keep your own counsel; you may be able to do more to your advantage in this way.
- If you are going to tackle someone on their private agenda, be absolutely sure of your ground and that you can handle it in the most assertive way possible.
- Look for a motivation – if you are suddenly flavour of the month with someone who is known to be ambitious, ask yourself why.
- Be vigilant – it would be naive to think that hidden agendas are not being worked out somewhere within your organization.

Negotiations

There are some very simple rules for conducting yourself effectively – and assertively – in negotiations.

Negotiations can fall into several categories. First, there are those taking place in the working environment with one other person such as your boss, a colleague or a member of your staff. Moving up in scale, the meeting room often witnesses negotiations among several colleagues whose views reside in different camps. Then there are those conducted between two opposing parties. When these two parties cannot agree, they may resort to the services of an arbitrator or mediator.

Whatever the situation, whether it is simple problem solving or a full-scale meeting between managers and a trade union, the basic rules for successful negotiating are the same. More often than not, it is merely a question of scale.

Negotiating in practice

Here are the basic steps for negotiating successfully:

- Know exactly what you wish to achieve and be absolutely clear on the level of your, and your opponent's, authority.
- Be assertive and use positive body language.
- Make sure that you understand the other's viewpoint.
- Convey your own viewpoint clearly and state your desired outcome.
- Look for areas of common ground to reinforce mutual interests and to develop a commitment to a satisfactory resolution.
- Listen actively and demonstrate understanding throughout the discussion.
- Never bluff, fudge, manipulate or lie.
- Never offer something you cannot deliver.
- If you are feeling pressured, ask for a recess.
- Communicate your proposals clearly and concisely and establish those of the other party.
- Summarize the areas of difference and explore the extent of these; identify the issues where compromise is possible.
- Having distilled out the main area of contention, discuss any concessions that you are both prepared to make.
- Summarize, agree and confirm in writing

Presentations

Presentations strike fear into the hearts of many managers, whatever their seniority. They are one of the most visible and exposed professional platforms and can leave your image enhanced, intact or in tatters.

Usually you will have advance warning of the requirement to make a presentation and will also, therefore, have time to prepare and practise for the occasion.

The two most important points are: *prepare* and *practise.*

Those who are 'naturals' at making presentations are the exception rather than the rule. Most good presenters are only good because they have invested time in preparation and practice. Everyone can do it if they try – and everyone can enjoy the experience.

There is nothing more satisfying than the glow of success when you step down from the platform having made an excellent presentation. It really is worth investing the time and energy to get it right.

Of course, much has been written on presentation skills, and clearly justice cannot be done to the subject in a few short paragraphs. However, here are a few pointers to help you add this mode of communication to the assertiveness toolkit that you are assembling:

Preparation and practice

- Make sure that you understand the purpose of the presentation.
- Have a clear impression of your audience, their level and their expectations; this will enable you to pitch your presentation correctly.
- Prepare your talk:
  - **beginning** – tell them what you are going to say
  - **middle** – say it
  - **end** – tell them what you have said.
- Most people will retain only about three points.
- Prepare visual aids:
  - **overhead projector slides** – these should be bold, clear and never more than a paragraph long
  - **handouts** – these can contain more detailed information along with copies of your slides. They should be of top quality
  - **35mm slides** – not always an advantage as you have to make your presentation in a darkened room.
  - **PowerPoint** has raised the standard of presentations and the level of expectation of audiences everywhere. Sound and animation features are available, but make sure they add to your message. Also, be comfortable with the technology, especially if you are projecting your presentation from your laptop on to a screen. If you plug in too early, your audience will be able to watch as you search your directory and open up your presentation.
- Prepare a set of cards with keyword prompts, facts or difficult names on them to help you if you are nervous.

- Practise – in front of a mirror, colleagues, friends and family. Make sure that you get the timing right and get your audience to fire awkward questions at you.

Making the presentation

- Wear clean, comfortable and unobtrusive clothes. If you don't, your audience will pay more attention to your attire than to what you have to say.
- Arrive in plenty of time; familiarize yourself with the equipment and check your slides are in the right order.
- Make sure that you have a glass of water handy in case your mouth dries up.
- If you are using torch pointers, telescopic pointers or infrared remote controls – practise (watch out for shake).
- Relax, by whatever means suits you.
- Tell your audience what you expect from them in terms of interruptions, discussion or questions; you may prefer to take these as you go along, or leave them to the end.
- Enjoy your talk but remain vigilant: it is too easy to be drawn into letting your guard down and saying something contentious. If you cannot answer a question, be honest about it and tell the questioner that you will find out and get back to them.
- Try to avoid jokes until you are a skilled presenter.
- Don't talk down to your audience but, equally, don't assume they understand the technicalities of your subject.
- Pause from time to time. This is a performance, and pauses are useful for dramatic effect – and to collect your thoughts.
- Of course, use assertive language and body posture.

Summary

By now you should have started to gather together some useful tools for developing your assertiveness skills. You may have had a chance to practise some of these techniques and found that they really do work. These early successes should increase your confidence and fire your enthusiasm to learn more, take control and have the courage to set your own goals.

Now that we're about two-thirds of the way through the masterclass, it may be worth checking your progress to see where you are with your assertiveness aspirations and what there is still left to do. You could, for example, ask for feedback from one or two of your trusted friends or colleagues.

It is very easy to slip back if something doesn't go according to plan, so find some support to shore you up in these moments.

You might like to write down your experiences and your learning. It will ensure that everything stays conscious, which is where you need it if you are going to take command of your own communication skills.

Fact-check (answers at the back)

Think about the following questions and use them to develop your skills in creating a public image.

1. Which statement is *incorrect* in respect of how you should build your brand?
   a) I build my brand in group or departmental meetings ❏
   b) I build my brand with clients, customers and suppliers ❏
   c) I build my brand among my colleagues who have similar expertise to me ❏
   d) I don't build my brand, it builds itself ❏

2. When you run meetings, which statement would suggest that you do so unassertively?
   a) I keep things to time ❏
   b) I leave with clear action points allocated to the appropriate members of the team ❏
   c) I tap into the creativity and problem-solving capability of the team ❏
   d) I always end up with all the action points! ❏

3. When you've completed a negotiation, what outcome would suggest that you did so assertively?
   a) I conceded too much ❏
   b) I was not heard or understood ❏
   c) I reached a satisfactory win/win solution ❏
   d) I do not know or understand the other party's position and goals ❏

4. Which statement about passive/aggressive behaviour is *false*?
   a) People agree (unconvincingly) and then take no action – or sabotage the outcome ❏
   b) Often, the body language is 'loud' in its message that the person wants to be anywhere but at the meeting ❏
   c) Passive/aggressive behaviour uses sarcasm ❏
   d) Passive/aggressive behaviour is a contradiction in terms and doesn't exist ❏

5. Which is the *wrong* step to take when you are preparing for a meeting?
   a) Make sure everyone knows where the meeting is, what time it's being held and how long it will last ❏
   b) Ensure that an agenda has been circulated and forewarn of any preparation that needs to be done ❏
   c) Arrange for minutes to be taken, circulated and agreed afterwards ❏
   d) Meetings are best when they are called spontaneously to address an emergent issue ❏

6. What is the effect of aggressive behaviour in a meeting? Identify the *false* statement.
a) It derails the purpose of the meeting ❏
b) It adds a drop of excitement to the proceedings and encourages everyone to contribute ❏
c) It may be effective in the short term ❏
d) People may be fearful of the aggressor and fail to contribute ❏

7. When confronting aggressive behaviour, what should you *not* do?
a) Be calm and listen carefully ❏
b) Acknowledge what is being said and offer your own view ❏
c) Argue with the aggressive person and try to convince them they're wrong ❏
d) If your comment is dismissed, come back again in a different way ❏

8. Which strategy is a passive/aggressive person *unlikely* to use to avoid taking responsibility?
a) They may tell you that you're paranoid ❏
b) They may deny that you read their signals correctly ❏
c) They may feign agreement and sabotage your plan later on ❏
d) They may apologize, tell you that you've read them correctly and take on a different stance ❏

9. In the event of suspecting someone has a hidden agenda, what should you do?
a) Accuse them of trying to 'get one over on you' ❏
b) Mention that you've noticed them trying to win favour with senior people ❏
c) Set up a 'trap' to see if they fall into it ❏
d) Give them feedback on your feelings and ask if they would clarify their motivations ❏

10. What good practice should you adopt as you step into the world of making presentations?
a) Telling 'good' jokes to get the audience laughing and 'on your side' ❏
b) Saying how nervous you are because you hate giving presentations ❏
c) Being technical to demonstrate how much you know ❏
d) Doing rehearsals to get you used to your voice and the timing of your presentation ❏

CHAPTER 20

Body language

The notion of 'body language' has drawn much attention and intrigue. It is tempting to think that words are the most important factor in communicating messages but, as we have seen, words form only a small proportion of the messages that are exchanged. You have only to think of a mime artist who has perfected the art of communication using the body to recognize the truth of this. Also, think of those people who are very still when they communicate. It is sometimes hard to 'read' them clearly and it may lead to misinterpretations or misunderstandings.

In this chapter we will look at the forms of body language that have the most impact on others. This is by no means an exhaustive study of the subject, but it will maximize the effect you can create when you communicate assertively.

The following areas will comprise the learning for this chapter:

- assertive body language
- the use of gestures
- developing rapport
- the use of verbal language
- interpreting body language.

Your body really can speak louder than words.

Assertive body language

Because your body conveys such a large proportion of what you are communicating, it is worth concentrating on this area for a short time and considering what it is we convey with our bodies and how we can be sabotaged by them.

It is a useful exercise to 'body-watch' – but try to be discreet. You will notice that when two people are engrossed in riveting conversation, they are completely unaware of their bodies. (Unless the conversation is skirting around sex, of course; in which case we are *very* aware of our bodies!) We use our bodies at the unconscious level to emphasize points or to transmit secondary messages.

Assertive behaviour is distinguished by the continuity between the verbal and the non-verbal. In other words, your body reflects precisely what you are saying when you are in 'assertive mode' – it is congruent with the intention behind your message.

Because of the restricted time and space available here for this topic, we will address only the most potent aspects of body language:

● personal space
● stance
● senses.

Personal space

We all carry around an egg-shaped exclusion zone which varies in size in direct proportion to our circumstances, purpose and level of comfort. As a point of interest, you can usually measure the size of someone's 'egg' by the length of their focal attention.

On an underground train, this is almost zero (people often look glazed or they focus on reading matter); at work, it can extend to include one person or a small gathering of people; at a large presentation, it can reach to the extremities of an entire hall.

Varying the size of the 'egg' is an instinctive part of our behaviour. However, it can be very useful to understand the nature of this 'personal space' so that it can be used to good effect.

Learning point I. *If we do not include people in our personal space, it is almost impossible to influence them.*

Notice how you 'shut down' when someone you dislike comes too close, or someone you're not sure about comes too close too soon. I'm sure that we have all experienced backing away from someone as they repeatedly trespass on our personal territory until the next step takes us through the window or into a cupboard.

Remember, too, a time when you were part of a large audience, and the presenter or entertainer made you feel as if you were the only person in the room. This was because they extended their personal space to include you.

Notice how you use your own space, and how you act differently with family, colleagues and those in authority. As an exercise, practise drawing your space in until its boundaries meet your body. Then try filling a room with your presence by expanding your space. You can do this by changing your focal point and placing your attention on the walls. Accompany this with a visualization of yourself as an extraordinarily confident and influential person.

Learning point II: *The more space you use, the more impact you will have.*

Tall people tend to have a natural advantage because they occupy a large amount of space. Yet they are often shy and withdrawn. This can show in their posture, which may be round-shouldered, or in their gait, which may be 'in-toed'.

Short people, who may not enjoy the same natural impact, can make up for their lack of size by expanding the horizons of their space and adopting a good assertive style. Indeed, a large number of short people are considered to be taller than they are because of this ability, and they have become extremely successful in the process. Unfortunately, their communication style sometimes overcompensates for their lack of physical stature and can become overly aggressive.

There are ways of sitting and standing that look 'big' and carry impact. By adopting some of the following techniques, short people can actually 'grow' in others' perceptions.

Here are some techniques for creating presence:

- **Assertive standing:** stand straight and 'think' tall. Try not to twine your legs around each other or stand with your weight upon one leg. Nothing destroys the image like crumpling on to the floor because you have overbalanced!
- When you wish to **communicate powerfully,** again, stand straight, feet planted firmly on the floor, body centred, hands at your side. If it is hard to push you over physically, it will be hard to push you around verbally.
- **Assertive sitting:** convey confidence by using as much space as possible while sitting. Sit with your body on the diagonal, bottom well back in the chair and lean slightly forward. Sit 'small' and you will be perceived as small.

Stance

Your posture will convey a huge impression, so it is important to get it right.

Everyone will notice someone who stands upright and walks well. This is a good habit to cultivate. It portrays confidence and authority.

Tall people are notorious for stooping and they always say it is because they can't get through the doors. However, it is an enviable gift to be tall; many would give their eye teeth for height – so, if you are tall, duck only when necessary. Stoop when you are young and you will have no choice but to stoop when you are old.

Short people can walk tall, too. In fact, people of under five foot three can look six foot tall if they have good posture. We often confuse confidence for size, so you can make the most of this misconception by cultivating your own personal stature.

Senses

Taking the liberty to touch someone in the working context conveys superiority. A boss can pat his or her staff on the back, but they probably wouldn't appreciate it if their staff reciprocated. A pat on the back is an authoritative action. When it remains unchallenged, a hierarchy is established.

A good way of putting things back on an even footing is to look for an immediate opportunity to touch them back in a different manner. You might say, 'Excuse me', as you pick a hair off their jacket, or 'You've brushed up against some dust', as you sweep their chest, arm or shoulder briskly with the back of your hand.

The use of gestures

Gestures can either reinforce your communication or they can draw attention away from what you are saying. They should be used prudently, therefore, to maximize their effect.

Gestures include everything from 'windmill' arms (sit on your hands if this is you) to almost imperceptible movements of the face, head, torso or arms – they rarely involve the use of the legs.

The most common gestures are made with hands alone and they serve to emphasize what is being said by the mouth.

The type of gesture you choose to use can indicate something about your personality. If you 'prod the air' more than artistically necessary, you will appear aggressive. Open gestures, arms out away from the body, can indicate an open and warm personality. Be too energetic and untidy with your movements and you will come across as shambolic and disorganized. This is especially true if the style of your dress also tends to be untidy or too casual.

TIP *Assertive gestures tend towards the moderate ground. Timing and relevance are crucial. They should flow smoothly and mirror as closely as possible what is being said.*

Developing rapport

Empathizing with another does not depend solely on the words you use. Much of the rapport is carried in your body language.

If you watch two people talking enthusiastically and unselfconsciously, you will probably notice that their bodies take on virtually the same demeanour. For example, both may have crossed their legs, put an elbow on the table and their chin in the palm of their hands. If they are drinking, you will often find that the drinks diminish at exactly the same rate. They will have *matched* and *mirrored* each other's behaviour. If you do this consciously, but subtly, you will find that your ability to build rapport will have improved greatly.

Should you find yourself in an unpleasant or fraught conversation and you wish to alleviate the tension, it is possible to do this also by matching and mirroring the other's body language. Having matched and held their body position for some time, you can start moving your own body towards a more relaxed position. You will soon find that they start mirroring you and the tension will fade. It is impossible to remain aggressive when you are physically relaxed.

TIP *Beware: if you are not sufficiently subtle in your mirroring and matching skills, it will look as if you are mimicking the other's behaviour. If this is the impression you create, it will be very difficult to make amends.*

Couple this technique with good eye contact, active listening skills, affirming head nods, 'Ah-has', 'Mmms' and so on, and you will be able to build rapport with the best of them.

Being able to empathize with someone involves understanding their feelings by getting beneath the surface. This can often be achieved by being able to relate what they are saying to a similar experience of your own. If you are at sea, however, with no common understanding, the mirroring and matching technique can be used to engender the same feelings in you that are being experienced by the other person. If the other person has lost confidence, for instance, and takes on the foetal position, try it out for yourself and see what emotions it brings up. You will probably gain a better understanding of their feelings and be able to empathize more effectively.

The use of verbal language

The words we choose and the way we construct sentences can assist us in the process of building rapport.

To illustrate this, think of the way we talk to children. We are constantly reflecting back to them the words they use themselves. It has to be said that sometimes we diminish their intellects, but nonetheless the principle is the same. Listen out for the kind of words used by the person with whom you are trying to build rapport and reflect this style of language back to them.

A manager often uses a distinctive language that is related to the function or specialism of his or her role. Finance, information technology, manufacturing, design and development all have their own language. If you use this language back to these specialists, they will feel comfortable with your style. Use a different language, and they will feel alienated.

Here are some examples of language compatibility:

- A **financier's** language includes words like: balance, bottom line, assets, investments, credit, etc.
- Some of the following words would be used by an **information technologist**: logical, image, capacity, network, hardware, upgrade, etc.

The same sentence can be constructed differently for each audience:

- To the **financier**: 'On *balance*, I feel it would be to our *credit*...'
- To the **information technologist**: 'It would seem the most *logical* approach to *upgrade* our *image* by...'

And to a **visionary designer** whose language may include words like see, impact, style, colour, create, proportion, impression, etc., say 'I can *see* that we could *create* the best *impression* by...'

Interpreting body language

BEWARE: this is not an exact science.

When watching someone for the tell-tale signs of a hidden message, don't engage only your brain; engage your senses, too. People often think that they are privy to the inner secrets of another person, but you have to be bordering on the telepathic to know, really.

However, here are a few guidelines to interpreting body language:

- **Be aware of the environment** in which you are making your observation. If it is cold, your subject may have a tense jaw or their arms may be folded tightly across their bodies. In these circumstances, they *may not* be either nervous or aggressive – but then again, *they may*.
- **Watch for 'leakage'.** One example of leakage is someone who is controlling their nerves extremely well, but subconsciously lets them escape through toes curling and uncurling at the end of their shoes; muscles clenching and unclenching round their jaw, grinding teeth, rattling change in their pocket and quivering knees. As resourceful human beings, we have many such outlets.
- Mostly, look for **discontinuity** and **coincidence.** If someone is pledging their unequivocal support but shaking their head as they do so – watch your back. If someone says 'I never lie' at the same time as moving their pointing finger from side to side – withhold belief in them for a while and watch them closely. This can be a gesture of denial. If someone says, 'I am not interested in scoring points with the boss' and yet is coincidentally around the boss at the most politically charged moments, watch you don't get sideswiped.
- **Watch people's eyes** – it sounds obvious to say that people look where their interest lies, but sometimes, during an unguarded moment, it is interesting to note exactly where this is – or who it is.
- Sometimes it is easier to **identify 'anti' body language** – people tend to be very clear when they dislike someone. You can see it in their eyes and in the way they orientate their bodies away from the object of their distaste. This is the opposite of mirroring. Sometimes their complete and habitual removal from the scene gives the game away.

When people like each other, they get into close proximity – into that personal body space that is circumscribed by 'the egg'. They may touch, they often have good and prolonged eye contact, and they smile, reinforce and reflect each other's behaviour. Sometimes you are aware of 'chemistry', when there are no identifiable body signals. It is interesting to observe this behaviour and speculate on what it is that causes this effect.

Summary

In this chapter we have briefly looked at a very powerful aid to communication – and the interpretation of communication. We have learned that the body will not lie for you. If there is any incongruence between your message and your intention, it will find its way to the surface through 'leakage'. This makes your (and others') motivation visible, much more visible than you probably realized.

Your body, including your eyes and voice – not words – carries about 90 per cent of any message you are trying to convey. Because the proportion is so large, this aspect of communication has powerful potential. If you use your non-verbal knowledge skilfully, you will find that your level of control increases significantly. Beware, however, that you don't treat this aspect of communication as if it were a definitive code. You need to remember to put in it into context so that any risk of misinterpretation is minimized. Also, be aware that you may be looking for confirmation of a story or fantasy you hold about someone. This will result in you force-fitting the outcome of your analysis into a premeditated conclusion, which will 'muddy the water' of your communications.

However, you should now be more aware and be able to body-watch from a more informed position.

Enjoy body-watching!

Fact-check (answers at the back)

Think about the following questions and use them to develop your body language.

1. Body language is a powerful channel for communication. Which of the following statements is true?
a) Communicating without the visual channel (without seeing the communicator's body) can be more revealing ❏
b) By definition, gestures are distracting and misleading ❏
c) Most of the message is contained by the words used ❏
d) Tone, pitch and volume of the voice are considered to be part of body language ❏

2. When someone in the work context pats you on the back to establish their seniority, what can you do to redress the balance?
a) Shrug their hand away and tell them you don't appreciate their touch ❏
b) Pat them back immediately in like manner ❏
c) Find an opportunity to make physical contact in a different, but appropriate way ❏
d) Stand on a chair to make them feel small! ❏

3. What are gestures useful for achieving?
a) Drawing attention to yourself ❏
b) Maximizing the drama of your message ❏
c) Emphasizing what you are saying ❏
d) Distracting people from what you're actually saying! ❏

4. Empathizing with another is very helpful in building rapport. What can you do to establish an initial connection with someone?
a) Tell them what you think they should feel ❏
b) Mirror and match their body language ❏
c) Share your story with them, assuming that your experience will match theirs ❏
d) Say: 'I know how you feel!' ❏

5. Most people use their own distinctive language in their communications. If you want to establish rapport, what can you do to make a connection with them?
a) Use your own distinctive language to draw their attention to your message ❏
b) Reflect back language similar to their own ❏
c) Say you don't understand what they're saying and ask them to speak in English ❏
d) Get out a dictionary and make a play of looking up their words ❏

6. Body language can be used to assist in the interpretation of someone's message. What is the secret of body language?
   a) It is an exact science and the code is well known ❑
   b) It points towards what's going on under the surface ❑
   c) It enables you to cover up what you're really saying ❑
   d) It enables you to tell when someone's lying! ❑

7. In terms of body language, what is leakage?
   a) The secretion of unpleasant bodily fluids ❑
   b) The release of stress in repetitive small movements ❑
   c) Spitting and spluttering during speech ❑
   d) Excusing oneself repeatedly to go to the bathroom ❑

8. What techniques can you use on the telephone to convey the signals that your body would send if you were face to face?
   a) Make exaggerated gestures to compensate for not being in front of each other ❑
   b) Signpost what's going on for you – 'I was quiet because I was distracted momentarily.' ❑
   c) Talk more loudly ❑
   d) Make use of your invisibility to sit with your feet on the desk ❑

9. What do you notice when two people are locked in great conversation?
   a) They both talk at the same time ❑
   b) They mirror and match each other ❑
   c) They each agree with everything the other person says ❑
   d) They finish each other's sentences ❑

10. Tall people have an advantage because...
    a) People are frightened of them ❑
    b) They take up lots of space and have natural impact ❑
    c) They can see over everyone's heads ❑
    d) They can walk faster than anyone else ❑

CHAPTER 21

Personal power

We have almost come full circle now, so to close the learning for this masterclass, we will discuss personal power – how to win it, how to hold on to it and how to succeed with it.

In the sense that we're using it, personal power is correlated with confidence and goal clarity. It's about believing in what you want and going out to get it. For those who are not naturally blessed with personal power, it is a quality that is worth striving for, and it does take some striving to acquire it. However, with consciousness and dedication, this prize can be won and used to enhance our lives and successes.

The interesting thing about personal power is that you don't have to be born particularly advantaged to have it. It is not dependent upon your looks, size, intelligence, wealth or talents. Some of these may help; but the good news is, anyone can acquire personal power.

Most, or all, of the following qualities are found in powerful people:

- clarity of vision
- well-defined values and beliefs
- confidence
- powerful communication
- an ability to build relationships.

Power remains only with those who respect it. There may be a short-term gain for those who win power through confidence tricks, but it is inevitable that their fall from power will be in direct proportion to the 'con'.

Let's take each element of personal power and examine it separately.

Clarity of vision

It is essential to create a framework upon which you can hang your power. It is only when you know where you are going and are 100-per-cent committed to getting there that you can plan the way forward to your success. It doesn't matter which path you take, or whether you change the route from time to time, as long as you keep your eye on the goal.

Identifying the goal in the first place does require vision. Once you have this, and this is usually acquired through self-knowledge, the rest will fall into place.

If you have difficulty establishing your primary goal, start with a series of smaller ones. These will soon form a pattern that will lead you towards an understanding of what you wish to achieve. Ask yourself where you would like to be in 10, 20 or 50 years' time. Is maintaining your present course and direction sufficient to give you long-term satisfaction? Don't be concerned if your goal is extraordinarily ambitious. All those who have succeeded started out with 'impossible dreams'. Equally, don't be ashamed if your goal is not particularly ambitious. This means that you are meeting your own needs extremely well and puts you way ahead of the game.

Visionaries take the following steps to create a framework upon which they can build their successes. They...

- identify personal goals
- see their goals clearly and imagine what it is like to have reached them
- make a commitment to achieve them by a certain time
- act as if their goals have already been achieved.

If you don't put a time limit on the attainment of your goals, your mind will always think of them as being in the future. Acting as if you have already reached your goals will help to bring them into the present.

Test out these steps for yourself. Start small to gain confidence in the process.

Well-defined values and beliefs

Know what you value and believe. This is really much more difficult than it appears because values and beliefs may change over time, especially if your circumstances change dramatically for one reason or another. Dig deep, though; these underpin all your behaviours.

In the process of getting to know your values and beliefs you will have to ask yourself certain questions. For example, what price are you prepared to pay for your success...

- **personally?** – intimate relationships (partner, family, friends)
- **ethically?** – what you feel is right or wrong; what you need to do to feel good about yourself
- **professionally?** – career progression, promotion
- **politically?** – being in the right place at the right time.

If you ask a successful person the question 'What price are you prepared to pay for your success?', they will often have a clear, well-thought-out answer that is right for them. They are absolutely comfortable living within the framework of their values and beliefs. Any conflict – and conflict will develop from time to time as the balance of their life changes – will be addressed in the light of this value set.

Confidence

Here, we get back to the basics of **successful assertiveness.** Respect and honour yourself. You are as worthy as the next person.

Self-worth is the precursor to building confidence. If you believe in yourself, others will, too.

True confidence enables you to handle any situation well. Even in situations that you have not met before, you will be able to draw on your experience and extrapolate from your past behaviour to meet the needs of the moment.

A sudden lack of confidence can petrify and paralyse the mind and all coping mechanisms disappear. This rapid evacuation of all that you have learned will undermine your attempts at building confidence and put you back to square one again. So be kind to yourself; know that these things happen to everybody and that you are still a worthy individual. Forgive what you perceive to be your mistakes and move on.

The more you practise assertive behaviour, the less often sudden losses in confidence will happen. As with your goals (gaining confidence may be one of them, of course), try believing that you have already succeeded and act that way. It will soon become a reality.

Powerful communication

Powerful people are often extremely good communicators. Their communication skills are characterized by typical assertive behaviour.

Having a vision is not enough. The only way a vision becomes a reality is through motivating others to play their part, and the only way to motivate is to communicate. Only in very rare cases are visions actualized in a vacuum; usually they are dependent upon someone, or many people, co-operating in some way.

Not many of us are natural orators but we can learn from those who are. Here are a few qualities that you can learn to develop in yourself.

- **vision** (remember Martin Luther King's 'I have a dream...' speech)
- **belief** – in your purpose, your own ability and the ability of your team
- **acute observation** (listening, watching, sensing)
- ability to develop **empathy**
- ability to judge the **mood of the moment** and respond appropriately (flexibility/intuition)
- a sense of **timing** and **theatre**.

Powerful communicators regard their public appearances as theatrical performances. They create an impact, build tension, move their audience and leave them on a 'high'.

An ability to build relationships

It is often difficult to build and maintain relationships at the best of times, but it is especially difficult when driven by the work environment. Nonetheless, this ability is crucial if you wish to rise to the top.

There is no magic formula for developing good relationships and they can be stamped with a variety of styles – friendly, nurturing, respectful, mysterious, controlling, aggressive and so on. Try to identify your own style and check out the impression you create with colleagues.

Professional relationships can be troublesome because they have to be developed with people who are imposed upon us, not chosen by us. Indeed, we might actively avoid some of our colleagues when out of the work environment. Building good relationships therefore demands patience, determination and the ability to step back and see things from a different perspective.

Most people do not try to be bad or difficult. If this is the behaviour that they exhibit, it usually indicates that they hold a belief that is being challenged. If you encounter this behaviour as a manager, you may need to spend some time delving below the surface to understand the problem. Beware, however; you cannot merely go through the motions, and you may learn some unpalatable truths about yourself in the process.

Much can be done to maintain relationships remotely (by telephone, letter, email, etc.) but first you have to know and understand the people who work around you. This is done usefully at times when the pressure is off or at times when you socialize together. There is a fine line to tread between being too involved and too remote. You will have to determine the best balance for yourself; but remember that power holders are often characterized by a certain amount of mystique.

Summary

In this chapter we have briefly touched upon the dominant features of personal power. You may want to seek feedback on how you come across. Sometimes we make the mistake of believing that others hold the same belief about us as we do ourselves – either positively or negatively. We may think that they don't see our lack of personal power because we spend time hiding it. Or we may think that they interpret our over-domineering style as powerful. It is worth getting feedback from a trusted source so that you know where your starting point is. It may be painful (or it may not!) but having clarity in terms of how you are seen is really valuable.

Fact-check (answers at the back)

Think about the following questions and use them to develop your personal power.

1. What is personal power?
a) It is 'Popeye' physical strength ❏
b) It is the confidence to know what you want and know what you need to do to get it ❏
c) It is the ability to dominate situations ❏
d) It is the ability to delegate ❏

2. What do people with personal power possess? Identify the odd one out!
a) Clarity of vision ❏
b) Values and beliefs ❏
c) A position high up in the hierarchy of an organization ❏
d) Ability to build rapport ❏

3. We are goal-oriented beings. What is your goal for the future?
a) 1–5 years from now ❏
b) 5–10 years from now ❏
c) Lifetime goal ❏
d) I don't have a goal ❏

4. Which of these statements about goals is true?
a) Goals get in the way of spontaneity ❏
b) Goals are pointless because they always change with circumstances ❏
c) Goals help us make relevant decisions and take appropriate action ❏
d) Goals are always out of reach ❏

5. How easy do you find it to articulate your vision?
a) I carry a clear vision for myself and can describe it easily ❏
b) I have a vision but it changes so regularly that I don't bother to talk about it ❏
c) People tend to laugh at my vision when I talk about it, thinking it's too fanciful ❏
d) Because I can't control events, I don't have a vision ❏

6. If your relationship building style were assertive, what should it look like?
a) Friendly yet firm ❏
b) Political and manipulative ❏
c) Wilful and commanding ❏
d) Easily biddable ❏

7. If you are engaged in a 'challenging' relationship, what assumption may help you get it back on track again?
a) They may feel misunderstood and unfairly judged ❏
b) They may be disruptive and difficult ❏
c) They may hold a grudge against you for no good reason ❏
d) They may be trying to make you look bad ❏

8. What feedback have you had about your personal power quotient?
   a) I'm often told I'm too aggressive ❏
   b) I don't receive feedback – and I don't ask for it! ❏
   c) I seem to enjoy healthy, co-operative and productive relationships and people tell me they enjoy working with me ❏
   d) People say that I'll never get anywhere being as quiet as a mouse! ❏

9. If you had to deal with a conflict in your team, how would you do so assertively?
   a) I'd tell the opposing parties to get a life and sort it out! ❏
   b) I'd encourage each party to listen to each other's point of view and find some common ground ❏
   c) I'd try to resolve the issue for them ❏
   d) I wouldn't get involved at all. It's not my business ❏

10. How satisfied are you with your assertiveness skills?
    a) I am assertive in my dealings with others and feel comfortable with this ❏
    b) I am assertive sometimes but need to practise more in 'difficult' situations ❏
    c) I am not particularly assertive but would like to be ❏
    d) I get hyped up and tend to dominate situations ❏

7 × 7

1 Seven key ideas

● Assertiveness is a choice. It's not something that you have to do all the time!
● Assertive communication is a win/win style of communication. It allows both parties to feel heard and acknowledged.
● Being assertive is contingent upon you knowing what you want to communicate and communicating it consistently.
● Finding and flexing an assertive communication style is the beginning of self-understanding.
● Sometimes being passive, or being aggressive, is assertive (inasmuch as you are choosing to communicate in the most effective way for a particular situation).
● Listening is a major part of being assertive. Indeed, the balance of listening to speaking should be, at the very least, 2:1 – if not 5:1!
● Assertive communication also allows you to raise your children and manage your pets effectively.

2 Seven best resources

● http://www.mindtools.com/pages/article/Assertiveness.htm –Assertiveness: Working WITH People, Not Against Them (Management Training and Leadership Training, Online)
● http://www.wikihow.com/Be-Assertive – How to Be Assertive
● *Assertiveness Pocketbook* by Max A. Eggert – full of good advice on how to overcome self-defeating beliefs, and deal with common problem areas
● *Brilliant Assertiveness: What the most assertive people know, do and say* by Dannie Lu Carr – practical and accessible, *Brilliant Assertiveness* examines what it means to be assertive and contains exercises and case studies to help you establish your assertiveness skills.

- iTunes app: *Confidence Booster: Self-Esteem and Assertiveness Training* by Sean Gohara – a walk-through guide on boosting self-esteem and assertiveness utilizing powerful techniques to take you through a full 'internal transformation'
- *How to Say 'No': Politely but firmly take back control of your time and your life* by Claire Shannon – if you find yourself trying to please everyone but, in doing so, fail to please yourself, this is for you!
- *Emotional Intelligence: 21 ultimate tips for gaining control over your emotions and becoming a boss of your thoughts and behaviour* by Joseph Sanchez

3 Seven things to avoid

- Try not to confuse aggression (you win, they lose) with assertiveness (you win, they win). Assertiveness does not always mean that you get your own way!
- Don't try to be assertive ALL the time! It can become a tyranny if you beat yourself up every time assertiveness eludes you – and you can become a 'communication tyrant' to others!
- Try not to expect everyone to have the same communication style as you. By listening and asking questions, you can help others express themselves more effectively.
- Beware of responding to emails emotionally and instinctively. Put them to one side while you think about what you want to say and how you're going to say it.
- Don't try to assert yourself at every opportunity. Sometimes, it's best to take yourself off duty and let things go. Ask yourself, 'Will my intervention make a positive difference?'
- Try not to criticize or judge others' approach to their communication. Remember what it was like when you were not consistently assertive and be generous to those who are trying!
- Expecting yourself to get it 'right' all the time. With the best will in the world, you're likely to find yourself falling back into your old habits from time to time. Just review what happened and try again!

4 Seven inspiring people

- Paloma Faith – a songwriter, singer and all-round performer. Paloma is distinctively herself, with no compromises. Yet she engages empathically with her art and those that surround her. A marvellous role model of international standing.
- HRH Prince Harry – another uncompromisingly authentic human being with a big heart for doing important work and having a great time. He is lovely to his grandmother, too!
- Angela Merkel, former Chancellor of Germany – conducts herself with great authority, consistency and genuineness in a tough political context as a minority representative of women.
- Dame Judi Dench – a brilliant and acclaimed actress who brings her personality fully to her audiences. She has endured serious personal loss yet acts as an exemplar of dignity, courage... and humour.
- Malala Yousafzai – a fabulously brave young Pakistani woman who defied the Taliban, after being shot, by advocating education for girls. At age 17, she became the youngest ever recipient of a Nobel Prize.
- David Beckham – formerly a footballer with Manchester United, he played for a number of clubs in Europe and America while also being the captain of the England team. He has been a Goodwill Ambassador for UNICEF since his early football career. A good father and a good role model.
- Sir David Attenborough – primarily known as a naturalist and broadcaster, he has travelled to the most remote parts of the world to bring unique images of animals and descriptions of their lives to television audiences. The enduring image of him being the plaything of two baby gorillas in Rwanda is perhaps defining!

5 Seven great quotes

- 'The difference between successful people and really successful people is that really successful people say no to almost everything.' Warren Buffett
- 'It's never too late to be what you might have been.' George Eliot
- 'If liberty means anything at all, it means the right to tell people what they don't want to hear.' George Orwell
- 'Get up, stand up / Stand up for your rights. / Get up, stand up, / Don't give up the fight.' Bob Marley
- 'Your playing small does not serve the world. There is nothing enlightened about shrinking so that other people won't feel insecure around you. We are all meant to shine.' Marianne Williamson.
- 'Be yourself; everyone else is already taken.' Oscar Wilde
- 'You may not control all the events that happen to you, but you can decide not to be reduced by them.' Maya Angelou

6 Seven things to do today

- Decide how you want to communicate and give yourself some early targets to achieve to get you going.
- Listen to yourself in communication with others and see whether you can identify your dominant communication style.
- Identify a role model, observe them in dialogue and see what they do that you could also do – authentically.
- Pick up a few sentences that allow you to open a 'difficult' conversation assertively.
- Read through your written communications and try to view them from the other person's perspective. Try to imagine the impression that they'll get from them.
- Tackle a difficult conversation that you've been putting off for a while.
- Ask a trusted friend to hear you rehearse some 'openers' or anticipated responses and give you feedback. Once

you've heard yourself saying things differently (and to your satisfaction), you'll begin to find your new style more easily accessible and familiar.

7 Seven trends for tomorrow

- With the increase of social media in all aspects of life (including the professional), think about how your communication style is conveyed in the 'sound bites' you choose. Without much context, meaning can easily be distorted.
- People tend to be accessible, online, all the time. This creates a willingness in them to interrupt face-to-face communication in order to respond to a ring or a bleep – or a theme tune! 'Instantaneousness' is the biggest disturbance in the communication field and can lead less assertive people to feel unimportant and uninteresting.
- Virtual working patterns are both a blessing and a curse for the unassertive communicator. They are a blessing inasmuch as there is often more time available to plan responses to questions or prompts. They are a curse inasmuch as messages are devoid of the physical clues and cues that allow appropriate responses to be given and it is easy to misunderstand and miscommunicate messages.
- The increase in multigenerational working environments means that different styles of communication are called for and different meanings are projected on to different communication styles. It seems that we must be multi-skilled and multi-talented in order to 'hold true to ourselves'.
- Globalization brings with it the need to communicate across multi-variant cultures and social divides. Being assertive in one cultural context may be received as aggressive in another. It is important to take some time to understand the social mores of those with whom you are communicating.

- Virtual, yet face-to-face, meeting options are increasing in popularity due to the cost benefit. This type of meeting requires a particular type of etiquette to compensate for the physical distance and atmospheric difference. To avoid confusion or mixed messages, communicators must be participative and their communication clear and unambiguous.
- A 'counter-trend' may emerge that addresses the issue of privacy and confidentiality. To avoid old photographs and 'sensitive' conversations from getting into the hands of those with few reasons to respect their provenance, people may go back to hushed conversations and contact prints!

PART 4
Your Memory Techniques Masterclass

Introduction

Memory is central to everything you do – and the great news is that it can be improved, quickly and easily. This Part will give you practical advice about taking control of every aspect of your memory and using it to the full.

When you know how to remember, how to tap into your brain's amazing power and apply it to all your learning needs, you feel confident about a range of challenges, at work and at home. You retain key information and access it easily, saving time and achieving more. Whether it's names, numbers, times, dates, individual facts or complex documents, you know how to remember everything you need, making you more organized and helping you in many different tasks. You impress people by remembering their names, improve your ability to communicate from memory, and do the right things to make other people remember you.

Memory training also helps your whole brain work better. The key techniques encourage you to organize your mind, improve your creativity and speed up your thought processes. You get a new awareness of what you can achieve, even under pressure, and see just how effective and enjoyable it can be to take charge of the complex set of processes that makes up your memory.

Small steps can make big differences. This masterclass begins with a guide to adopting the right mindset, revealing how any negative thoughts that have been holding you back can quickly be replaced by a confident and open approach to memory. You may well have got out of the habit of engaging with information and enjoying the learning process, but that can easily change. By exploring how your memory works, and adapting your learning techniques to match, you can activate the full power of your brain and start making your mind do exactly what you want.

Most of the strategies explained in this Part have been around for thousands of years, but they're more relevant than ever. All of them can make you better at the things you need to do today. You'll learn how to switch on your imagination, use the power of pictures, tell stories and go on mental journeys... to engage with the very real and important information you have to handle every day. Improving your memory is a fun process with seriously big benefits.

There are challenges we all face: dealing with the ever-rising tide of information, taking on new roles, coping with change. We also have our own particular learning needs, at work and at home, predictable and unexpected, enforced and chosen. Memory skills don't just help you survive the tests you face every day – they inspire you to set ambitious new targets, and to shine in everything you do.

CHAPTER 22

The right frame of mind

How you feel about your memory can have a big impact on how you use it. All your learning experiences up to this point have given you an opinion about your memory: the way you use it, how well it works, what sorts of things it can do. There will be some positive points, but it's likely that there are also plenty of negative ideas: for example, from the times when memory has felt hard or seemed boring or just plain let you down. It's easy to think that you've explored every avenue for your memory, when you've probably only scratched the surface; yet the thought habits are ingrained, and they're probably limiting the way you use your memory now.

If you can open your mind, you can re-evaluate your views and change your habits, breaking down barriers to learning that you may never even have noticed were there. It can seem like going backwards, because you may have to unlearn certain behaviours and recapture an approach that used to come naturally. But it's the way forward, and the necessary first step in setting up your thinking skills for success.

Brain power

There's never been a time when memory power was so important, and so neglected. It's undeniable that the workplace is changing at a pace never before witnessed. All of us are inundated with new information: new names, techniques, procedures, rules, facts, ideas. Stress levels are high, the need to communicate quickly and to think creatively is greater than ever – and yet few people feel mentally equipped to deal with it all.

How often do you hear or, worse, find yourself uttering the following mantras:

- 'I've got a terrible memory'
- 'I can't cope with this new software'
- 'I can't remember where I left that package'
- 'Everything's just too chaotic'

Stop. Within your head is more than enough brain power to cope with all the new data you face, all the changes you encounter in your working life. Your brain can deal with millions of pieces of information in the blink of an eye. You just have to use it properly.

Learn how your brain works, practise making it do what you want, and you can start tapping into its enormous potential.

The first step will always be to focus on the present – the way you try to think, learn and remember now. It's important to consider your current approach to learning, in order to highlight the bad habits and start focusing on the things that can be changed. Here's a learning task that you're unlikely to have to do in real life, but one that can help you to see the memory strategies you naturally employ.

> How would you go about memorizing the following number?
>
> 2821594434142463122635724

You have one minute to learn as much of the 25-digit sequence as you can. When the minute has passed, cover up the numbers and see how much of the order you can recall. This chapter ends with a technique for remembering the whole sequence with ease; but let's begin by considering what might currently be stopping you making the most of your brain's potential.

Negative mindsets

You are the product of your experience. From childhood you've been on the receiving end of lessons, instructions, guidance and orders, from a number of sources. Parental influence led to that of teachers, your wider family, other adults, peer groups, and society at large. From that array of experiences, your view of yourself and the world has been formed.

The problem is, you almost certainly received far more negative messages than positive ones. Research suggests that, on average, 90 per cent of the messages a child hears are critical or negative. It's hardly surprising then that many adults have deeply rooted negative beliefs about themselves, and life in general. How often do you hear people say things like 'I'm not clever enough for that', 'I always failed in that in school', or 'I'm too long in the tooth to change' – and how often do you secretly agree with them?

> **'Whether you think you can or whether you think you can't, you're right.'**
> Henry Ford

One of the inevitable outcomes of a negative mindset is that you're setting yourself up for failure even before you start. In many cases, you never even try something: fear of failure keeps you trapped in a familiar – but limiting – 'comfort zone'.

Yet we've all read about or spoken to people who are not limited by negative thoughts, not held back by fear of failure, not frightened to try something new. Focus on your negative ideas and challenge them.

The latest research calls into question the assumption that memory automatically deteriorates with age. If you can use it properly and keep it in trim, your brain can do things you never thought possible – and *keep* doing them.

Habit

Humans are creatures of habit in what they do, and how they think. We like routine, doing things the way we've always done them – too often not the best way, just the way we've got used to. Generally we don't even realize that we're operating in an habitual way, cutting ourselves off from options that could dramatically improve our success.

Think of a habit you've broken in the past. A habit has to be learned, so it can be unlearned. It might have been tough, it might have taken a while, but remember the satisfying feeling of success when you achieved it.

To improve your mental performance, and to start learning and remembering effectively, you need to identify the ways of *thinking* that serve no useful purpose; thinking that might be holding you back; thinking that you would like to change.

As an example, imagine you'd decided to do something about your habitual failure to remember people's names. The process of change would be built on the following key steps:

- *Accepting that your thought processes are simply habitual*: you've got into the habit of forgetting, and have no extra memory strategies to help you out.
- *Telling yourself that this particular habit serves no useful purpose*: even when you struggle and strain to remember, you still fail to recall key names at the crucial time.
- *Acknowledging that you can change, because you want to*: a habit learned can be unlearned.
- *Knowing that you can change, however old you are*: ingrained habits are harder to shift, but it's never impossible. Remember, the longer you've failed at something, the greater the benefits will be when you start to succeed.

- *Seeing the advantages of change*: in this case you'd concentrate on the social and professional situations where remembering names is crucial. Imagine the feeling of confidence you'd enjoy, and the sort of impact you could have on others.
- Confirming to yourself that, from this moment on, you'll actively work on remembering names, using the techniques explained in this Part.

Congratulations: you're on your way!

The way you've been taught in the past

When it comes to taking in new information, people have different natural tendencies. Three key learning 'modalities' have been identified:

1 **Visual** – seeing
2 **Auditory** – hearing
3 **Kinesthetic** – doing

Although we all rely on a mixture of the three, we have our particular, preferred learning styles.

Imagine you'd been given a barbecue kit to put together. How would you go about it? Would you read the instruction booklet? Would you ask someone to read the instructions to you? Or would you feel happiest simply playing around with the component pieces, exploring their construction through trial and error?

Your choice reveals a lot about your preferred modality. However, there are those who use all three to great effect. In doing so they're practising a form of holistic learning.

It makes sense to know which is your preferred modality so that, in any learning situation, you try hard to engage with information in that form.

It's also a good idea to practise other modalities in order to strengthen the learning and train your brain.

By taking a multi-modality approach, we can become progressive thinkers, creating a self-perpetuating circle of creative, challenging thoughts and positive feelings about ourselves.

To recap:

You have at your disposal an enormously exciting mechanism for learning and remembering – your amazing brain. But you may well be limiting your brain power because of:

- a negative mindset
- force of habit
- trying to use it in the wrong way.

So much for blockages to remembering and learning. What are the steps forward – the starting points for making this master-class work for you?

You need to be motivated

You won't succeed in anything if you can't see what's in it for you. Just as an athlete limbers up before an event and focuses on the goal, before you begin your journey to effective memory you need to prepare yourself mentally.

What will you get out of improving your brain? Your list might include:

- dealing with information more quickly and more effectively
- saving time
- impressing others
- enjoying learning
- using new skills to boost promotion prospects
- increasing confidence.

Spend a few minutes compiling your own motivating list, and make a point of looking back at it regularly.

You need a multi-faceted approach to learning

There was a time when we knew instinctively how to get it right. Think about the ways small children assimilate new information. They:

- engage all their senses
- give their imagination free rein
- ask lots of questions
- have little or no concept of failure
- remain enthusiastic and positive
- become totally engrossed in an activity
- try a variety of approaches.

This is sometimes called 'global learning', since it involves the whole brain: the left, logical side, which deals with organized thinking, decisions and lists; and the right, random side, which attends to imagination, creativity, pictures and ideas.

As adults, we tend to limit our thinking processes, designating one thing as a problem requiring logic, and another as a challenge requiring imagination. The trick to effective memory and learning is to use both sides at once, and to benefit from all the options available.

You need the right learning environment

Today's workplace is often open-plan, busy, full of noise, movement and interruptions. It's fine if you can concentrate in that sort of environment – some people even prefer it – but it makes it difficult for those who need peace and quiet to think effectively. Just as we all take in information in different ways, we also have our own preferred places and conditions for learning.

Whenever possible, you need to take control of your learning environment. What sort of place would be ideal for you? Would it be:

- noisy or quiet?
- a small room or a large, open office?
- inside or out?
- heated or air-conditioned?

Experiment with the conditions, and be aware of all the tricks at your disposal for boosting focus and concentration.

- Tackle important information when you're most alert.
- Let people know when you need private time and space to think.
- See if a particular kind of music boosts your thinking power.
- Surround yourself with visual images that please you, and be aware of how colours affect your mood.
- Keep your workplace as organized and as calm as possible.

You need to practise

All too often we abandon something without giving it a fair chance of working. We don't try as hard as we might to change an old habit and replace it with a new strategy, and reach for excuses to avoid practising it and putting in the work: 'I'm too busy', 'It's too difficult', 'Nothing's happening'. Suddenly the old, safe ways seem very appealing.

There's no magic wand or instant fix. Look back at your 'motivations' list – the things you could get out of having a powerful brain. Isn't it worth a little effort?

PMA – Positive Mental Attitude

We've already highlighted the debilitating effect of the negative drip-feed many of us have been on. The following points will help you start to change negative into positive, and begin building the right attitude to learning.

Remember:

- change is possible
- the techniques for tapping into your true mental potential are simple to learn
- learning can be fun
- the benefits of a trained brain are immense.

Stop:

- limiting yourself
- talking yourself down
- expecting failure.

Start:

- trusting in your abilities
- seeing problems as challenges
- enjoying the rewards of your efforts.

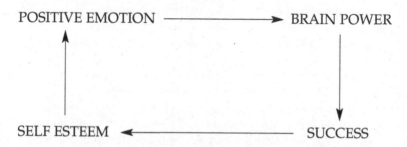

POSITIVE EMOTION ⟶ BRAIN POWER

SELF ESTEEM ⟵ SUCCESS

So, you need to ask yourself five key questions:

1 What's in this for me?
2 How do I learn best?
3 Where do I find learning easiest?
4 How can I start to practise?
5 How can I boost my beneficial thoughts?

Answer each of these questions in a positive way and you take a big step towards becoming a powerful and effective learner.

Learning habits may be deeply ingrained, but they can be changed – and when they are, the results are dramatic.

Near the start of this chapter you tried to learn a sequence of digits, using the approach that came naturally to you. Now, try learning it in a different way. It's possible to change information: to make it memorable. In this case, changing the numbers into words. All you need is to remember the first two lines of a couple of very famous songs:

'I'm dreaming of a white Christmas,
Just like the ones I used to know'
and
'Should old acquaintance be forgot
And never brought to mind'.

Spend a few moments repeating the lyrics from memory, checking you can recall them accurately. If you can, then you now know the complete number sequence. Simply write down the number of letters in each word.

'I'm' has two letters, so you write down 2.

'Dreaming' has eight letters, so the next number in the sequence is 8. 'Of' has two letters, so next you write down 2... and so on. See how quickly you can write out the entire 25-digit number from memory.

This is clearly an artificial experiment, but it proves an important point. By adopting the right frame of mind, and showing a willingness to learn in a new way and to change information into a more memorable form, you can remember anything. It's even easier when you're motivated, and learning real information that's useful to you.

You've made a commitment to finding new and improved learning techniques – and now it's time to get to grips with how your memory works.

Summary

To round off this chapter, plan your targets for the future – they need to be realistic but also aspirational, reflecting your growing confidence in what you might be able to achieve.

Think about how you'd like to feel about your memory. What would it be like to have confidence in your memory skills generally, but also to succeed at particular tasks? Choose one area of your life where memory is a problem and imagine yourself in control, enjoying the benefits of a trained brain.

Next, consider some of the rewards of memory improvement. Which aspects of your life would benefit most from stronger learning skills? How exactly would the pay-offs appear? Think about things like time saved, stress reduced, promotion, better pay – and impressive results.

Finally, just how good do you want your memory to be? Which are the main areas you want to work on, and how will you benchmark your improvement? You might want to be able to memorize a phone number without writing it down, recall five work tasks, or give a ten-minute talk from memory. Your targets can change in time, but setting some clear goals now will focus your efforts and boost your motivation to give memory your best shot.

Fact-check (answers at the back)

The following questions are designed to help you set your priorities:

1. Which of the following areas of memory do you worry about most?
   a) Memory loss with age ❑
   b) Forgetting facts and figures ❑
   c) Losing possessions ❑
   d) Failing exams ❑

2. When you were at school, how good was your memory?
   a) Can't remember ❑
   b) Poor ❑
   c) OK ❑
   d) Strong ❑

3. How confident are you about learning new skills?
   a) Not at all ❑
   b) Unsure ❑
   c) Fairly ❑
   d) Very ❑

4. How good are you at remembering names and faces?
   a) Terrible ❑
   b) Not bad ❑
   c) Confident ❑
   d) Perfect ❑

5. What state is your mind in at the moment?
   a) Chaotic ❑
   b) Untidy ❑
   c) Quite neat ❑
   d) Well-organized ❑

6. How do you feel about inventing creative stories?
   a) Negative ❑
   b) Uncertain ❑

   c) Interested ❑
   d) Excited ❑

7. Which of these skills would you like to improve most?
   a) Speaking from memory ❑
   b) Revising for tests ❑
   c) Remembering people ❑
   d) Learning facts ❑

8. How often does your faulty memory cause you big problems?
   a) Regularly ❑
   b) Often ❑
   c) Occasionally ❑
   d) Never ❑

9. How memorable do you think you are to others, as a writer and speaker?
   a) Not at all ❑
   b) Slightly ❑
   c) Reasonably ❑
   d) Very ❑

10. How much confidence do you have in your ability to train your memory?
    a) None ❑
    b) A little ❑
    c) Quite a lot ❑
    d) A great deal ❑

CHAPTER 23

Your amazing brain

Whatever you've come to feel about your memory, advertising agencies know that you have an amazing capacity to learn and remember – as long as the right things happen to activate it. Spend a moment thinking about a few adverts that have stuck in your mind: on TV, at the cinema, in magazines or on billboards. Whether or not you've actually bought these products or heeded the messages, these communications have worked because they've created lasting memories. So how did they do that?

- They must have captured your attention in some way. How?
- They probably engaged with several of your senses. Which ones?
- They're likely to have triggered your short-term memory. With what?
- Their creators have worked hard to make your memory work. What did they do?

As well as remembering these adverts, see where your memories go next. When you first saw them, how did you feel, where were you living, what was your life like? Use the adverts as starting points and see what other information comes to mind. Start exploring your unpredictable, interconnected memory, ready to begin the process of learning how it works – and adopting the habits that will make it do what you want.

Your approach to learning

All knowledge is but remembrance.
Plato

If I had six hours to chop down a tree,
I'd spend the first four hours sharpening the axe.
Abraham Lincoln

What's *your* approach to learning? Like Lincoln sharpening his axe, how do you prepare for a memory task, to make it as easy, enjoyable and efficient as possible?

Imagine you had to learn the following shopping list of ten simple items:

> chocolates, potatoes, soap, milk, paper towels, coconut, bananas, cheese, wine, bread

Spend a few moments now trying to learn this list as you would normally. As you do so, make an effort to notice what you're doing. What habits have you picked up? How do you try to remember?

By the end of this chapter, you'll be able to learn a list like this with ease, and recall the items forwards or backwards. In fact, you'll be capable of learning a list twice as long.

To learn how to do that, you need to understand how your memory works. We'll examine the physical mechanisms of the human brain, to get a glimpse of how this amazing resource works, and how it must be fuelled and operated.

First, though, we need to ask a fundamental question: Why does it work sometimes, but not always?

Factors affecting recall

Almost everyone claims to have a terrible memory, but they don't seem to think that it's *always* terrible. In fact, they're in no doubt that it works very well for them sometimes.

A man who forgets his wife's birthday every year may be a doctor with a mental database crammed with thousands of medical facts. A woman who says that she can't remember telephone numbers could easily be a keen musician, and know countless pieces of music off by heart.

One of the most important steps in memory improvement is simply realizing that some things are easier to remember than others. Our brains do work, and we demonstrate our learning skills many times every day – but not every type of information sticks easily. Like Lincoln and his axe, you need to invest time preparing for the task, altering information to make it memorable.

We do this already. Everyone at some time will have made use of mnemonic tricks. 'Thirty days hath September'; 'Every Good Boy Deserves Favour '; 'Richard Of York Gave Battle In Vain'. Perhaps you remember certain numbers by spotting patterns, noticing significant digits – your age, for example, or your house number. Unfortunately, few people ever get to know about the really powerful memory techniques – the ones that let you change *any* kind of information to make it compatible with the way your mind works.

To discover what they are, you need to test your memory. Use the following experiment to find out the characteristics a piece of information needs to have if it's going to be memorable. Read through this list of 25 words once or, if possible, get someone to read them out to you. As soon as the list is finished, see how many of the words you can write down from memory, in any order.

> shoe, watch, flower, Madonna, chair, lion, kettle, ball, pin, firework, pencil, tiger, phone, warm, puma, hill, time, sharpener, mugger, cheetah, hat, car, apple, book, kite

What's most interesting about this test isn't how many words you remember – but which ones. It's possible to predict with surprising accuracy which words most people recall.

book, *kite* – you're likely to have remembered the last two words on the list because there was very little time to forget them. No new words appeared to confuse you, so you were able to carry them in your short-term memory for long enough to write them down.

shoe, *watch*, *flower* – the words from the very start of the list are also likely to have stayed with you. When the experiment began, your mind was fresh and alert. You were interested in the sorts of word that might be included, and it's likely that you were making a special effort to remember.

On the other hand, the words from the middle of the list are a great deal harder to recall. Your interest wanes, your mental energy drops, your concentration wavers and the whole task just seems too difficult and confusing.

lion, *tiger*, *puma*, *cheetah* – most people who try this test spot the four linked words – the big cats – and remember them all as a group. Perhaps you found that this also worked for *pencil* and *sharpener* – two words that you could easily link together in your mind.

Madonna – when a words stands out from a set of information, is noticeable and unusual, it's much easier to remember.

firework – being able to picture a word is a vital part of remembering it. In this case, the word also conjures up sounds and even smells, making it particularly powerful, especially compared with the abstract words in the list such as *warm* and *time*.

mugger – this word is likely to have provoked an emotional response, making it much more memorable than bland words such as *pin*, *phone* and *hill*.

From this simple test, key factors about memory are revealed.

You remember:

- when your mind is alert, you're interested and motivated, especially at the start and end of any learning period
- when material is patterned or connected
- when information is unusual
- when you can picture what you have to learn
- when the information makes you feel something.

You forget:

- when you lose interest and motivation, especially in the middle of a learning period

- when the material has no shape or connections
- when information is dull
- when it's difficult to picture the material
- when what you're learning doesn't provoke any emotional response.

If you consider these points in terms of your day-to-day memory experiences, you'll see that they make sense. The sort of information you tend to remember is:

- material you're interested in, or really motivated to learn, such as statistics about your favourite sport, or material to help you make money
- songs, tunes and poems – connected into memorable patterns of sound and rhythm
- stories, also based on connections, with one event causing another, one scene linking to the next
- faces – you know you've seen a person before
- unusual events – the days when you did something out of the ordinary
- embarrassing moments, times of happiness, fear, surprise – all occasions made memorable by strong emotions.

Of course, most information we have to learn doesn't conform to these points. We waste so much time struggling to remember things that – as they're presented – simply aren't memorable:

- numbers – abstract, hard to visualize or connect
- names – you recognize the face, but what's the name? Again, the name is abstract, easily confused and forgotten.
- everyday jobs – you don't feel particularly motivated, the information is dull and uninspiring, and so you regularly forget it.

So the best-kept secret of memory is this: if information is difficult to learn, you need to change it, to make it memorable.

Making it memorable

It may well be a step that you've never really considered before, but it will revolutionize your learning. Learn something well enough the first time, and that's it – you don't have to relearn it endlessly. Information is changed to make it compatible with the way your memory works, and so learning it is easy and efficient, saving you time in the long run and boosting your confidence and success. Well-learned information is there whenever you need it, wherever you are – and in a form in which it can be explored, organized and then produced in the most effective way.

So how do you make *any* kind of information memorable? There's a one-word answer to that: **IMAGINATION**.

The Emperor Napoleon once said that 'imagination rules the world'. We all have powerful imaginations, seen in dreams and fantasies, and used when we're reading books, listening to radio plays and working through problems.

It's imagination that allows us to take information and change it, to make it memorable. As long as you can return it to its original form when the time comes, it simply makes sense to explore and learn it in a form that your mind can handle.

It's time for a little imagination training. Below are four everyday words. Spend a few moments picturing each one in your imagination. In the first instance, simply try to imagine each object with as much clarity and in as much detail as possible.

- box
- tree
- car
- cake

Next, return to each item, and imagine picturing it from different angles. Can you imagine walking round it, seeing it from above, even getting inside it and looking out?

Now try adding some sense information. Imagine touching the item: what does it feel like? Is there any smell, sound or taste? Add as many details as you can to your imaginary pictures.

Next, practise making information unusual. Anything is possible in the imagination, so make each of your four images as unusual as possible. You could visualize the objects in a strange place, or doing odd things, or becoming very large or incredibly small. Exaggerate to make the images bizarre and memorable. These skills are vital when it comes to powerful learning and remembering. You take control of information in your imagination, make it visual and unusual, and give yourself a range of sense triggers.

Feelings are also important. To practise the skill of inventing emotional reactions to information, go back to the first word, *box*. You should already have a memorable image in your mind – but your task now is to imagine *destroying* it. How would you go about wrecking the box? What would your feelings be as you ripped it up, set fire to it or attacked it with a chain saw?

Next, imagine you're scared of the *tree*. How could you use your imagination to make this tree the most frightening thing in the world?

Turn the *car* into a source of hysterical fun. How could you picture it so that it made you roar with laughter?

Finally, invent an embarrassing moment involving the *cake*. Involve yourself in the action, and imagine the feeling of utter embarrassment.

> Visual
>
> Unusual
>
> 3-dimensional
>
> Stimulating to the senses
>
> Stimulating to the emotions

As soon as a piece of information has been given these characteristics it can be connected with others in a memorable pattern. It's like inventing a story about your material.
Each item becomes one step in the story, prompting you to remember the next.

One item can transform into another, or explode and release the next image. You can imagine joining items together, putting one thing on top of another, or seeing an object come to life and do something bizarre and memorable to the next item on the list. Remember, anything is possible in imagination. The story doesn't have to have any real logic – only the connections you create.

To link these four words together in a story, you might imagine opening the box to find a tiny tree inside. You could take the tree and fix it to the rear view mirror in your car, and then drive off – straight into a giant cream cake sitting in the middle of the road.

- Think of the *box*, and you'll remember finding the *tree*.
- Think of the tree, and you'll recall fixing it in your *car*.
- Picture driving off in your car, and you'll remember how you felt when you smashed into the giant *cake*.

BOX → TREE → CAR → CAKE

However long a list is, you only need to deal with one item at a time. Make each link strong enough and it'll take you to the end of your story.

The structure of the brain

To help you appreciate just what your brain is capable of, let's take a look at how it's structured.

St Augustine said, 'People travel to wonder at the highest of mountains, at the huge waves of the sea, at the long courses of rivers, at the vast compass of the ocean, at the circular motion of the stars and they pass by themselves without wondering.'

Inside our heads we are wondrous indeed. In fact, the more we explore our amazing inner universe with all its range and its complexities, the more we realize there is to discover. There are three clearly defined areas of the brain:

1 *The Reptile brain.* Also known as the stem brain, it oversees the primitive survival mechanisms such as self-protection, reproduction, nourishment and shelter. It's also responsible for understanding physical reality, collected via the senses.
2 *The Mammalian brain.* This brain area represents a quantum leap in terms of evolutionary development. It's here that feelings, emotions, memories and experiences are assimilated. It's also the part of the brain that deals with

bodily needs and functions such as hunger, thirst, sexual desire, body temperature, metabolism and immunity. Having collected a vast array of information via the senses and bodily sensations, it then passes that knowledge on to the largest part of the brain, the thinking part.

3 *The Cortex*. This part makes up around 80 per cent of the total brain. Here resides the intellect, where reasoning, decision making and linguistic ability result in purposeful voluntary actions. It's here too that many believe the sixth sense of intuition can be found. This is the part of us that is able to perceive information that is not picked up by our other senses. It's the superior qualities of the cortex that stand us apart from all other living things and make us unique as a species.

As well as this tripartite brain there's another division into the left and right hemispheres. These are responsible for the different modes of thinking, and they specialize in particular skills.

The left hemisphere. This works in a logical, rational, linear and sequential manner. It takes responsibility for such things as speech, writing, details, facts and organization.

The right hemisphere. This part of the brain works in a disorganized, random but more holistic way. It relies on intuition, and deals with feelings, emotions, visualization and aspects of creativity. Although each part of the brain has its own particular responsibilities, all the parts communicate and interact with each other. If we delve at a more microscopic level into how the brain works, it becomes even more fascinating.

There could be 100 billion neurons in your brain. These cells pass messages back and forth throughout the brain to the central nervous system. They're able to do this via electrical and chemical reactions. Under the microscope a neuron could be mistaken for a minute creature from the deep. It consists of a central body with feathery tentacles known as dendrites. The dendrites have attachments called synapses, where the exchange of chemical signals takes place. Once stimulated by a chemical signal, a dendrite sends an electrical impulse to the cell body. This triggers a larger electrical pulse onto the axon, which acts like a lightning conductor. It channels the signal at great speed through its length, and out to other cells in the brain. An outer coating of the fatty protein myelin helps enhance the speed at which the message travels. The final stage of the process occurs at the synapse, the junction between one neuron and another.

Neurons store information and act together to cause actions and reactions. They work in assemblies, each with specific tasks. Some deal with the outside world through the senses and movement, while others are responsible for internal communication between the areas of the brain to ensure we can think, imagine, create and be aware. These assemblies communicate with each other, simultaneously sending and receiving messages over great distances and at phenomenal speed, while also being aware of the needs of the whole body.

Each neuron can have thousands of connections to others. Add to that the fact that each cell can react or fire up around 500 times a second, and it's clear that the human brain is breathtaking, and its capabilities awesome.

Where memory fits in

Memory is complicated, to say the least. Most scientists now accept that memory is a set of systems operating in different parts of the brain. There are also different types of memory.

Procedural memory. This is the unconscious ability to do such things as run, drive a car, ride a bicycle, play a piano or juggle.

Semantic memory. This is where our knowledge of the world is stored. For example, it's your semantic memory that knows that kangaroos come from Australia and that Sydney has an amazingly designed opera house.

Episodic memory. This is the memory that records and stores past events, but is not always reliable. For example, your semantic memory might record facts about Australia, but you might not be able to remember all the details of a holiday you spent there.

Prospective memory. This is the system that lists the things you have to do in the future. It's one of the most unreliable of our memory systems.

So human memory is phenomenally complex – and yet the techniques for using it better and getting more out of it every day are remarkably simple.

Storytelling

Let's return to the list of words at the start of this chapter:

> chocolates, potatoes, soap, milk, paper towels, coconut, bananas, cheese, wine, bread

Here's an example of how an imaginary story could be created to turn each item into a memorable picture, and then to link each one to the next.

Imagine...

...opening a box of expensive chocolates, only to discover to your horror that each one has been replaced with a potato! You investigate further by starting to peel one of the potatoes, and you discover when you bite into it that it's made out of soap. You need to get the taste out of your mouth, so you take a long drink of milk, but unfortunately the carton has a leak, and the milk pours all over you, and out across the floor. More and more milk is pouring out, and you try to mop it up with some paper towels, but it's no good. The level is rising fast. Sitting on top of the towel rail is a coconut. As you watch, it grows and grows, until it's big enough for you to sit on and float on top of the milk. A banana floats by, and you fix it on to your coconut boat as a mast – then use a large triangular piece of cheese as a sail. You find a bottle of red wine on board, and use that to paint a colourful design on your sail. Unfortunately, though, you've been a bit rough and a number of holes have been torn in the sail – which you try to patch up with pieces of bread.

Read the story through again, trying to picture it all vividly. After that, see how many of the ten shopping list items you can remember. Simply go back through the story in your mind, link by link, and write down each item as it appears.

It began with a box of *chocolates*. Inside that were *potatoes*, which turned out to be made of *soap*. You tried to get rid of the terrible taste with *milk*, but the carton leaked and you used *paper towels* to mop it up – in vain. As the milk levels rose, you used the huge *coconut* as a boat, and fitted it with a *banana* mast and a *cheese* sail. You painted the sail with *wine*, tearing it in the process – and the story ended with you repairing the holes with pieces of *bread*.

It might help to imagine filming the strange events. Your mind's eye becomes a camera, able to zoom in on key details, move with the action, and explore everything that's going on. When you replay the mental film, you'll be able to recreate all the details of the story.

Put the technique into practice. Lay aside any other strategies or habits you might have picked up. Most important of all, be positive. Don't be tempted to think that the following list is too long to learn. You're only dealing with one item at a time, so it could be *any* length, and you'd still be able to remember it.

Bear in mind all the key points. As you go along, each item needs to be visualized, made unusual and memorable, and then connected vividly to the next. Abandon all normal logic, but make sure there's a strong reason for you to remember the next item on the list – and the stranger, more exciting, frightening, embarrassing, violent or funny the link is, the better. Exaggerate, and let your imagination run riot.

Here's the list: 20 everyday words. Take as much time as you need to transform the list into a memorable story, then play it back in your mind's eye and see how many of the words you can write down, in order. There's no reason why you can't even do the same thing in reverse. Simply follow the chain of events back to the start.

> television, clown, rabbit, fire, tea, pocket, scissors, snake, bin, castle, slide, bush, money, newspaper, ant, sandwich, ring, basin, coal, cat

Summary

Return to the adverts you explored at the start of this chapter. Do you have some clearer insights now into why they stuck in your brain – maybe for decades? It wasn't chance: they were designed to be memorable, just as you can design all the real information you want to learn and fix it in your mind.

Think about some of these key themes.

Imagery. How do you think the images were chosen, and why did they have such impact?

Structure. Were different bits of the advert held together by a story, song, or some other means?

Senses. Which of your senses were activated, and how?

Emotions. What reactions were the advertisers hoping for? Humour, surprise, nostalgia, desire...?

And when you've considered what the advertising agency did, think about what you did to make the memories last: visualize the images, put yourself in the picture, tell someone about the joke, whistle the jingle...

Many of these key aspects of memory will be central to the strategies and systems you learn in this Part as your brain training gathers pace.

Fact-check (answers at the back)

Try these questions to test your ability to learn a list of words: in this case, 15 office items. Give yourself five minutes to commit the words to memory, in order, using the techniques you've explored in this chapter; then cover them up and see how many of them you can recall. Answer all the questions before checking your success.

> photocopier, chair, coffee machine, bin, pen, telephone, computer, stapler, filing cabinet, shredder, paper-clip, calculator, desk, ruler, calendar

1. What is the third word on the list?
a) computer ❑
b) ruler ❑
c) coffee machine ❑
d) chair ❑

2. What comes between *computer* and *filing cabinet*?
a) stapler ❑
b) coffee machine ❑
c) calendar ❑
d) telephone ❑

3. Which word is after *paper-clip*?
a) shredder ❑
b) pen ❑
c) chair ❑
d) calculator ❑

4. What comes before *pen*?
a) stapler ❑
b) bin ❑

c) desk ❑
d) filing-cabinet ❑

5. Can you recall the tenth word?
a) shredder ❑
b) paper-clip ❑
c) stapler ❑
d) calendar ❑

6. Which word comes before *telephone*?
a) bin ❑
b) pen ❑
c) coffee machine ❑
d) computer ❑

7. What is between *desk* and *calendar*?
a) shredder ❑
b) chair ❑
c) stapler ❑
d) ruler ❑

8. What is the second item on the list?
a) coffee machine ❑
b) pen ❑
c) desk ❑
d) chair ❑

9. Which of these words is somewhere on the list?
a) printer ❑
b) photocopier ❑
c) scanner ❑
d) lamp ❑

10. What was the 11th word you saw?
a) paper-clip ❑
b) shredder ❑
c) calculator ❑
d) ruler ❑

CHAPTER 24

Think like a genius

It's very easy to get trapped into narrow ways of thinking, limiting the way you use your brain and preventing you from realizing your full potential. If memory feels hard and learning seems boring, if each mental challenge is just another struggle to overcome, if success means simply avoiding catastrophe... then something has gone badly wrong, and needs to change. You have to take a very different approach, but it's worth it. The benefits are fantastic.

Great learners enjoy what they do. They take an active approach, tackling each challenge in an energetic and entertaining way. Whatever the information they want to learn, they take control and mould it into a form that suits the way their memory works. And they're liberated in their thinking, bringing all their mental skills to bear. They're strategic and organized, so they save time and achieve real results; but they're also imaginative, they have fun with their learning, and they get much more out of the process than just remembering something. Their powerful approach to memory lets them engage with it more fully, understand it more deeply, and do really clever things with it as a result.

Global thinkers

Many of history's most famous thinkers and achievers have a key trait in common – the ability to use all of their brain.

Thumbing through a book that explores the sketches of the artist Leonardo da Vinci, one is struck by his breadth of subject matter and inventiveness. He was not only a highly gifted artist, he was also an engineer and military expert, possessing a degree of curiosity and ingenuity that made him outstanding. Lewis Carroll made his living teaching mathematics at Oxford University, but he also tapped into the power of his imagination when he wrote *Alice's Adventures in Wonderland* and *Through the Looking Glass*. Albert Einstein – still one of the figureheads in the world of science – also explored the world of philosophy. He once said, 'Imagination is more important than knowledge. It is a preview of life's coming attractions.'

What these exceptional men had in common was an approach to thinking that is described as *global*. As outlined in the previous chapter, as well as the brain being divided into three parts, reptile, mammalian and cortex, it's also divided into two sides, left and right. The left side is responsible for logical, rational, linear and sequential thought, while the right side looks after the more intuitive, holistic, random side of our thinking.

Da Vinci, Carroll and Einstein did not just tap into one side of their brain, they capitalized on both. Although specialists in their fields, they widened the scope of their expertise, whether it was to paint sublime pictures and design flying machines, or work on the intricacies of mathematics while writing about a young girl walking through a mirror into another reality.

Although we all do tap into both sides of our brains, we tend to prefer to use one side or the other. We shy away from pushing out of our comfort zones to explore and practise ways of thinking we consider difficult. We're leaving so much brain power untapped.

A global approach means that the brain is being utilized fully. Learning becomes easier, more can be achieved, thresholds and limitations challenged. The saying, 'None of us is as good as all of us', could well be applied to how we approach using our brain's capabilities. What we need to do is to develop our right-brained modes of creative, intuitive thinking, as well as the left-brained skills of verbal and written communication, organizational and rational abilities – and, crucially, start putting the two sides to work *together*.

Global learning is further enhanced by using the senses and by immersing oneself in a subject. By diving in and becoming engrossed and asking the who? what? why? when? how? questions, understanding is enhanced and learning becomes even more effective.

The advantage of adopting this global approach is that it also produces positive emotions via increased brain power, and encourages us to be even more adventurous in our thinking.

More memory practice

Don't worry that you'll get confused between the different mental pictures you create and the stories you invent. Your memory is unbelievably powerful, and it's able to keep all the different batches of information separate.

Put this principle to the test by learning another list of words, and then checking that you can still remember the 20 words you learned at the end of the last chapter. Here's the new list of words:

> grass, elephant, computer, matchbox, mirror, football, rocket, biscuit, caravan, fence, spade, cow, tent, cloud, lamp, shorts, basket, train, sun, glass

Remember the key characteristics of memorable information. These words need to be visualized in as much colour and detail as possible, exaggerated and given sense and emotion triggers, then linked together into an unusual, connected story. Give yourself a maximum of ten minutes to commit this list to memory – to *make it memorable*. As soon as you've completed your story and checked that you can remember all 20 words, return to the first list, and read out *those* 20 words – beginning with *television*.

You now have 40 items committed to memory, in two distinct mental 'files'. As long as each story is built on strong links, they won't overlap or become confused. In each case, the first word is all you should need to start off the chain of images – and you'll find that you can recall the list backwards as well as forwards.

> Memory techniques like these may seem disordered and fanciful, but in fact they create a real sense of organization and precision.

Picture clues

So far you've worked with lists of objects, each of which provided a definite image. You know that you can memorize lists of shopping or presents, or all the items to be taken on holiday – but what about information that's harder to visualize? What happens when you need to remember words that suggest no obvious pictures?

The trick is to use *picture clues*. You think up a picture to remind you of your original information. It may well be very different from the actual word you're trying to learn, but it'll be enough to jog your memory. Picture clues can be based on how a word sounds, what it looks like, or on an image that it suggests. You can use any picture that works for you.

As an example, imagine you had to learn the following list:

> *First ten U.S. presidents since World War Two*
> Truman, Eisenhower, Kennedy, Johnson, Nixon, Ford, Carter, Reagan, Bush, Clinton

Here are some suggestions for picture clues but the best ones are always those that you think up yourself.

- *Truman*: perhaps a cricketer, like Freddie Truman, or someone taking a lie-detector test to prove that they're a 'true man'.

- *Eisenhower*: maybe you simply think of 'ice' – or it could be an 'ice shower'.
- *Kennedy*: you could picture Barbie's boyfriend Ken, or maybe a rocket being launched from the Kennedy Space Centre.
- *Johnson*: the image here could be of Johnson's baby powder, or the actor Don Johnson.
- *Nixon*: perhaps a Nikon camera, or a thief 'nicking' something.
- *Ford*: a river-crossing or a Ford car.
- *Carter*: a man pulling a cart.
- *Reagan*: a ray gun.
- *Bush*: a bush.
- *Clinton*: Clint Eastwood perhaps.

Spend a few moments coming up with an image clue that works for you, for each of the ten presidents' names. Once you have your images, learning them is as easy as learning the items on a shopping list. Simply take each one in turn, connect it with the next, and build up a memorable story.

You might imagine...

...Freddie *Truman*, still wearing his cricket gear, climbing into an ice-cold shower – *Eisenhower* – only to find Barbie's plastic boyfriend Ken – *Kennedy* – in there already. Ken is covering himself with Johnson's baby powder – *Johnson* – before he poses for photographs taken using a top-of-the-range Nikon camera – *Nixon*. The photographer races off to get the pictures printed in his *Ford* car, but he's driving so fast that he crashes into a *Carter*. Enraged, the carter pulls out a ray gun – *Reagan* – and the poor photographer tries to hide in a nearby *Bush* but Clint Eastwood – *Clinton* – is already using it to hide from the Indians.

Whatever kind of story you create, run though it a few times in your mind, checking that you can remember all ten picture clues and that each one links clearly to the next.

When you're confident with your imaginary tale, use it to write down the names of the ten presidents from memory.

Check that you can still remember the two lists of 20 words – one began with *television*, the other with the word *grass* – and the ten-item shopping list. All the pieces of information should be there in their individual files: already that's 60 pieces of data memorized with ease.

Image illustrations

With practice, you'll get used to thinking of a picture to represent any kind of information. Often you don't need to worry about every last bit of the original material – just think of a picture that's going to jog your memory. After all, without these techniques you'd probably remember the information eventually. It's in there *somewhere* – you just need a prompt to retrieve it when you really need it.

Say you wanted to learn the following list of jobs to do in a day at work:

- Set a date for the office party
- Order new calendars
- Buy a present for Paul
- Arrange a game of squash
- Pay cheques in to the bank
- Book your holiday.

You might come up with the following image 'illustrations' for each job:

- The party itself, full of sounds, tastes and feelings
- A large, colourful calendar
- Paul, holding his present
- A squash racket
- Large cheques
- A sun-baked beach.

You could then connect the images into a story like this:

The office party is in full swing, and the noise is so great that all the calendars fall off the walls. One hits Paul as he's opening his present and he collapses, unconscious. You prod him with your squash racket to check he's OK, then write him a cheque for compensation, which he uses to pay for a holiday in the Caribbean.

If you ran through that chain of images a few times on your journey to work, you'd have a powerful memory story to help you organize your day. You could consult this mental checklist wherever you were, and make sure that all the key tasks were completed by the end of the day.

Numbers

So far we've concentrated on remembering words and phrases, but it's also possible to use the same basic techniques to memorize numbers.

These days, most of us don't need to remember large amounts of numerical information. What we need to get to grips with are PIN codes, burglar-alarm settings, addresses, extension numbers, birthdays, times – all mostly made up of just a few digits. Having a strategy for learning these small groups of numbers saves a great deal of time and trouble.

As with the lists you've learned so far, the trick is to think in pictures. You need to invest a little time deciding on a picture to represent each of the ten digits, 0–9, so that you always have an image clue to use.

On a blank piece of paper, jot down the ten digits, with enough space alongside each one to write a brief description – or make a quick sketch – of the image you give it.

You could base your images on what a digit looks like. In that case, you might draw a ball next to 0, or write 'sun' or 'orange'. Next to the number 1 you could write 'pen' or 'pencil', or draw a needle or pin. You just need to think of one key image for each digit.

You might base some of your images on what a digit sounds like, choosing something that rhymes with it: 2 could be 'shoe', 3 might become 'bee', 4 'door' and so on.

Another possibility would be to make use of the significance a digit might already have. If you were born on the sixth day of the month, for example, you might illustrate 6 as a birthday present, or write 'birthday cake' on your piece of paper; 7 could become one of the Magnificent Seven; 8 an After Eight mint.

When you've come up with an image for each of the digits, check that no two are so alike that you'll get confused. You can also fine-tune your system as you use it, so don't be afraid to develop and improve your set of ten images.

Using this number system is simple. To learn a group of numbers, you just transform each digit into the image you've assigned it, then connect the images together into a scene or story. The one crucial extra step is to make the scene appropriate to your reason for learning the numbers in the first place.

For example, if the code to disarm your burglar alarm was 3264, then your number system might give you these four images:

BEE SHOE BIRTHDAY PRESENT DOOR

You could imagine a huge honey-bee landing on your shoe. You try to flap it away with a birthday present you're holding, but the bee flies off and out of the house through the open front door.

Bee on *shoe*, threatened with *birthday present*, flying through *door* – this simple scene gives you the four important numbers: 3264.

The final step would be to connect this scene with your reason for learning the four numbers. You might imagine sounding the alarm as the bee escapes – to remind you that these images give you the code for the alarm.

Perhaps you want to remember that the PIN code on your bank card is 7205.

For 7 you might have an image of *heaven* (rhyme); 2 might be represented by a *swan* (shape); 0 could be a *football* (shape); 5 might turn into a *hook* (shape).

You might picture yourself standing in heaven, when you see a majestic swan. You climb onto its back, and enjoy flying – until you realize that people on the ground below are pelting you with footballs. To get your own back, you burst every one you can catch, using a large metal hook.

To connect this strange tale with the original numbers, you might imagine seeing an animated version of it on the screen of a familiar cash machine. Every time you use a machine for real, you'll remember the cartoon – and see yourself in *heaven*, climbing onto the *swan*, being pelted with *footballs* and bursting lots of them on a *hook*: your bank card PIN must be 7205.

Practise using your own number system by memorizing the following historical dates.

Step 1: *Turn each digit into the appropriate image.*
Step 2: *Connect the images into a short story.*
Step 3: *Connect the story with your reason for remembering.*

Dates:

Gunpowder Plot: 1605

Death of Ovid: 17

Battle of Waterloo: 1815

Henry VIII born: 1491

Ruin of Pompeii: 79

Below are five UK dialling codes. See how quickly you can use your system to commit them to memory – and remember you don't need to worry about the first two digits each time, because all STD codes begin with 01.

Dialling codes:

Newcastle: 0191

Liverpool: 0151

Oxford: 01865

Peterborough: 01753

Birmingham: 0121

Any kind of information can be given a picture clue, and those pictures can be linked into memorable stories. The information is simply being made compatible with the way human memory works.

Summary

To round off this chapter, think about the implications of the skills you've learned. You've seen how to get your brain in gear and start learning lists of words; and what you can do to make numbers easier to recall. So how is that going to benefit you in real terms? What does this sort of memory training mean for your life, in work and out?

If you can learn lists, you can start organizing the practical tasks you want to achieve and take more control of your time and effort. You can remember directions, processes, targets, skills; the key points in documents or presentations; notes for meetings; priorities in negotiations. You can also make long-term plans, including less tangible ideals: skills you'd like to learn, experiences you want to have, aspects of your character you're working on, dreams you want to turn into realities.

With strategies for learning numbers you can fix vital details into your memory: times, dates, serial numbers, security codes, document references, financial projections... You can cope better with the facts and figures you need to know, but you can also choose new, ambitious ways to use and show off your memory skills.

Fact-check (answers at the back)

Use the first five questions to practise remembering names.

You have three minutes to learn the following people. Don't worry about the order of names. You'll need to be able to match first names to surnames, so use the techniques you've been practising to commit them all to memory.

> Walter Black, Chrissie Webster, Eileen O'Reilly, Scott Gardener, Mike Rembrandt, Charlie Wu, Karen Baker, Len Windsor, Tina Strong, Ronnie Martinez

Now, from memory, fill in the missing names.

1. Eileen _____
   a) Black ❑
   b) Wu ❑
   c) Windsor ❑
   d) O'Reilly ❑

2. _____ Gardener
   a) Scott ❑
   b) Charlie ❑
   c) Mike ❑
   d) Ronnie ❑

3. _____ Rembrandt
   a) Mike ❑
   b) Scott ❑
   c) Chrissie ❑
   d) Ronnie ❑

4. Karen _____
   a) O'Reilly ❑
   b) Wu ❑
   c) Baker ❑
   d) Windsor ❑

5. _____ Strong
   a) Len ❑

   b) Walter ❑
   c) Tina ❑
   d) Scott ❑

Now test yourself on a sequence of numbers.

Give yourself three minutes to learn the following serial code, using the method you learned in this chapter.

948371092758

Cover the numbers and answer these five questions:

6. What is the third number?
   a) 5 ❑
   b) 6 ❑
   c) 7 ❑
   d) 8 ❑

7. What comes before 0?
   a) 1 ❑
   b) 2 ❑
   c) 3 ❑
   d) 4 ❑

8. Which number comes after 3?
   a) 6 ❑
   b) 7 ❑
   c) 8 ❑
   d) 9 ❑

9. What is between 0 and 2?
   a) 6 ❑
   b) 7 ❑
   c) 8 ❑
   d) 9 ❑

10. Which of these numbers does not appear in the code?
   a) 5 ❑
   b) 6 ❑
   c) 7 ❑
   d) 8 ❑

CHAPTER 25

How to remember anything

You're approaching the halfway point in this memory techniques masterclass, so pause to consider any changes you've noticed already. Have you found any opportunities to use the memory techniques for real? By putting them to work you'll embed them in your learning and improve your thinking habits. The more they pay off, the more you'll want to hone your skills further.

Keep an eye out also for any of your existing strategies that work. Notice when you tie a knot in a handkerchief, go to a particular place to help you remember, run through the alphabet until one letter kick-starts your brain... Now you can also think about why these behaviours work, and what they tell you about your memory. If they work, keep doing them; otherwise, replace them with the tactics you learn in this masterclass.

And celebrate your successes. It's easy to underestimate the skill involved in scoring full marks on one of the memory tests, or the achievement of remembering things you've struggled with for years. Pat yourself on the back every time you prove you can use your memory well. Enjoy the learning challenges you're given – especially the things you now choose to do with your developing memory skills.

Recapping your learning

One of the best things about the sort of learning described in this Part is that it cuts out wasted repetition. Once you've created pictures and stories to remind you of a set of information, you never have to start again from scratch.

You can quickly recap the material even if you haven't used it for months, simply by reminding yourself of the key images – and every time you do so you're strengthening the memories, rather than just learning the same material again.

Spend a few minutes now recapping some of the information you've learned so far in this Part, the images and stories that allow you to recall:

● the ten-item shopping list, beginning with *chocolates*
● the list of 20 words beginning with *television*
● the list of 20 words beginning with *grass*
● the first ten U.S. presidents since World War Two
● the dates of:
  – the Gunpowder Plot
  – the death of Ovid
  – the Battle of Waterloo
  – the ruin of Pompeii
  – the birth of Henry VIII

● the dialling code for:
  – Newcastle
  – Liverpool
  – Oxford
  – Peterborough
  – Birmingham.

You're able to remember any kind of information by making it memorable, and so far you've learned more than 70 distinct pieces of information.

Practice makes perfect – so try memorizing the first ten numbers in Japanese. Don't be tempted to think that this is too difficult. The technique is one you're well used to by now. You simply invent an image-reminder for the way each number sounds, then link all ten together.

1	ichi	6	roku
2	nee	7	nana
3	san	8	hachi
4	she	9	q
5	go	10	ju

Image ideas:

1 and 2 – itchy knee
3 – sand
4 – sheep
5 – 'go' sign
6 – rock
7 – bananas
8 – a sneeze (it sounds like 'hatchoo!')
9 – a queue
10 – juice

Perhaps you imagine yourself...

...rubbing your itchy knee in the sand, when a flock of sheep rushes at you, knocking you flying across the beach. You try to get rid of the sheep by holding up a large sign saying 'Go', but it's no good: they're all settling down for the day on rocks by the shore, and opening up their picnic boxes – which are all full of bananas. Unfortunately, sheep must be allergic to bananas because they all start sneezing – 'hachi!' – and form a long queue at a stall selling juice, which they hope will wash away the offending taste.

> itchy... knee... san(d)... shee(p)... go... rock(u)... (ba)nana... hachi... q(ueue)... ju(ice)

Ten images, each jogging your memory about a Japanese number.

The best images and stories are always the ones that you think up yourself, so spend a few minutes putting your imagination to work on this list. Check it through a few times, reinforce or change difficult or confusing parts – then test yourself by covering up the list and reading all the numbers back from memory. If you were to recap your story a few times every day, within a week you'd know this list by heart.

The best-kept secret

Stories are powerful tools for giving otherwise abstract and unconnected pieces of information a memorable structure. But there is another strategy – one that has been called 'the best-kept secret' about your memory. It makes learning faster and easier, it works in the way your brain likes to work, and it has been used with incredible success for centuries.

Ancient Greek legend has it that super-rich Scopas threw a huge banquet, during which disaster struck. His banqueting hall collapsed on his hundreds of guests – among them Simonides, the poet, one of a handful of survivors. Identifying the bodies would have been impossible had it not been for Simonides' trained memory. By closing his eyes and mentally rebuilding the banqueting hall, he was able to connect every guest with their location in the room, and provide a perfect guest list and seating plan from memory.

This tale comes from a time when memory systems were taught and celebrated. How else could one teach, speak, argue cases of law or compose epic poetry without a practised ability to do it from memory? By Roman times, using mnemonic strategies came as second nature to great orators such as Cicero, who is known to have addressed the senate for days on end from memory. Before they were taught what to remember, students were taught how to remember it – and the central element of every memory system was what has come to be known as the 'Roman Room' concept, or the 'Memory Palace'. Simonides used the framework of a banqueting hall to contain the information he needed to remember the guests, and you too can use the frameworks – buildings, golf courses, towns, walks – of your everyday life to store vast amounts of information in an incredibly usable way.

It's a natural tendency of the human brain to think spatially, and to connect abstract information with concrete places. Have you ever got to the top of the stairs and forgotten what you were coming up for? If you return to the spot where you were standing when you had the urge to go up, your memory may well kick back into action. Detectives often take eye witnesses back to the scene of a crime to help them remember exactly what they saw. If you listen to music as you drive around, it's likely you can recall where you were the last time a particular song or piece of music came on. The Roman Room technique capitalizes on this strong link between memory and location. It makes use of the fact that you already know from memory many hundreds of mental frameworks into which information can be slotted and stored.

The route system

Step 1. Pick a building you know well. This technique also works well when you use walks, car journeys – even golf courses – but it's easiest to start with a simple building: your home, where you work or perhaps a hotel you visit regularly.

Step 2. Divide this building into ten separate areas. It often helps to sketch a quick plan on a piece of paper. The areas could be rooms, particular features or whole floors – just however you think the building can best be divided into ten zones.

Step 3. Decide on a route, from Area 1 to Area 10. It's important that you're sure of the route, because you'll always take the same mental walk around this building. What would be the most logical way of getting from the first area to the last?

Step 4. Close your eyes and imagine moving along the route. Start by picturing yourself standing in Area 1. What can you see? What does this place smell like and sound like, and what details set it apart?

From there, visualize yourself moving to Area 2. Again, bring this zone to life in your mind's eye. Keep doing this, going from place to place and spending a few moments in each one, until you arrive at the end of your route.

Step 5. As a final check, see if you can imagine making the journey in reverse. This shouldn't be a problem: in real life you have no difficulty remembering the way out of your house or back home from work. It's just a good way of making sure that you're fully confident with this memory route.

When you've completed these five steps, you're ready to put your route to use. It's been time well spent: you'll be able to use this mental structure many times, to help you remember many different types of information.

To use a route, you simply locate a different piece of imagery in each of the ten areas. These are exactly the same sort of image clues used to remember words, names, ideas or numbers. The route system just removes the need for a story to link them together; instead, the connecting structure is already decided upon. All you have to do is slot in the images.

Use your imagination to fix each image in place as powerfully as possible. As you make the mental journey around this building, think of unusual, funny, violent, memorable ways of placing an image into each room.

As an example, here's a sample route around a typical house:

1 front porch
2 hallway
3 living-room
4 dining-room
5 kitchen
6 laundry
7 staircase
8 bathroom
9 bedroom
10 study

If you were using this route to memorize a shopping list – apples, coffee, cakes, butter, sugar, oranges, mineral water, salt, treacle, cereal – you could imagine...

...stepping into the front porch, and finding a huge *apple* filling the room. You have to squeeze past it to get into the hallway, which is flooded with hot *coffee*. Imagine the smell, and the feeling of the hot liquid as you paddle out into the living-room. Here, all the furniture is made out of *cake*: a cake sofa, cake dresser – even a cake TV. You walk into the dining-room, where a meal has been set out on the table – but the only thing on every single plate is a block of *butter* – hardly a balanced meal! In the kitchen, every cupboard, tin and pan is full of *sugar*. Imagine opening up a high cupboard, and being showered with an avalanche of sugar.

The next area on this route is the laundry. Here, *orange*-trees are growing amongst the clean clothes – and the whole room is painted bright orange. The staircase has been turned into a cascading waterfall – but a very expensive one, using gallons of *mineral water*. There are three rooms upstairs. In the bathroom, the bath is full to the brim with *salt*. Imagine what it would feel like to take a bath here – and how it would taste if you accidentally got a mouthful! Lying down in the bedroom is just as uncomfortable, because someone has spilled sticky *treacle* all over the bedclothes. Your journey ends in the study, where the books on the huge bookcase have been removed – and replaced with packets of *cereal*. There's cereal all over the carpet, and the desk – it's even got into the expensive computer.

In practice, filling up a route like this is extremely fast. Once you've done it a few times, you'll be able to imagine moving from room to room with ease, and take just a few seconds to visualize fixing each image in place. Try it, and you'll find that retrieving the images is almost unbelievably easy.

In the example route, you'd instantly remember:

- the apple blocking the porch
- the coffee flooding the hallway
- the cake furniture decorating the living-room
- the butter served up in the dining-room
- the sugar filling the kitchen
- the oranges growing in the laundry
- the mineral water cascading down the staircase
- the salt filling the bath
- the treacle spilled in the bedroom
- the cereal all around the study.

Design a route of your own. Follow Steps 1 to 5, then put your framework to use straight away to learn the following list of items to pack for an imaginary holiday.

> sunglasses, suncream, swimming costume, passport, travellers' cheques, camera, sandals, maps, tennis racket, toothbrush

It's useful to have several routes organized in your mind, so that you can use them in rotation. Once used, you'll find that the images have disappeared from each route by the time you come to use it again. On the other hand, you can fill a route with information of lasting value to you, recap it every so often, and retain it as a permanent resource.

Take time now to design a second route. Make it memorable, different from the first, but follow the same five steps. When you're confident of this second mental structure, practise using it by committing the following information to memory:

> *Bodies of the solar system, in order from the Sun:*
>
> 1 Sun
> 2 Mercury
> 3 Venus
> 4 Earth
> 5 Mars
> 6 Jupiter
> 7 Saturn
> 8 Uranus
> 9 Neptune
> 10 Pluto (now 'downgraded' to a dwarf planet, but still worth knowing about!)

As with the lists of U.S. presidents and Japanese numbers, you first need to come up with an image clue for each of these heavenly bodies. Here are some suggestions, but feel free to think up your own:

1 Sun – your son, or the *Sun* newspaper
2 Mercury – a thermometer
3 Venus – goddess of love
4 Earth – a pile of muddy earth
5 Mars – a Mars bar
6 Jupiter – perhaps a duplicator, or a 'dew pit'
7 Saturn – Satan
8 Uranus – uranium
9 Neptune – sea god
10 Pluto – Mickey Mouse's dog

Once you've got your ten image clues, you simply fix them into place around your route. Always be on the lookout for appropriate ways of slotting them into place, and try to make use of things already present in your mental structure – items of furniture, for example, as 'hooks' to hang them on.

If your second route was based on your workplace, for example, you might imagine pages from the *Sun* newspaper pasted across the window of your office; a thermometer fixed to the control panel in the lift; a pile of earth in the middle of the boardroom table, etc.

Give yourself enough time to fix each of the ten images in place, then see how quickly you can write them all down, in order, from memory. If you have trouble recalling any of them, simply leave a space and go on to the next area. It may take a little time to recall a few stubborn images, but all the clues are there somewhere.

When you're confident with this new data, spend a few minutes recapping the other information you've learned:

- the ten-item shopping-list, beginning with *chocolates*
- the list of 20 words, beginning with *television*
- the list of 20 words, beginning with *grass*
- the first ten U.S. presidents since World War Two
- the dates of:
  - the Gunpowder Plot
  - the death of Ovid
  - the Battle of Waterloo
  - the ruin of Pompeii
  - the birth of Henry VIII
- the dialling codes for:
  - Newcastle
  - Liverpool
  - Oxford
  - Peterborough
  - Birmingham
- the first ten numbers in Japanese
- the ten items to take on holiday
- the ten items on the shopping list beginning with *apples*.

Along with the solar system list, that's 110 separate pieces of information, neatly arranged in mental files. Every time you recall them like this, you fix them even more firmly in your mind.

One of the most powerful benefits of the route system is that whole sets of information can be fixed into each mental space. This means that you could easily create a single route to hold details of all the projects you were working on, or all the jobs you wanted to get done in a given week, month or year. The route system gives you the power to be highly organized – but, within that framework, to be creative too, adding and removing images whenever necessary.

Memorizing sets of information

Using the 'house' route described earlier, here's an example of how *sets* of information can be included and memorized.

You might decide to make the front porch your 'staff training' room, if that was a key part of your work. You could decorate it with picture clues to remind you of:

- the outdoor activity course you need to book (rope swings and balance beams fitted around the porch)
- the names Judy and Roy, staff members you need to see about their appraisals (Judy might be performing a Punch and Judy show in a cupboard, and Roy could be sitting on the window-sill dressed as Rob Roy)
- the date 1st July, an important deadline (the digits to remember are 1 and 7, and this might give you the images paintbrush and heaven – so you could imagine using the paintbrush to create a dramatic illustration of heaven on the front door).

Whenever you return to the front porch in your mind, you'll find it filled with image clues for all the key details to remember about staff training. You can add new pictures when necessary, and remove those that are no longer required. To do that, either visualize the old images being removed or rubbed out, or simply stop highlighting them in your mind, and let them slip away naturally from your memory.

You might decide to make the bathroom your area for remembering details about the key tasks you need to accomplish before the end of the month. You could imagine:

- finding the bath full of old door signs (since you need to order new ones)
- flushing computer disks down the toilet (to remind you to replace a key software product)

- discovering Ben Hur using the shower to wash his golf clubs (to make sure you remember to organize a game of golf with your colleague Ben)
- seeing Ben Hur use his shoe to kick oranges around the bathroom (giving you the digits 2 (shoe) and 0 (orange), and thus a reminder to arrange the match for the 20th).

The mental routes you create can also help you read, digest and remember texts and documents. As you read, get used to breaking the information down into key points. You're going to be illustrating each point with an image clue – so what *are* the key points? How much detailed information do you need to retain, and what images would jog your memory about each main point?

As you're reading, jot down key words or phrases that would act as a sufficient 'crib sheet'. Reading a memo about a change of premises, for example, you might jot down:

- moving
- 5 December
- Derby
- 3 new jobs
- Paul in charge of project.

When you'd finished, you would give each point an image clue. Perhaps you imagine choosing slides to illustrate this information in a visual presentation. What picture would be appropriate for each idea?

You might choose:

- a removal van
- someone using a hook (5) to pull a nail (1) out of a shoe (2) – 5/12
- a Demolition Derby
- worker bees (3)
- the dome of St Paul's Cathedral.

Fixing the images into one of your memory routes, you might imagine:

- a removal van crashing into the porch
- a cobbler at work in the hallway, using his hook to prise a nail from a shoe

- a Demolition Derby taking place in the living-room
- three worker bees eating at the dining-room table
- the kitchen transformed into St Paul's Cathedral.

As always, the process written down looks more complicated than it is in practice. You could easily slot images into your route as you read through the text, and the habit of thinking in pictures is an easy one to pick up. Soon you'll be condensing all the material you read automatically, and coming up with memorable illustrations with ease.

Reading like this is almost certainly slower than you're used to – but how often have you 'read' a whole page without taking in a single piece of information? *Active* reading is much more focused, so it feels more tiring to begin with, but you do it in shorter bursts – and get out exactly what you put in. Give it a try, and soon you'll be reading not just for the sake of reading, but to understand and learn.

A newspaper article analysed a report about the things people liked least about their working life – and how they would go about making changes if they could. It broke the 'moans' and 'wishes' into two lists of ten key points – just as you could have done if you were presented with the entire research document.

To practise illustrating ideas picked out of larger texts, and fixing the images into a route, try coming up with a picture to represent each of the ten 'wishes' printed below, then arranging them around one of your mental frameworks.

> *Top ten wishes*
>
> 1 to work shorter hours
> 2 to change 'company culture'
> 3 to work flexible hours
> 4 to avoid commuting
> 5 to work from home
> 6 to change job
> 7 to have more staff
> 8 to earn more
> 9 to retire
> 10 to have less stress

Summary

Things you can do to back up your memory skills and establish yourself as an effective, active reader:

Preview a document or book, using the information on the cover, reviews, recommendations, and then skim-read to get a sense of what it's about. It really boosts your memory if things feel even a little familiar when you start to read, and this will also get you asking questions, drawing on prior knowledge and thinking about the best learning strategies to use.

Make notes while you're reading – either on the text itself, or in a notebook or laptop. Record your responses as much as the key ideas. Use colours, draw pictures, write questions – anything that helps you engage with and understand the text, and combine it with what you know. The notes will help you set up long-term memories of the important points, but keep the paper version too, as a handy memory-jogger.

Keep thinking about *why* you're reading something: for pleasure, to confirm your understanding, to learn new stuff... Set yourself a target, decide the level of detail you need and the amount of information to absorb, then choose memory strategies to match. Be sure to recoup your investment from every bit of reading you do.

Fact-check (answers at the back)

These questions will challenge your ability to learn a list – of jobs you need to get done today. It's important to remember them in exactly the right order.

Study this list for three minutes, using the strategies you've learned so far to fix it in your memory.

1 Unlock safe
2 Call Andy French
3 Update website
4 Book meeting room for Tuesday
5 Order lunch
6 Meet Pippa Redwood at 3.45 p.m.
7 File receipts
8 Change printer cartridge
9 Finish writing report
10 Lock office

Make sure you can't see the list as you answer the following ten questions:

1. Who do you need to telephone?
a) Alice Andrews ❏
b) Andy French ❏
c) Frank Anderson ❏
d) Fiona Finch ❏

2. What should you file?
a) Invoices ❏
b) Letters ❏
c) Forms ❏
d) Receipts ❏

3. When do you need the meeting room?
a) Monday ❏
b) Tuesday ❏
c) Wednesday ❏
d) Thursday ❏

4. What should you do after making the phone call?
a) Book meeting room ❏
b) Update website ❏
c) Change printer cartridge ❏
d) Unlock safe ❏

5. What job comes before locking the office?
a) Finish report ❏
b) Change printer cartridge ❏
c) Order lunch ❏
d) Book meeting room ❏

6. Who are you meeting?
a) Pippa Redwood ❏
b) Paula Robinson ❏
c) Pauline Redmond ❏
d) Pat Rimmer ❏

7. What is the fifth job on the list?
a) Update website ❏
b) Finish writing report ❏
c) Lock office ❏
d) Order lunch ❏

8. What comes before the telephone call?
a) Change printer cartridge ❏
b) Update website ❏
c) Unlock safe ❏
d) Order lunch ❏

9. What sort of task comes before ordering lunch?
a) Filing ❏
b) Telephoning ❏
c) Updating ❏
d) Booking ❏

10. What time is your meeting?
a) 3.30 ❏
b) 3.45 ❏
c) 4.15 ❏
d) 4.45 ❏

CHAPTER 26

Learning
to learn

Have you stopped complaining about your bad memory yet? Too many people write off their memory skills, practically boasting about how poor they are. In the process they set themselves up for failure, missing even simple opportunities to help themselves and never exploring the practical strategies that could make all the difference. Of course, these same people are also constantly showing off the miraculous things their memories can do – but they only concentrate on the occasions when their brain lets them down. They make memory difficult and dull; but by now you should have seen the light and adopted a much more positive approach.

Memory training is a lifelong process. As a child you were able to do some of it really well, but you still had a lot to learn. As an adult, there are things that might have become tricky, but you also have many advantages in the level of mental maturity you've achieved. Some techniques in this masterclass will prove their worth straight away, others may well take a while but keep trying, keep experimenting, keep thinking about the best ways to make them work for you. And don't give up if the going gets a bit tough. Nothing worth doing was ever completely straightforward.

Preparing for success

You have a test approaching, your emotions are in a turmoil as you realize you have just so much to remember. Your mind appears blank as you spin into panic. There's an important presentation looming, you feel stressed and anxious, convinced you will forget everything and make a fool of yourself. The radio interview that will give you the opportunity to talk about your company and its work is tomorrow, but how will you remember your name, let alone get your message across? Such responses are typical: we've all had that sinking feeling. Somehow it seems that whatever it was we did know has been lost in the recesses of our brain.

However it doesn't have to be that way. If you begin to put the following advice into practice and do the necessary preparation, you'll be putting yourself in the best possible setting to meet with success. It's good to know that by regularly using these tips and techniques you can enhance your ability to learn, remember with ease, get those answers right, interview with high impact and make a memorable presentation without reading from copious notes.

Step 1: put yourself in the best learning environment for you.
There's little point struggling to learn effectively if where you're working is too noisy, too quiet, too hot or too cold, too untidy or too bare and unwelcoming. Whatever is best for you, try to create it before you start to tackle whatever it is you have to learn and remember. The colour of the room you're in, the music you might be playing, the smells you're inhaling, the pictures on the walls, even how you're sitting, can all have a profound impact on your emotions and therefore your attitude to your work.

Step 2: ensure you're in a positive frame of mind.
Feeling good about yourself and your abilities and anticipating a good outcome to your endeavours is very important. Just as no athlete worth their salt would dream of approaching the starting blocks of a race with a negative mindset, so you should see a successful outcome to your work. Recognize negative self-talk and replace it with something more constructive and positive.

You might find using creative visualization techniques could help you here. This is a method of relaxing and mentally creating a positive outcome to whatever it is you're about to embark on. It's a way of setting yourself up for success, not failure.

Other techniques include using affirmations. This is a method of repeating positive statements about yourself and your abilities. There's also the reframing technique. Here you choose to banish negative self-talk and select the positive way of viewing something.

Remember everything has a positive aspect to it if you really look hard enough. Choose to view your abilities and your approach to learning in a new way.

Step 3: see what's in it for you.

Now that may be easier said than done, especially if you have to deal with information that does not exactly excite you. But whatever you're tackling, you're much more likely to remember it if you can see how it will help you. In this way you become an active, not a passive, learner. Remember, there's a positive gain in everything, if you're prepared to look for it.

Step 4: be prepared to relearn.

We're creatures of habit in the way we think, and so we can limit ourselves by the mental boundaries we've set ourselves as a result of past experiences. Reframing, thinking outside the box, accepting there might be other ways of approaching a subject, and seeing the big picture, all help to encourage a more proactive stance to learning and retaining information.

Remember, too, the importance of the global approach to learning that we covered in the previous chapter.

Step 5: be courageous and don't be defeated by past mistakes or learning problems that seem insurmountable.

It could be the case that the way you were taught in the past didn't suit you, but you can do something about that now by knowing and using a wider range of learning styles. It's all too easy to stay in one's comfort zone rather than going out and trying new ways of learning and trying new ways of learning. Don't limit yourself or subscribe to the 'Better the devil you know' mentality.

Step 6: celebrate your successes.
Realizing how much you already know can really boost your confidence. Be willing to look back at past successes to see how far you've come already. Why not make a list of what you've achieved so far? Keep a notebook that celebrates your achievements; stick up pictures, photographs, certificates, anything that's a reminder of positive learning experiences.

Step 7: keep yourself in tip-top condition by eating and sleeping well and taking regular exercise.
A balanced healthy eating programme not only helps prevent unnecessary wear and tear on your body, it also energizes you and helps you keep mentally fit. Getting enough good-quality sleep should also figure in helping you operate at your optimum level. If you're not sleeping well, consider how you can relax and let go before going to bed.

Do you need to invest in a new mattress? Would using essential oils on your pillow help? or playing relaxing music? or using ear plugs? Also try to ensure you're taking regular exercise, at least twice a week. Sometimes just getting up a little earlier for a brisk walk can help set you up for a more energetic and positive day, and certainly after a day full of pressure, exercise helps to burn off excess stress.

So how can you begin to take action to ensure you incorporate this advice into your everyday life so that you're in the best possible frame of mind to learn and remember? List these questions in a notebook and next to each one jot down what action you need to take to improve things.

1 Are you in the best learning environment? What changes can you make?
2 Do you have a positive mental attitude? What improvements can you make?
3 How can you get the most out of any learning experience? What's in it for you?
4 What mental barriers have you set up? Identify a limitation around learning or memory that you have imposed on yourself. Where has it come from? How can you change it?

5 What is your preferred learning style? How could you improve your abilities in the other modalities? Mentally revisit a mistake or failure. How can you now regard it in a more positive way?
6 List five recent successes in order to appreciate your abilities. List five more you want to achieve.
7 How can you improve your diet? How can you improve your exercise regime? Are you getting good-quality sleep? Are you taking time for relaxation?

Recapping your learning

To conclude this chapter, let's see how well you've remembered the lists from previous chapters.
What are:

● the ten-item shopping-list, beginning with *chocolates*
● the list of 20 words, beginning with *television*
● the list of 20 words, beginning with *grass*
● the first ten U.S. presidents since World War Two
● the dates of:
  – the Gunpowder Plot
  – the death of Ovid
  – the Battle of Waterloo
  – the ruin of Pompeii
  – the birth of Henry VIII
● the dialling codes for:
  – Newcastle
  – Liverpool
  – Oxford
  – Peterborough
  – Birmingham
● the first ten numbers in Japanese
● the ten items to take on holiday
● the ten items on the shopping list, beginning with *apples*
● the top ten 'wishes'?

Summary

Think about the role that other people play in your ongoing memory training. It's not always positive. Are you still being held back by things that people have said about you as a learner, maybe in the dim and distant past? Do you work or live with people who give you negative messages about your memory now? You may need to reprocess some of those ideas, old and new, and find ways to turn down the volume on any negative noises you hear. Maybe there are also issues with the way people give you information, or the conditions in which they expect you to learn. Don't let poor practice by others hold you back.

On the positive side, make the most of people who can help you improve. Which people inspire you to use your brain brilliantly? Who could you work with to strengthen your learning skills? It's also worth thinking about the people you're doing this for, because an improved memory won't just be good for you. Who will you impress, support, inspire? How might your new memory confidence change things for the better at work or in your home? You can be more organized, creative, accurate, efficient... and those benefits can quickly rub off on the people close by.

Fact-check (answers at the back)

Here's a mixed set of questions, requiring you to use techniques you've learned so far.

For the first three, give yourself three minutes to learn this set of words, in order.

> finance, leadership, mentor, portfolio, committee, stock, brochure, charity, holiday, contract

1. What is the fourth word on the list?
   a) stock ❑
   b) brochure ❑
   c) portfolio ❑
   d) finance ❑

2. What comes between *committee* and *brochure*?
   a) stock ❑
   b) finance ❑
   c) mentor ❑
   d) charity ❑

3. Which of these words is not on the list?
   a) contract ❑
   b) holiday ❑
   c) leadership ❑
   d) secretary ❑

To answer the next three questions you'll need to learn another list: this time, countries, and once again in perfect order. Give yourself three minutes.

> United States, France, Spain, Italy, Greece, Turkey, Kenya, Australia, Germany, Sweden

4. Which country is between Kenya and Germany on this list?
   a) France ❑
   b) Australia ❑
   c) Spain ❑
   d) Italy ❑

5. What is the last country on the list?
   a) Germany ❑
   b) Sweden ❑
   c) France ❑
   d) Spain ❑

6. Which of these countries is not on the list?
   a) Portugal ❑
   b) Turkey ❑
   c) Greece ❑
   d) United States ❑

For the final four questions, study this numerical information carefully. You've got four minutes to fix these facts in your brain.

> Boss's birthday: 9/1
> Trip to Denmark: 6/5
> Summer holiday begins: 28/7
> Board meeting: 13/2
> Presentation to staff: 8/8

7. When does your summer holiday begin?
   a) 26/6 ❑
   b) 27/8 ❑
   c) 28/7 ❑
   d) 29/6 ❑

8. What is the date of the board meeting?
a) 6/5 ❑
b) 9/1 ❑
c) 13/9 ❑
d) 13/2 ❑

9. What's happening on 8/8?
a) Training course ❑
b) Presentation to staff ❑
c) Office party ❑
d) Trip to Denmark ❑

10. When is your boss's birthday?
a) 15/6 ❑
b) 3/8 ❑
c) 9/1 ❑
d) 11/12 ❑

CHAPTER 27

People skills

So much of the information we juggle these days, at work and at home, is about people. Computers and phones bring us into closer contact with other people than ever before, we know more about them, want them to know more about us, and we're constantly challenged to process names, numbers, jobs, addresses, birthdays, partners, likes, dislikes... for individuals, and amongst groups of interconnected colleagues and friends.

Personal information is particularly hard to handle because it's often communicated in an extremely unmemorable way. In noisy rooms, in the middle of other activities, out of context, late at night... You need a repertoire of robust memory skills to cope. But if you can, the benefits are great, allowing you to get so much more out of business events, social occasions, and just the daily interplay between all the people in your life, online and face to face.

Remembering names

One of the traditional party-pieces of the stage memory performer is remembering the names of every member of the audience. American magician and mnemonist Harry Lorayne made it his trademark, reciting theatrefuls of names night after night.

Many great military leaders, politicians and businesspeople have demonstrated equally breathtaking abilities to remember names. And yet for most people, remembering even one new name at a time is too much.

Perhaps you know what this feels like: you're at a conference, talking to a colleague, when a recent acquaintance comes over to join them and it's up to you to introduce them to each other – and suddenly you cannot remember either of their names. But imagine the opposite effect. Think how powerful it would be to be able to put names to faces at meetings and parties; how effective to remember key facts about the people you do business with; and how useful to know enough about memory to make everyone you meet remember you.

Step 1 is to listen, to hear people's names when you're introduced to them. Slow the process down: practise asking people to repeat their name if you missed it. Give yourself time to take it in.

Step 2 is to be interested in every new name you hear. Ask where it comes from, what it means, how it's spelled.

Step 3 is to switch on your mind's eye and visualize the name. Spend a couple of seconds imagining what the name would look like written down, or how it might come out as a signature.

Step 4 is to think of picture clues. What images come into your head when you think of the name? You're only looking for image triggers, so you might pick just part of the name to turn into a picture – an object, place or animal. Perhaps you think of a well-known person who shares the name, or a friend or relative of yours. You're making a vital memory move – moving away from abstract names to images that are real, unusual, interesting, colourful and memorable.

As the pictures start to emerge, **Step 5** is to try to make some connection with the real person in front of you. Imagine them holding whatever image has occurred to you, standing in the place that came to mind, or turning into the famous person you thought of. Think of their name as *illustrating* them in some way, and use your imagination to connect them with the image clues their name suggests.

For example, if you meet John Butcher, his name might well suggest meat, knives, chopping boards, roast dinners. As you talk to him, picture him taking out a huge meat cleaver and chopping great hunks of meat. As always you can involve your senses, switching on every facet of your memory, fixing your new friend in your mind with some powerful memory joggers.

With practice you can carry out these five steps quickly, without them getting in the way of conversation, and learn to give yourself enough memory clues to negotiate a meeting or party. Afterwards, it's up to you how many of the new names you choose to remember permanently. You can invest time in rehearsing the most important names and adding extra details so that you remember them long into the future.

Here are some more examples of image clues:

Surnames

- Anderson: perhaps someone hiding in an Anderson air-raid shelter, wearing a gas-mask
- Shelley: covered in sea-shells
- Rowling: constantly performing forward rolls
- Jones: singing in the style of Tom Jones
- Cathcart: pulling a cart piled with cats

First names

- Leo: lion
- Kate: kite
- Mark: covered in dirty marks
- Mike: holding a microphone
- Donna: prima donna ballerina

Leo Shelley could be visualized roaring like a lion *and* covered with shells. Mike Rowling could be trying to talk into his microphone *and* do hundreds of forward rolls. The trick is to build up a set of images, using all the time at your disposal to add extra reminders.

Every new piece of information can also be given an image and added to the mental scene. You might picture Kate Jones flying a kite while singing Tom Jones songs – at the same time as working out on an exercise bike and reading a book – representing the two hobbies she's told you about. If you recalled an image of Donna Anderson dancing around her air-raid shelter – and talking to a man in a fig-leaf – you'd remember that her husband was called Adam.

Remember people's names a few times by using these techniques, and you'll soon find that you know them off by heart. The strange imagery fades away, and you'll have forgotten *why* you know them – you just *do*.

Don't worry about getting names wrong. There are plenty of jokes about people confusing mental images and making embarrassing gaffes, but in reality this rarely happens. Mnemonic techniques just give you extra chances for learning more names – and when you get in the habit of remembering, that feeling of confidence is often enough in itself to make you remember.

Printed below are ten names, along with an extra fact about each one. Learn them all by using one of your mental routes. Think up images to jog your memory about each first name, surname and personal fact, then fix them in the spaces around the route.

Tom Bird: enjoys fishing
Sheila Walker: comes from India
Richard Welsh: works with computers
Arnold Donald: has a wife called Jean
Tracey Cole: keen tennis player
Jane Webster: American
Ronald Smith: enjoys cooking
Tara Singh: accountant
Shaun MacDuff: keen horse-rider
Juan Domingo: married to Maria

To recover the information, simply retrace your steps, moving from room to room in your mind. Each area on the route should contain clues to three key pieces of information: first name, surname and personal detail.

When you're confident with the imagery you've created, see how much of this information you can write down from memory. You may not remember every single person you meet, but these techniques will certainly help you feel more confident about keeping track of the important ones.

Thinking creatively like this is also a good basis for creative conversations. If you get used to thinking in pictures from the first moment you meet someone, then you're in the perfect frame of mind to discuss ideas and possibilities, and to solve problems. You'll also be aware of what it takes for other people to remember *you*. Give them time to hear your name and take it in. When you're talking about yourself, try to speak in pictures and stories, suggesting images and emotional responses for them to latch on to.

It can only benefit you if people remember you, and even simple strategies like these can be more effective than the most expensive business card.

Communicating effectively from memory

Talks, interviews and presentations

What you've already learned about how the brain functions, and how we learn and remember best, can stand you in good stead when it comes to performing in the public arena. You can tailor-make your message to appeal to all of your audience by considering the following nine points.

1 Ensure you paint pictures with the words you use. Remember how the brain likes unusual, dramatic, exciting images. Make use of similes and metaphors.
2 Tap into the three modalities by giving your audience something to see, hear and do.

3 Include such information, and present it in such a way, that it will appeal to both the left and the right sides of the brain. Give your talk a logical structure, but fill it with creative ideas – and try to engage as many of your audience's senses as possible.

4 Put yourself in the shoes of your audience. Carry out some research. How do they think? Help them to make connections with things they already know in order to lead them into new territories, and if possible, personalize the messages you're sending them. Tap into what will move or influence them emotionally.

5 Know that the way you open and close your presentation is important in terms of the powerful images you create. People pay most attention at the beginning and end of an interview or presentation, so it's also crucial to ensure your audience doesn't lose interest in the middle of what you're saying. Pay special attention to how you structure that part. Again make use of images, paint pictures, tell a story, give your listeners something to see, hear and do. Make links and connections with what's already been said and signpost where you're taking them next.

6 Before you begin any presentation or interview, anticipate success by visualizing how it will be. See yourself being well prepared, dynamic and interesting and being well received by your audience. See and feel how receptive and appreciative your audience is. Experience how great you'll feel as you pat yourself on the back! Now practise and rehearse to perfect your performance. Imagining is powerful but certainly not enough on its own.

7 Using the learning and memory techniques you've been introduced to in this Part, you can now create your whole presentation mentally by organizing the key information in one of your chosen routes. Take along memory joggers by all means, but just think how impressive it will be to give your performance without once losing eye contact with your audience or fiddling with pages of notes. We are always impressed with those who show they know their subject so thoroughly that they speak without a script.

8 If you're going to use visual aids, remember to make them colourful and meaningful to give them impact. Use images and few words. Don't forget, 'a picture paints a thousand words'!

9 Remember the importance of positive self-talk. Cultivating a positive mental attitude not only transforms the way you feel about yourself, it also gives a new and powerful dimension to the way you appear to others. Energy and conviction are qualities that make your audience sit up and listen. Don't forget: your best visual aid is you!

So what action can you now take to improve the impact you will have when you next give a talk, interview or presentation?

Checklist

1 How can you improve the language you use?
2 How can you tap into the three modalities?
3 How can you appeal to left- and right-brained thinkers?
4 How can you engage the senses of your listeners?
5 How can you empathize with their points of view, their needs and their emotions?
6 How can you open and close powerfully?
7 How can you keep them interested in the middle?
8 Can you visualize success?
9 Can you select the key points of your presentation, interview or talk and place those points in one of your mental routes or settings?
10 How can you improve your visual aids?
11 Finally, what positive messages can you send yourself about your abilities and skills as a presenter or interviewee?

Summary

You're now in a position to be able to think through every aspect of a talk or presentation. You've got the strategies you need to communicate your message from memory, and you know how to make your audience remember what you say.

Think about memory as soon as you start planning your speech. Turn your key points into a list, choose an image for each idea and then connect the images into a memorable story or place them around a route. Practise using these clues to give your performance from memory. Rehearse it out loud, but also use your powers of visualization to see yourself in action, speaking with confidence and flair.

The real benefits will be clear when you do it for real. You'll be fluent and flexible, able to talk to time, answer questions, make eye contact, and never again worry about losing your notes or having your computer presentation break down. You'll also be presenting an organized argument, talking in pictures, being funny, interesting, believable... and so using your understanding of memory to activate all the other memories in the room.

Fact-check (answers at the back)

Here are ten questions to help you practise your memory for names. Learn the following ten people, in exactly the order they appear here. This is the order in which they're due to speak at tomorrow's conference, and it will be your job to introduce them.

> Simon McDonald, Lou Chesterfield, Will Sharp, Katie Douglas, Angela Mann, Kevin Brown, Phil Downing, Wendy Lee, Gavin Shah, Harry Dale

1. Who's the first person on the list?
a) Kevin Brown ☐
b) Katie Douglas ☐
c) Simon McDonald ☐
d) Lou Chesterfield ☐

2. Who is due to speak immediately before Katie Douglas?
a) Will Sharp ☐
b) Wendy Lee ☐
c) Harry Dale ☐
d) Gavin Shah ☐

3. Who comes after Wendy Lee?
a) Simon McDonald ☐
b) Katie Douglas ☐
c) Will Sharp ☐
d) Gavin Shah ☐

4. Who will speak between Katie Douglas and Kevin Brown?
a) Harry Dale ☐
b) Wendy Lee ☐
c) Angela Mann ☐
d) Simon McDonald ☐

5. What is Mr Downing's first name?
a) Paul ☐
b) Phil ☐
c) Peter ☐
d) Perry ☐

6. Who is eighth on the list?
a) Wendy Lee ☐
b) Katie Douglas ☐
c) Kevin Brown ☐
d) Angela Mann ☐

7. What is the final speaker called?
a) Kevin Brown ☐
b) Angela Mann ☐
c) Harry Dale ☐
d) Simon McDonald ☐

8. What is Lou's second name?
a) Chipperfield ☐
b) Chesterton ☐
c) Chesterfield ☐
d) Champion ☐

9. Who will speak after Angela Mann?
a) Kevin Brown ☐
b) Will Sharp ☐
c) Gavin Shah ☐
d) Wendy Lee ☐

10. How many of the first names on this list begin with the letter K?
a) 1 ☐
b) 2 ☐
c) 3 ☐
d) 4 ☐

CHAPTER 28

Lifelong learning: your personal memory improvement plan

Take a moment to remind yourself of the goals you set yourself earlier. Look back at the answers you gave at the end of Chapter 22. Can you now see the way forward – the way you'll start moving your memory skills in the right direction, changing the way you feel, and achieving what you want in each of the key areas of learning? Maybe you've already seen some real benefits from the work you've been putting in. Now is the time to plan properly for the future, to make sure these gains continue and you get the most out of your growing confidence and strengthening skills.

To start this chapter, spend a moment looking at yourself. Produce a mental picture of yourself now, beginning to use these techniques every day, at work and in your life outside. In your mind's eye, watch yourself gaining real benefits from your memory training and starting to find new ways to make them work. And as you do so, think about how you're going to keep this momentum going and turn the improvements you've already made into a life's work.

Becoming a lifelong learner

The term 'lifelong learning' seems to be on everybody's lips these days. However, it's something that has always been practised by high achievers and those who have become great and inspiring role models over the centuries. Such people have naturally high curiosity and great enthusiasm for knowledge. They automatically keep their minds stimulated, challenged and exercised, as we saw earlier with the likes of da Vinci, Carroll and Einstein.

The very fact that you're reading this masterclass puts you in the category of lifelong learning already. To continue the process, here are some suggestions.

See the advantages

As a result of committing to lifelong learning, you're likely to:

- continue to build and maintain high self-esteem
- stretch your mental muscles
- push out of your comfort zone and explore exciting new realms of knowledge
- develop new skills
- keep fresh, stimulated and motivated
- create and sustain a positive learning energy cycle
- improve your knowledge
- improve your earning potential
- become more creative
- use more of your brain
- feel more excited by life and all it has to offer.

How to do it

How can you ensure that lifelong learning becomes part of your everyday existence?

- Create the space to learn. Make use of travelling or waiting time to gain new knowledge. Get up a little earlier than usual and combine jogging with an MP3 player or an exercise bike with a book!

- Read in the bath and in bed. Turn the television off more often.
- Sign up for some classes, or another professional qualification. There's so much on offer these days. Learning with others can be stimulating and fun.
- Identify the need. What could you learn that will give added benefit to the work you do or the quality of your life?
- Is your learning environment as beneficial as it could be?
- Could you create a space where you know you'll be in the best possible atmosphere to learn? Remember, too, that you will have a preferred time of day for learning, and that the short intense burst approach might be better for you than taking huge chunks of time for studying.
- Try to immerse yourself in your chosen subject or subjects. Be wide and deep in your approach. Be aware of how much you already know – and build on it
- Check out your health. Do you need to make changes in your diet? Are you fit? Do you need a routine medical check? Are you sleeping well?
- Are you using your preferred learning style? Make sure you're absorbing new information in the way that's most beneficial to you. At the same time, try to build your strengths in the other modalities to enhance the global approach.
- Always try to use both sides of your brain to capitalize on global learning. Be logical, but give your imagination all the licence it needs.
- Keep hold of a positive mental attitude and don't pul yourself down when you make mistakes. Be enthusiastic and excited by the rich process of boosting your memory and improving your knowledge and skills.

Tips for retrieving stubborn memories

Work has been done to highlight strategies for improving the recall of eye-witnesses to crimes – and it reveals tips for retrieving stubborn memories. There are four key points:

1 *Recreate the initial conditions*
Witnesses to crimes or accidents are often asked to
try to remember exactly what the weather was like.
How warm did the air feel? Was it windy? They also try
to bring back their own feelings. Were they hungry or
thirsty, sad or happy, excited or bored, on the day the
incident occurred?
This is also useful when you're trying to recall images from
a memory story or route. Try to tap into general memories,
and to recall feelings, and you may well recover the precise
images you're looking for.

2 *Concentrate on details, no matter how unimportant they seem*
We've seen that the brain works on a pattern of
interconnections, and that information needs to be patterned
and connected to suit it. It follows then that any details you
remember can be used as a starting point, to begin a chain
of associations back to the detail you're trying to recall.
If, for example, you return to an area on one of your mental
routes and remember a detail that seems unimportant
to the main image you're looking for, it's still worth
concentrating on it and seeing what it yields. It could
suggest something else; that might link to another
thought – and suddenly the key image appears.

3 *Visualize a remembered scene from another point-of-view*
Witnesses to bank robberies might be asked to imagine
what the robbers must have seen – and you can use the
same principle to boost your recall. Get used to visualizing
a mental route, story or scene from different angles, and
letting your mind's eye search out the detail you're missing.

4 *Replay a memory in reverse*
After road accidents, eye-witnesses are sometimes asked
to replay the events backwards: visualize the crashed
cars... then describe what happened just before the crash...
and what led to *that*...
It's a particularly useful strategy when you're trying to
remember by using a story or route. If it doesn't work
perfectly one way, try recalling it in reverse.

Your personal action plan

No matter how much you read about a subject, or how inspired you become, the only way to make any knowledge work for you in a purposeful way is to actually put it into practice.

You've already discovered that by using some of the exercises in this Part. You've been able to remember nearly 200 things so far. There's nothing like doing something for it to have impact. All too often though, after finishing a course or a book, we put the written material away on a shelf and carry on as before.

That's why preparing a personal action plan is such a good idea. Give yourself written goals and timelines, put your plan somewhere where you'll see it regularly, and you'll be far more likely to take and *sustain* action.

Select from the following as guidelines, adding more if you need to, then lay out the information to suit you. For example, when considering 'Continue lifelong learning', you might have several topics or areas that you want to tackle under the **How?** heading, with a number of timelines under **When?**

What? How? When?	
● Become a more positive thinker	● Adopt a global approach
● Continue lifelong learning	● Move out of comfort zones
● Acknowledge recent successes	● Obtain optimum health
● Find time	● See the advantages
● Knock down mental barriers	● Reward yourself
● Pamper yourself	● Practise and review
● Develop your imagination	● Memorize useful facts
● Memorize useful numbers	● Develop new routes for remembering

Tests

You should now feel confident about your memory, and aware of what you have to do to make it work. The basic principles are simple, and the applications are endless.

Give the information you have to learn:

- imagery
- emotional triggers
- exaggeration
- pattern.

Anything can be made compatible with the way your memory works, and represented as a set of linked pictures: jobs, names, times, dates, facts, presentations, interview answers, memos, reports. In the right form, your brain can hold unlimited amounts of data.

To confirm the progress you've made since starting this Part, take part in this final set of tests. Use any of the techniques you like, individually or in combination. You can make up similar tests yourself in the future to help keep your memory in trim.

Test 1: word list

Memorize the following list of words. Try to do it in less than five minutes, then check your success.

sword, handbag, curtain, custard, rake, bomb, trombone, shark, mountain, dragon, leaf, cafe, biscuit, tablet, boot, comb, gate, ice, oven, camera

Test 2: job list

Learn this list of jobs. Again, give yourself a maximum of five minutes.

1 order new letterheads
2 take laptop to be repaired
3 arrange meeting with Kelly
4 cancel trip to India
5 go to bank
6 submit invoices
7 play squash
8 call Chris (ext. 263)
9 lunch with Andy
10 book holiday, starting 25 August

Test 3: numbers

Use your number system to memorize the following imaginary extension numbers. You have ten minutes.

Scott: 8305

Rita: 1876

James: 2236

Pam: 4907

Daniel: 9301

Test 4: names

Below is a list of ten people you'll be looking after at a conference. You have ten minutes to learn all their names, so that you can write out the entire list from memory.

Jack Braine, Holly Harper, Christian Attley, Ashley Verne, Debbie Green, Frank Shepherd, Ray Oates, Helmut Schreiber, Dougal MacMillan, Hattie Chandler

To finish the tests, see how much of the information you've learned throughout the book is still fresh in your mind.

● ten items on the shopping list beginning with *chocolates*
● 20 words on the list beginning with *television*
● 20 words on the list beginning with *grass*
● the first ten U.S. presidents since World War Two
● the dates of:
  - the Gunpowder Plot
  - the death of Ovid
  - the Battle of Waterloo
  - the ruin of Pompeii
  - the birth of Henry VIII
● the dialling codes for:
  - Newcastle
  - Liverpool
  - Oxford
  - Peterborough
  - Birmingham
● the first ten numbers in Japanese

- the ten items to take on holiday
- the ten items on the shopping-list, beginning with *apples*
- the top ten wishes of workers in the research document.

That's a lot of information – and it's still just a glimpse of your memory's infinite power.

Remember:

1 It's important to understand how you learn best.
   What's your preferred learning style? Are you a left- or right-brained thinker?
   Do what you do well, but try to harness the full range of your learning possibilities.
2 You need to organize your learning.
   Look for the easiest ways to arrange the information you have to learn.
   Organize your approach to learning to make the process smooth, quick and fun.
3 You should tap into your imagination.
   Children have a naturally fertile imagination and so can you.
4 Adopt the best mental attitude.
   Be positive. Break bad thinking habits, motivate yourself, reward and encourage yourself.
5 Find the right learning environment.
   What surroundings will encourage you to be at your most receptive?
6 Match your healthy mind with a healthy body.
   Eat well, exercise regularly and get a good night's sleep.
7 You're never too old to learn.
   Don't be tempted to use age as an excuse for not continuing to learn and remember. You have more brain cells than you need, however old you are.
8 Practise.
   Do it! Start using the techniques you've learned in this masterclass, and they'll soon become second nature.
9 Be a lifelong learner.
   Keep your brain stimulated and use it to go further in everything you do.
10 Your brain is amazing.
   Never underestimate your learning power. Its potential for storage and creativity is immeasurable.

Summary

You've done lots of very specific, strategic learning in this masterclass, and you know how to choose the best techniques for every challenge. But what about some of the knock-on benefits? Will your training have an impact on other, less 'directed' areas of your memory?

In the coming months, notice any improvements in your 'natural' memory: your instinctive recall, your ability to find the right word, the ease with which you connect with moments from the past. See if your short-term memory improves, for ideas, names, conversations. Are you making fewer slip-ups, avoiding confusion, finding that fewer things get caught 'on the tip of your tongue'?

Explore moments from your distant past. Are they any clearer, now you're more aware of using your senses and following connections?

And do you have clearer ideas about your future? When you think about the things you want to achieve, see if you're creating more vivid 'memories' of future successes – because your brain is simply better at forming ideas and exploring them in detail.

Try to recognize everything that changes for the better. As well as tangible improvements at work and beyond, celebrate the less obvious but equally important developments to your memory as a whole.

Keep up the good work and enjoy this new relationship with your amazing brain.

Fact-check (answers at the back)

Use this set of questions to gauge the progress you've made.

1. How much confidence do you have now in the strength of your memory?
   a) None ❑
   b) Some ❑
   c) Quite a lot ❑
   d) A great deal ❑

2. What is the likelihood of you remembering the name of someone you met last month?
   a) Impossible ❑
   b) Unlikely ❑
   c) Likely ❑
   d) Certain ❑

3. How organized are you about all the jobs you need to remember?
   a) Not at all ❑
   b) Fairly ❑
   c) Very ❑
   d) Completely ❑

4. Which of these skills needs the most practice now?
   a) Learning lists ❑
   b) Remembering names ❑
   c) Recalling numbers ❑
   d) Memorizing speeches ❑

5. When you read a document, how much of it can you remember the next day?
   a) None ❑
   b) Some ❑
   c) Most ❑
   d) All ❑

6. Which area of your memory improvement has impressed you the most?
   a) The things I can learn ❑
   b) The techniques that work ❑
   c) The power of my brain ❑
   d) My capacity to keep improving from here ❑

7. How good are you at using imagination to strengthen your memory?
   a) Terrible ❑
   b) Not bad ❑
   c) Good ❑
   d) Brilliant ❑

8. How do you feel now about speaking from memory?
   a) Very nervous ❑
   b) Uncertain ❑
   c) Fairly confident ❑
   d) Assured ❑

9. Are other people likely to remember the things you do and say?
   a) Definitely not ❑
   b) Reasonably ❑
   c) Very ❑
   d) Completely ❑

10. How committed are you to being a lifelong learner?
    a) Not at all ❑
    b) Quite ❑
    c) Increasingly ❑
    d) Very ❑

7 × 7

1 Seven key ideas

- Everything you need to improve your memory is at your fingertips. Daily life offers you a wealth of resources and opportunities to help you stimulate and grow your memory power.
- Remembering well is all about getting into the right habits. With commitment and energy you really can change the way you operate, embedding new habits of thinking and behaving that will revolutionize the way you learn.
- Success with memory depends a great deal on *unlearning* a few ingrained habits, too. It's time to start challenging any negative things you've told yourself about your abilities. Break down the barriers to learning that your own attitudes and activities have put in the way.
- Many interesting and inspiring things have been written about memory. Use these insights to help you reflect on your own learning journey – and try to memorize some of them, to hone your skills and help you share your insights with others.
- Don't put off improving your memory. The benefits will kick in as soon as you start taking control of the way you use your brain, and there are some small steps you can take to make big gains – so start taking them today.
- The world is changing quickly. The need for a trained brain is only going to get greater. Prepare yourself now to cope with the ever-increasing demands on your memory, and enjoying developing skills that can give you a real edge.
- Keep up with the science of learning. Many discoveries from the last few decades still hold true, guiding the key principles of memory improvement; but new advances are being made all the time, so keep your eyes open for information that might redirect your approach and shape your personal plan.

2 Seven best resources

- **Everyday places.** There are opportunities all around for flexing your memory muscles, wherever you find yourself. Take a traffic jam. You could sit in the queue and fume... Or, you could look around and use memory techniques to learn the company names and nationalities of lorries; or specific cars, their colours, occupants, registration plates... Don't waste time: use it, and the information around you, to keep your memory skills in shape.
- **Search engines.** Another way of practising the key techniques in this Part is to start a random memory trail online. Load up a search engine, type in something that comes to mind, and see where you can take it from there. Typing in 'stamp collecting' might take you to a stamp auction site, where there's a stamp showing a humpback whale – so next you could search for information about the history of whaling, then explore more detail about one of the countries mentioned.... As you move along the information trail, use memory techniques to remember your 'journey'; and later, see how many of the links in the chain come back to mind.
- **The neighbourhood.** You might already have a fairly good knowledge of your local environment, but exploring it on foot and creating a number of memory 'routes' will strengthen your capacity to learn more. Walking also creates free thinking time in which you can let your creative juices flow, reviewing key memories from the past, or using stored information to help you plan for the future.
- **Walls and fridges**. Decorate your working and living spaces – using walls, fridges and other useful spaces – with visual triggers for the information you're trying to learn: key points for presentations, foreign vocabulary, useful facts and figures. Get used to looking at the details as you pass by, sometimes repeat them aloud, and see if you can start anticipating them. Objects, images, even items that give out fragrances or sounds – they can all be used to rehearse and reinforce memories.
- **Book shops and libraries.** We're creatures of habit, but it's good for us to try new things too. So the next time you're in

a favourite book shop or your local library, be consciously curious. As well as checking on your usual favourite authors, or reading up on subjects you already know something about, try selecting at random. Take a seat, enjoy a coffee, question, explore, make some lucky dips... and enjoy the new connections and discoveries that emerge.

- **Children**. Young children already practise many of the habits we recommend in this Part – so watch them at work (and play). See how they live in the present, focused and absorbed. Observe their creativity and imagination; the way they engage all their senses; their lack of self-criticism, restraint and fear of failure. See if some of it rubs off on you!

- **You.** Too many people underestimate their own power. The human brain is astounding in its capacity and often vastly under-used – unless it's trained and cared for. So make sure you're getting good quality sleep. Eat the foods that make you feel healthy, and keep well-hydrated. Exercise and get out in nature; breathe deeply; and do everything you can to be playful, positive, and *powerful*.

3 Seven habits to adopt

- Start remembering people. Get into the habit of actively *listening* to names, *repeating* them in your head, and using *images* and *associations* to fix important names in your brain.

- Chase elusive memories. If something is 'on the tip of your tongue', it's still in reach – so don't give up until you've got it back.

- Try delivering at least *part* of every presentation or speech from memory. With preparation and practice you'll be amazed at what you can achieve – even under public pressure.

- Don't just *cope* with the new information that comes your way; actively seek out interesting and important information to commit to memory.

- Put more effort into *streamlining* and *organizing* information – and you'll automatically make it much easier to remember.

- Look for fun opportunities to keep your memory strong. Many video games, word puzzles, number challenges, and

competitive pastimes like chess and bridge, exercise your mental muscles and help to keep your memory sharp.
- Instead of criticizing yourself when you occasionally forget, celebrate your success every time your memory does you proud.

4 Seven mistakes to avoid

- Don't neglect your own memory in favour of gadgets. Yes, use all the tools at your disposal – but don't forget the uniquely creative, insightful and intuitive power of your own brain.
- If you catch yourself looking at a document, email or manual without taking anything in... *stop* – and only start again when you're able to read actively and effectively.
- Guard yourself against information overload. If it feels like there's simply too much coming your way, do whatever you can to stem the flow and only tackle manageable memory tasks. This has to be better than forgetting *everything*!
- Stop missing opportunities because you're worried about your memory letting you down. A trained memory will actually help you to do everything better – so seize every chance you get to put yours to use.
- Challenge the myth that memory inevitably gets worse. Your memory may well change over the years; but, with positivity and practice, there's no reason why many important aspects of it can't change for the better.
- Make sure that poor diet, lack of exercise and insufficient sleep aren't limiting your power to learn.
- Instead of simply *recording* information – on paper, in computers or online – see what happens when you use your memory to *engage* with it in clever and creative ways.

5 Seven great quotes

- 'Memory is the treasury and guardian of all things.' *Marcus Tullius Cicero, Ancient Roman politician and philosopher*

- 'If you want to win friends, make it a point to remember them. If you remember my name, you pay me a subtle compliment; you indicate that I have made an impression on you. Remember my name and you add to my feeling of importance.' *Dale Carnegie, writer*
- 'Lulled in the countless chambers of the brain, our thoughts are linked by many a hidden chain; awake but one, and in, what myriads rise.' *Alexander Pope, English poet and satirist*
- 'We have forgotten to remember, and just as importantly, we have forgotten how to pay attention. So instead of using your smartphone to jot down crucial notes, or Googling an elusive fact, use every opportunity to practise your memory skills. Memory is a muscle to be exercised and improved.' *Joshua Foer, author*
- 'You should always be taking pictures, if not with a camera then with your mind. Memories you capture on purpose are always more vivid than the ones you pick up by accident.' *Isaac Marion, author*
- 'Practising is not only playing your instrument... it also includes imagining yourself practising. Your brain forms the same neural connections and muscle memory whether you are imagining the task or actually doing it.' *Yo-Yo Ma, musician*
- 'Memory is the mother of all wisdom.' *Aeschylus, Ancient Greek playwright*

6 Seven things to do today

- When you wake up, try to remember what you dreamed about. Some days the images and experiences will come back to you, some days it will all be a complete blank... but it's great brain exercise to try to recapture your dreams – especially later in the day.
- Change one of your passwords – to something creative and cryptic that you can remember, but nobody else could guess.
- Picture a room you know well; and into it, place images to remind you of the important jobs you need to do today.

- Spend a few minutes exploring an enjoyable memory from the past – from some different mental angles and through as many senses as you can.
- Set yourself a mental maths problem to stretch your 'working memory' – the part that juggles new information while you do something with it. What is 23×34...?
- Choose something you want to do later today – then see if you remembered to do it. If you didn't, pick something different tomorrow... and keep exercising your 'prospective' memory capacity.
- Redesign your business card or email signature to make it distinctive, eye-catching and *memorable*.

7 Seven trends for tomorrow

- Jobs will be increasingly flexible and bespoke, allowing us greater scope to design our own working lives – but giving us greater responsibilities than ever to be organized, efficient, and in control of everything we need to know.
- More of us will have multiple careers – so we'll need to be confident about learning new skills, working with new people and thinking flexibly about our ever changing roles and responsibilities.
- Entertainments like TV series, films and video games will become increasingly complex, challenging us to engage on new levels and to use our memories like never before.
- Instead of owning everything we'll *share* more things – like lawnmowers, desks, cars... so we'll need to be organized and accurate about remembering who, what, where, when...
- Our passwords will need to be more complex, and we'll only be able to store them in our brains if they're to be truly secure.
- We'll need to work until we're much older – so we'll need to stay mentally sharp for longer, with lasting confidence in our memory skills.
- Opportunities for *lifelong* learning will inspire many of us to stay mentally fit well beyond our retirement from work, continually seeking our new learning challenges.

Answers

Part 1: Your Personal Impact Masterclass

Chapter 1: 1d; 2c; 3b; 4c; 5a; 6d; 7b; 8d; 9d; 10a

Chapter 2: 1b; 2d; 3d; 4d; 5d; 6d; 7a; 8d; 9d; 10b

Chapter 3: 1c; 2c; 3c; 4a; 5b; 6c; 7a; 8d; 9c; 10c

Chapter 4: 1d; 2d; 3d; 4c; 5d; 6d; 7d; 8b; 9d; 10d

Chapter 5: 1a; 2a; 3d; 4b; 5d; 6d; 7d; 8a; 9d; 10d

Chapter 6: 1a; 2b; 3a; 4d; 5a; 6b; 7d; 8d; 9d; 10d

Chapter 7: 1d; 2d; 3c; 4d; 5c; 6c; 7b; 8c; 9b; 10d

Part 3: Your Assertiveness Masterclass

Chapter 15: *Individual responses*

Chapter 16: 1a; 2c; 3d; 4c; 5c; 6c; 7c; 8a; 9d; 10d

Chapter 17: 1d; 2d; 3d; 4d; 5d; 6c; 7b; 8c; 9c; 10c

Chapter 18: 1b; 2d; 3c; 4c; 5c; 6c; 7c; 8b; 9c; 10d

Chapter 19: 1d; 2d; 3c; 4d; 5d; 6b; 7c; 8d; 9d; 10d

Chapter 20: 1d; 2c; 3c; 4b; 5b; 6b; 7b; 8b; 9b; 10b

Chapter 21: 1b; 2c; 3 *individual response*; 4c; 5 *individual response*; 6a; 7a; 8 *individual response*; 9b; 10 *individual response*

Notes